BOOK OF OUTDOOR LORE

Clyde Ormond

Drawings by Ernest Kurt Barth

with animal sign drawings by Douglas Allen

OUTDOOR LIFE · HARPER & ROW
NEW YORK

Lithographed in the United States of America

CONTENTS

Introduction   3

1. Hiking into the Outdoors   11

Treacherous terrain • How far each day
• Footwear for hikers • Foot care for
hikers • The hiker's clothes • The laundry problem.

2. The Hiker's Pack   28

Pack basket—tumpline • Packboards •
Go-light gear • Cold-weather gear •
Packing the load.

3. Water Travel   47

Water displacement • Building the raft
• Rubber life rafts • Boats for wilderness travel • Development of the canoe
• How to paddle a canoe • Packing and
portaging • Rough-water tactics • Repairing the craft.

4. Finding Your Way 71

    Maps • The compass and how to use it • Finding north star • Shadow stick • Route sketching • Blazing the trail • Using nature's signs • Getting lost.

5. Forecasting the Weather 90

    The atmosphere • Cloud formations • Weather signs • Wildlife behavior • Dangerous weather.

6. A Shelter for the Night 104

    Tarp shelters • Lean-tos and other frame shelters • Desert and seacoast shelters • Rock shelters • Cave shelters • Selecting a campsite • Animal pests.

7. Firemaking 123

    Hazards of fire • Fireplaces • Building a cooking fire • Keep your matches dry • Fire without matches • Extinguishing the fire.

8. The Water Problem 140

    Purifying water • Locating water in the mountains • Water in the desert.

9. Meat for the Pot 150

    Firearms • Hunting with a sling • The slingshot • Steel traps • Box trap • Snares • Skinning small game • Dressing small game • Cooking small game • Preparing big game.

Shirt-tail flies • Emergency lures •
Emergency tackle • Cleaning fish • No-
utensil cooking • Frying fish • Fileting
• Baked fish • Smoked fish.

11. Edible Plants   194

Emergency foods • Edible plants •
Wild berries • Edible nuts • Emergency drinks.

12. Knots and Lashings   222

Hemp and nylon rope • Stopper knot
• Whipping and burning • Turkey-
head knot • Braiding • Knots • Lashings • Care of rope.

13. The Ingenious Outdoorsman—
What He Can Make   246

Camp lights • Potato-sack pack • Camp
table • Camp bed • Raised fireplaces •
Camp coolers • Washstands • Clock-
compass • Emergency snowshoes and
binding • Birchbark kettles • Camper's
soap • Preserving animal skins • Eskimo tanning methods • Catgut •
Leathercraft.

OUTDOOR IDENTIFICATION SECTION

I. Tree Identification   287

Classification of trees • America's forest
areas • Ash • Aspen • Basswood •

Beech • Birch • Cedar • Chestnut •
Cottonwood • Cypress • Elm • Fir •
Gum • Hemlock • Hickory • Larch
• Magnolia • Maple • Oak • Pine •
Redwood • Saguaro • Spruce • Syca-
more • Walnut • Willow.

II. Signs of the Animals   345

Elk • Whitetail deer • Blacktail deer •
Mule deer • Moose • Caribou • Ante-
lope • Rocky mountain bighorn • Des-
ert bighorn • Dall sheep and the Stone
sheep • Rocky mountain goat • Black
bear • Grizzly bear • Brown bear •
Polar bear • Gray wolf • Fox • Coyote
• Cougar • Bobcat • Beaver • Badger •
Raccoon • Muskrat • Porcupine •
Woodchuck • Squirrels • Opossum •
Weasel • Marten • Mink • Rabbits •
Skunk • Javelina • Snakes.

INDEX   483

Foreword

By Don DeHart, big-game guide and outfitter, who conducts hunts from Alaska to Mexico with clients from all over the world.

Clyde Ormond has traveled the trails and rivers up and down the North American continent for over thirty years, hunting, fishing, and absorbing the lore of the unspoiled wilderness of our vast and beautiful land. He is a natural woodsman and the keenest, most observing person I have ever traveled with.

I have known Clyde for a good many years, and we have spent weeks at a time in the mountains and hills. From Alaska's arctic wastes on the ice packs of the polar seas to the mountains of the North and Southwest, we have tramped and ridden the trails together. He has tremendous ability in observing and recording what he sees, either by camera or notebook, and what he files away in his memory is fantastic. When he starts to write, he is able to call upon a veritable filing cabinet of valuable information. And he is always very sure that what he writes is absolute fact. So, I can truthfully say, I know of no man better equipped to write a book on outdoor lore.

Clyde is no armchair writer. On our treks in the far back country, I've seen him spot the tracks of a wolf or wolverine on a sand bar, or sight a moose or a grizzly bear from a distant mountain. He is able to see game at a distance long before the average man can. Some of my professional guides, on seeing him for the first time, have remarked, "'Spose we better take it easy with this dude writer." Much to their surprise and chagrin, at the end of a long day's hunt this "dude" writer will come into camp in the lead.

I believe this book to be one of the best ever written on the subject. In my judgment, it will fill the need for a basic guide to the outdoors. It is not only interesting reading, but may serve as a serious textbook, and will stimulate those who read it to heed the "call of the wilderness" that has long been an inspiration for many of us.

Don DeHart
Slana, Alaska

Complete Book of
Outdoor Lore

Introduction

To most people the outdoors means that part of our country which has not yet been exploited by buildings, industry, or agriculture. To the more imaginative the outdoors also means an escape from the prosaic cares of the day, where the human spirit may find complete physical change and freedom. We go into the outdoors for a physical and spiritual uplift, and it is with this aspect that this book is concerned.

The North American outdoors may be broadly divided into its mountains, forests, seacoasts, deserts, and its swamps and bayous.

The appeals of rugged mountains are many and varied—the blue spires reaching to the heavens; the cool clean air of high altitudes; the vastness and tenacity of mountainous upheavals. To each the appeal is different, but I have yet to find a person who didn't, in some personal way, love the mountains.

I have stood on thin shelving ledges on the face of Idaho's Sawtooth Mountains where the slip of a boot meant a plunge to eternity; and the sudden sight of a Rocky Mountain goat, staring at me from above like some venerable patriarch, was worth the climb. In the remote, foggy Aleutians, the day's hard climb to a

3

mountaintop was adequately rewarded by nothing more than the feel of whipping rain and wind, mixing in vortex between two oceans. In the primitive Wind River Mountains, the difficult trek over glacial wash above timberline has been amply repaid by the sudden sight of ink-blue lakes in the innumerable pockets of rock below.

The surprises of mountain country are myriad and diverse: Wild flowers splashing in color at the base of melting glaciers. The thump of a deer, startled and flashing gray among the timber. Pug marks of the wary cougar in the dust of a trail up a switchback. Red-frosted acres of ripe blueberry bushes on an Alaskan slope. Grizzly spoor in a wild raspberry patch. Peaks of eternal white in the Canadian Rockies. The laughing trickle of an ice-cold creek, quenching to the thirst and soothing to the ear. A bright outcropping of mineral on the bare face of a cliff. The sheer inspiration of unscalable peaks.

These are the things the observing person sees in mountain country; and America is blessed with mountains.

The rugged Rockies stretch from southern New Mexico to northeast Alaska. Many of the peaks reach fourteen thousand feet in elevation, with Mount McKinley thrusting over twenty thousand feet upward into the sky. This great curving range generally parallels the western seacoast. With such secondary ranges as the Coastal Range, the Wasatch Mountains in Utah, and the Bitterroots bounding Idaho and Montana, the pleasures of mountains are within convenient access to anyone in the western portions of the continent.

Similarly, the Appalachian system of mountains parallels the eastern seacoast, extending all the way from the St. Lawrence River southward to Alabama and Georgia. With such smaller ranges as the Green, White, Black, Adirondacks, Blue Ridge, Alleghenies, and Smoky Mountains, the Appalachian system combines to offer the joys of mountains to those living in the East.

Mountains and living forests go together like trout and a fly rod. There are no smells quite like green pine needles or the campfire smoke of dry aspen. Few sights are more inspiring than the carpets of tall conifers on the mountain slopes. There is no simpler lesson in courage and tenacity than a strong oak. What music can compare with the low moaning of wind in pine tops or the hush of a breezeless forest at dusk?

The sights, sounds, and smells of the forest are innumerable and coupled with surprises: The burst of a grouse from almost beneath one's feet. The chatter of a tree squirrel which has detected the invader's presence. The sudden sight of a lake below the trail, with the dark shadow of a moose nosing beneath the surface for food. A chipmunk's nearly inaudible patter as he races away on fallen maple leaves. The V of a mallard brood, swimming out into a river.

As with mountains, America has a priceless heritage of forests. To the city dweller or one who lives in a plains area, it is hard to realize that approximately one-third of our total land area is composed of forests. In the United States, excluding Alaska, there are 625 million acres of forest land. These forests are sufficiently spread throughout the country so as to offer enjoyment for all. As one example, there are now National Forests set aside in forty-one of the states.

Canada, too, has an amazing acreage in forests, with one million square miles of forested lands. Alaska has coniferous forests over the majority of its land area, and Mexico has areas of forests along its "spine" and in its tropical lowlands.

All these vast orchards of the Almighty offer pleasures and deep joys to those who will but take time to explore them.

The seacoasts, those almost limitless, tenuous lines where land is wedded to water, also offer varied forms of enjoyment to the outdoorsman.

My first real acquaintance with an ocean came some years back. I had previously flown over two oceans, fished offshore for big-game species, and had watched the fearless divers at Acapulco dare the sea by diving from the high cliffs above. I had swum in the ocean's languid, salty brine off a protected beach. I had skirted the open leads of the Arctic by dog team.

But the ocean first revealed part of its true character to me late one night off a rocky shore. The weather was wild and boats had been kept offshore for two days. All that night, the roar of the breakers could be heard for miles. They rolled in to smash upon the rocks below us, their rebellion and torture dying in rhythmic undefeat, in sprays of falling water.

This is the appeal and fascination of the seacoasts for many—the magnetism of awesome and often brutal power.

Others enjoy the seacoasts for the offshore fishing, the skin diving, boating, and swimming in sheltered bays and inlets. Still others love the seacoasts during hot summers for the feel of warm wet sand on bare feet, the sun's warmth on near-nude bodies. Many camp in trailer communities on shore, where they can hear the continuing pound of the surf.

Seacoasts bound the entire continent, ranging in

latitude from the warm beaches, caves, and harbors of Florida, California, and Acapulco, Mexico, through the rocky shores of New England, to the ice-bound coast of the Arctic, where anchor ice prohibits any use of the coastline for most of the year.

Another considerable part of our outdoors is the desert. To many people a "desert" is a hot, dry, inhospitable place, devoid of all life. A true desert is, of course, so devoid of water that plant and animal life are either scant or nonexistent. But North America has only one true desert—the Mojave Desert of California.

The modified deserts and arid regions are an integral part of the continent's playground. These broad areas of limited rainfall reach from central New Mexico to north-central Canada, with east-west boundaries highly irregular, and often overlapping forest and mountain areas.

During the intense heat of midsummer, the arid regions lie dormant. With spring rain, the desert comes vividly to life. There is no more beautiful sight than the Southwestern desert in full bloom. Few colors are more lovely than the yellow blossoms of the prickly pear, or the rainbow hues of Arizona's Vermillion Cliffs. Few plants are more awe-inspiring than the giant saguaro cactus reaching its spiny arms towards heaven. And with the cool of evening, the desert's own forms of animal life become active.

Just last month I traveled a section of desert near the Mexican border. At first glance, the rolling scrubby acres appeared lifeless. But by timing the trek for four o'clock in the afternoon and later, we moved about in the waist-high prickly pear and saw javelina, quail, whitetail deer, and one large rattlesnake before darkness had set in. The desert's "people" had come to life after the day's siesta.

To those outdoors-loving people who have learned that the deserts are not dead, our arid lands provide a wealth of enjoyment, offering such pleasures as rock-hunting, exploring, prospecting, and color photography.

The swamps and bayous are the mysterious lands of the continent. In no area can a person lose himself more completely than in the heavy foliage along winding waterways. Few sounds are more eerie than the call of birds and wild animals in such hushed, unfamiliar settings. Nothing torments the imagination faster than the solitude of swamps and bayous where vision is limited and legend takes on reality.

Swampland is, of course, terrain which is inundated by water until its soil becomes spongy. Marshlands are low, level lands whose drainage has been hindered or prevented by heavy vegetation, hard subsoil, or large areas of adjacent level lands. In flooded lands of this type, rivers won't maintain a single channel, but cut away into numerous offshoots which drain into a lacelike network of waterways called bayous.

The principal swamp-bayou areas are the Delta regions of the Mississippi, in Florida, and Louisiana; in the Great Lakes region between the U.S. and Canada; along the eastern Coastal Plain, including Florida's Everglades and the Dismal Swamp country of North Carolina and Virginia; and oddly enough, in the Far North. Opposite factors of climate and weather produce both the swamps of the South and the muskeg of the North.

Warm weather, rain, and river runoff produce the swamps. In Alaska and Canada, permafrost and hardpan soil act as a shelf under the summer runoff of melting snows headed for the Arctic and Pacific. With the lush growth of insulating moss between, water has no place to go, forming the boglike muskeg which is comparable to the swamplands of the South. This makes any extended travel most difficult.

I have an old trapper friend in British Columbia who, before the advent of the Alaska Highway, made six separate annual trips for supplies with pack horses from Fort Nelson to Fort St. John. These laborious overland treks were in bush and muskeg country, over a distance of more than two hundred and fifty miles each way. Naturally, he came to learn the route of least muskeg and bog. Later, the military flew this man over the same horse route while he dropped flags indicating his course. The pilot road for the Alcan, now called the Alaska Highway, followed that old horse trail.

Swamplands attract the waterfowl hunter, he who thrills to the cry of a dog pack on the trail of a varmint, whose heart leaps to the gobble of a wild turkey. For others, the interest may lie in exploring, poling a thin boat along an old trapping route, in photographing the wild grace of jumping mallards, or in reducing to canvas the resigned desolation of mangrove trees in a sepulchral setting.

As with any worthwhile pursuit, the full enjoyment of the outdoors entails certain fundamental hazards. In forests deep enough to impart the full flavor of the wilderness, there is the mild hazard of becoming lost. In mountainous regions, this danger may be accompanied by the possibility of falling, of sudden avalanches, or of encountering a dangerous animal. The desert's dangers are thirst, sunstroke, and the poisonous insects or snakes. In the seacoast and swamp areas, there is always the hazard of traveling on water, and, along the ocean, the dangers of storms.

Such dangers are relative. The tendency has always been to accent the hazards of being in the outdoors, rather than to stress the deep pleasures and benefits which are the real reasons for going. This is understandable, largely because hazards are tangible. The inspirations, pleasures, and deep benefits are intangible and harder to explain; but they are satisfying beyond description.

It is true that the hazards of any area or endeavor should be understood, so that they may be avoided. We learn to handle automobiles so that we may have the benefits of transportation. We use hammers, axes, and knives for their utility in keeping with the purposes for which they were developed. This should be our fundamental attitude in the enjoyment of the outdoors. The inspiration, benefits, deep joys, and real communion with the Almighty far, far outweigh the hazards.

Many have discovered, that two weeks' retreat into the outdoors from the business world, in the company of majestic mountains and chattering creeks, breathing the redolence of pine needles and wild huckleberries, is sufficient to rejuvenate them for the remaining fifty weeks indoors. For millions the tug of a trout on a flyline, the unexpected flash of wild game, the enduring honesty of great trees and rivers, and a sense of nature's unrelenting life cycle, feed both body and soul. They realize that the farther man travels down that long, complex road out of the wilderness and into the air-conditioned cells of comfort he calls office and home, the greater his periodic need to return.

CHAPTER 1

Hiking into
the Outdoors

Hiking across the uneven terrain of the outdoors, unlike everyday walking on the concrete sidewalks of cities, is something of an art. It was an art practiced with perfection by the American Indian as he stalked game along wilderness trails before the white man came. From the Indians the early mountain men learned the lore of wilderness travel, and it has been passed on through generations of outdoorsmen.

The art of hiking is basically a matter of learning to conserve your energy, of discovering the easiest way of navigating across rough terrain, often while wearing a heavy pack, without tiring yourself unduly. The pace at which you travel, the routes you select along the way, and the ease with which you traverse difficult or dangerous obstacles—these are the signs of how expert a hiker you are.

First of all, if you intend to hike a considerable distance, set a comfortable pace. If you are hiking with a friend, the slower should never try to match the pace of the faster. Trying to keep up with a fast walker is the surest way to tire yourself and spoil your excursion. It is better to set your own comfortable pace, lagging behind if necessary, and catch up while the faster one rests.

It is a cardinal rule in outdoor walking that the steeper the elevation, the shorter your steps should be. The same applies to rough terrain. The more rocky or obstructed the going, and the more slippery the surfaces, the shorter should be your steps. Nothing will tire you quicker than taking long, fast steps uphill; and taking long, fast steps downhill over slippery logs, grass, or rocks is inviting a fall.

Another vital rule in hiking is to step over and around obstructions. It takes the same energy to lift your body a foot off the ground as it takes to walk approximately 13 feet on the level. When confronted by blowdowns, large rocks, or other obstructions on the trail, the experienced hiker steps over them and conserves his energy. The same applies to small objects on the trail, which are apt to roll and unbalance the hiker. It is always better to plant the feet between the innumerable rocks, twigs, and mounds—even though it entails breaking stride—rather than chance a fall.

Another rule of hiking in any kind of terrain is to follow the route of least resistance. It is wise to take advantage of the routes selected by those who have previously traveled the same course. In regions of true wilderness, where few if any humans have been, the best routes are generally marked in some fashion by wild game. There are no better engineers for finding the easiest way through wild country than such animals as deer, sheep, elk, and caribou.

Often the trails left by these road builders will be faint, but the observant outdoorsman will spot them. Sometimes a trail through heavy forests will be pockmarked by deer in their seasonal or daily movements.

In areas of the Far North, trails will be worn a foot deep, like separate "buggy-tracks," by brown bear; or cut deeply into the high ridges by caribou. Often the routes of the wild animals will show only as openings through bush, worn grass at a creek crossing, or faint dung along a ridge. The experienced hiker looks for such signs, and gives thanks to the game for reducing his effort.

In the mountains the least obstructed routes generally follow the ridges. Before leaving one crest, the experienced hiker carefully scans the valley or canyon bottom, locates the longest, lowest ridge across to the opposite mountain, and marks it as his route. It is wise when hiking in the mountains to keep as much as possible of the elevation one has gained. Often the easiest opposing ridge won't be straight across but along a longer route following a mild course around an entire canyon apex. Just as it is always less laborious to step around a small pocket in the terrain, so it is with valleys and canyons. Hiking *around* their apexes—depending upon the ultimate objective, of course—often is less tiring in the long run than "loping down, and puffing up again." One reason for traveling along ridges in mountain country is that less blowdown timber occurs on ridges than on either side of the mountain.

The seasoned outdoorsman soon learns to glance at any mountain and tell, from its steepness, whether it is negotiable or not. Some mountains are simply not worth the effort to climb, unless you are hunting goats or sheep or are equipped with mountain-climbing gear. A good guide for any hiker is the "angle of repose"—the degree of inclination at which it is too steep for foliage to grow, and slides and bare earth appear. Generally speaking, one shouldn't try to climb these areas, but find a more gradual, though round-about, route.

On any mountainside that can't be climbed along a man-made or game trail, the best procedure is to zig-zag upward rather than take a straight course. That is, one should climb in an angling route for a few rods; then, where the thinness of foliage or absence of rocks suggests, turn sharply and climb a few rods in the opposite direction before reversing. This technique utilizes the muscles of the right and left side of the body evenly, and gives the sides of the feet, which must dig in on the uphill side with each step, a chance to rest.

TREACHEROUS TERRAIN

One of the best tools to help in crossing treacherous terrain is a staff about 4 to 6 feet long and 1½ inches in diameter. Light, dry wood, such as a small jack pine cut to suitable length makes an adequate one. A staff becomes a third leg in uncertain footing and often prevents a nasty fall. With such a staff, you can poke firmly into a stream bottom and, by moving either one leg or the staff at a time (never both together), always have two "legs" to give you balance. You can probe for holes, big rocks, or soft spots in the bottom of muddy streams. If you are with a partner, you can hold the staff between you and support each other.

In crossing the glacial creeks of the Far North, a staff of driftwood or scraggly timber found on the spot often represents the difference between crossing or staying on the same side. Such creeks, even in midsummer, have their source only a few miles away in the high glacial fields above. When you ford them in early morning, the creeks are low and clear, the flow reduced by the cold of the night. After a warm day, they are roaring, muddy demons, three times as deep, and vicious enough to roll rocks of glacial wash the size of buckets down in a seething boil that can often be heard for miles.

A good rule for crossing creeks and streams is to ford them either at the slow end of a deep pool or just before a long stretch of placid water breaks into a riffle. At these two places the water will be shallower and the current slower. Usually this is the widest part of the stream.

A hiking staff is also useful in desert areas. In some desert country, like portions of Arizona, there is a saying of the oldtimers that "everything that grows either sticks or bites you." This isn't literally true, but poisonous snakes and insects, and the various forms of cacti, keep the hiker constantly on his guard. He must continuously wind in and out among the sharp-tined cacti plants, some of which would penetrate the tough hide of a horse's leg, and be on the watch for harmful reptiles. A staff is useful for breaking an occasional spine out of the way or for defending yourself against desert rattlers.

A staff also is valuable when crossing swampland, muskeg, or other spongy ground. With it you can probe ahead in treacherous places for uncertain footing. You can use it as a pole for literally vaulting potholes you could not otherwise jump.

In crossing such watery areas, a fact to remember is that most swampland, if negotiable at all, has some solid high ground. Generally this ground borders the actual water level and permits travel between areas of inundation. Often small lakes, channels, and boggy areas are joined by necks of relatively solid footing.

These must often be crossed in a series of jumps between hummocks of vegetation. The point to remember is that the ground is most solid in those parts where vegetation roots appear. For instance, in boggy areas having such vegetation as moss, grass, and sparse willows, the most solid footing occurs at the roots of the heaviest foliage—in this case, the willows. I have crossed Canadian muskeg, either on foot or horseback, where small spruce trees would wiggle as far as 20 to 30 feet ahead of me. Yet by sticking to the footing afforded by these spruce and the smaller arctic birch, crossing was fairly safe. However, had I stepped where only caribou moss grew among the water puddles, I would have sunk in. In those areas, incidentally, the hardpan creating the boggy situation was approximately 4 feet below the surface.

Finally, when a mishap does occur in boggy country, and you fall through into muck or water, a staff long enough to catch solid footing on at least one side can be a lifesaver. If you do fall in boggy terrain, try to land "spread-eagle"—that is, with arms and legs outspread. This distributes the body's weight over a greater surface. I have an Eskimo friend who has twice saved his own life in this fashion when falling through thin ice in the Arctic. He landed with arms outstretched, holding his short *oonok,* or hunting pole, in his mittened hands. The pole, anchoring on ice at either side, held his weight sufficiently so that he could inch his way back to safety by squirming along the ice on his belly.

This trick of landing spread-eagle often saves a life in steep, mountainous country. If you slip on a steep slope, trying to keep your feet may tumble you over a cliff or down the slope. If you land spread-eagle, friction and a low center of gravity help to halt your slide.

HOW FAR EACH DAY

How far a hiker should walk in a day depends on such factors as the season of the year, the difficulty of the terrain, his age and physical condition, the purpose of the hike, and the amount of weight he needs to carry.

Some adults, unused to walking, cannot hike a half-mile without being tired. Others, hardened by outdoor living and mountain climbing, can walk all day and still be in fair shape. According to the standard set by President Theodore Roosevelt, a U.S. Marine should be able to walk a total of fifty miles in twenty hours. This is no reason for the beginner to attempt anything of that nature. Actually, pack horses average only two and a half to three miles per hour on mountain trails. That pace is too fast for a man. And there is little need for any outdoorsman, ever, to walk fifty miles in one around-the-clock period. Actually, one hikes for pleasure. When this is diminished by too strenuous an effort, the purpose is largely defeated.

On any trip, plan the hike so you reach your objective early in the day. If the hike is to be four miles round trip, you should be at the end of two miles well in advance of the half-day mark. You should rest, then turn back while there is still more than a half-day left, or before you are excessively tired. The hike back, on a single day's trek, invariably takes longer and is more tiring. Where the entire day is spent hiking towards a given objective, the last half, similarly, takes more time and energy than the first. This should be remembered so that a margin of strength may be left, and the full hike made more enjoyable.

This is especially true of hiking through deserts, swamps, or muskeg areas. In the desert the midday sun saps energy fast, and the afternoon portion of the day is hottest. Similarly, in boggy or muskeg areas the soft underfooting unexpectedly takes the hiker's energy before he is aware of how tired he is.

A good way for any beginning hiker to approach the matter of how far to hike in a day is not to set too definite an objective on his first hike—that is, not decide to hike to Clear Creek and back but see how far he can pleasurably hike toward Clear Creek before getting very tired, or in less than half of his available time. If he makes it to the creek, pleasurably, fine. If not, he should head back, then try for longer distance the next time.

Generally speaking, any person in good physical shape and health should be able to hike from three to five miles a day in easy country. Seasoned outdoorsmen can hike ten to twenty in rolling forest country, if necessary, with no pack or just a light load.

FOOTWEAR FOR HIKERS

Shoes or boots are the most important single item of clothing for hiking, since the feet take the most punishment. Generally speaking, hiking shoes should be 6 to 8 inches high, light in weight, and have a "cord" type of sole. Heavy boots, cowboy boots, oxford-type shoes, canvas sneakers, calked boots, or boots having no heels (wedge type), are not good for prolonged hikes.

Hiking shoes should be light, as the weight of heavy boots, multiplied by the thousands of times the feet must lift them, requires an excessive expenditure of energy. Cord soles are the best yet developed for holding firmly to most surfaces—rocks, wood, sand, and grass. Leather soles are not good for mountain

A light, rugged boot suitable for hiking.

hiking as they tend to slip on rocks and smooth surfaces. The same is true of wedge-type soles—they become miniature skis in mountain country. Where terrain is consistently swampy or filled with muskeg, a good choice is the rubber-bottom, leather-top pac. These, too, should be light, about 8-inches high, and have heels.

Many Canadians use moccasins for hiking. Once the feet are hardened to their use, these are fine in country that is rolling, wet, or has a moss or muskeg surface. Work moccasins that tie on and come high over the ankles are the most useful. For use in snow these are often supplemented by a rubber "slipper" with cleat soles. Good moose-hide moccasins will dry out

Moccasins are good for hiking in wet or muskeg terrain, but the feet must be toughened to their use.

at night without being stiff in the morning—and that's a decided advantage.

For serious hiking only good-quality shoes should be worn. The intermittent wetting, constant twisting and bending, and uneven wearing to which shoes used in outdoor hiking are subjected will not only ruin poor-quality footgear quickly, but will cripple the wearer. Seams will part; heels will loosen; tacks will work their way into the feet after several wettings; inner soles will become lumpy. Too often the front ends of such shoes, after being dried a few times, will lose their shape and resemble the curled front ends of skis. Some dry out hard as rocks. The results can even be disastrous when such a boot goes to pieces while the hiker is afield.

Hiking shoes should be purchased a half-size and a width larger than a person's dress shoes. Under the hiker's constant weight, feet spread out laterally to a considerable degree. After long hours of walking, the feet also swell slightly. All this takes up the extra half-size. Also, a thicker sock should be worn in a hiking shoe than in a dress shoe. In fact, when fitting a hiking shoe, it is a good policy to take along an extra-heavy sock and try on the new shoe over it.

Once the new shoe is taken home, it should be broken in by stepping into a tub of water, with the shoes fully laced, for three to five seconds. Then the shoe should be worn until it dries thoroughly on the foot. This shapes a new hiking shoe to the foot, and loosens and flexes leather and stitching to the point where it is wearable. After this initial wetting and drying, a good shoe grease or dressing should be applied, unless the shoe has been pretreated with a silicone preparation which makes it fairly waterproof. Broken in in this manner, the shoe should be worn for several days in advance of a long hike—even a few hours each evening around the house will help.

Good hiking shoes, conditioned in this manner, will take repeated wetting and drying in the outdoors without too much damage. After a wetting, shoes should be dried slowly at night near a camp stove or campfire. Treated with another coat of shoe dressing, they will be ready for wear the next day.

Too many people spoil good shoes by trying to dry them too fast. Often they set them in back of the camp stove or too near the fire and go about something else. When the odor of burning leather greets their nostrils, it is too late, and the shoes are practically ruined.

Instead, shoes should be dried slowly. They should be set considerably away from intense heat and off the ground where they would draw additional moisture. Good ways to dry shoes are to hang them from a tree limb in the sun or from the ridgepole of a tent, or set them against the sunny side of a flat rock. Hanging shoes upside down allows them to drain as well as dry.

FOOT CARE FOR HIKERS

An outdoorsman can patch up a minor burn or cut, or a blister from swinging an ax, and still enjoy himself. A small wound on his foot will cripple him. Proper foot care is essential to the enjoyment of any hike.

The difficulty with getting your feet wet on a hike is that sand and gravel often get into your shoes along with the water. Such gritty particles lodge between the toes and between folds of the skin, particularly at the underside of the first toe-joints. They also stick to the socks and work into the weave of the knitting. They grate against the foot's tender skin like sandpaper. Also, wet socks—particularly cotton ones—wrinkle, lose their shape, and gradually work down inside the shoes, where they quickly blister the feet.

The best way of caring for the feet after getting them wet is to thoroughly wash shoes, socks, and feet. Next, shake the shoes till they are as free of water as possible. Wring the socks dry and shake out further moisture. Wipe the feet dry with a handkerchief. Lacking a handkerchief, use the wrung-out socks to dry the feet, then wring the socks out again. Put socks and shoes on and continue hiking. There will be ten times less damage and discomfort to the feet if these precautions are taken.

In desert hiking, where the feet are not apt to get wet but do heat up, to prevent galling it is wise to stop occasionally, remove shoes and socks, and for several minutes fan your feet with your hat to cool the skin. When putting on the socks again, put the left sock on the right foot, and vice versa. This helps eliminate creases and makes the socks wear more evenly, thus prolonging their resistance against holes. Similarly, in forest hiking, when you come to a creek after an hour or so of hot hiking, it is refreshing to take off shoes and socks and dunk the feet into the cool water.

A final suggestion: Make certain never to wear socks with holes in them on lengthy hikes. The material around the edge of a hole in a sock, once dampened by perspiration, tends to roll, forming a hard ring which is sure to cause blisters.

THE HIKER'S CLOTHES

The season of the year and the expected weather determine the hiker's clothing. Usually, the majority of hikes are made in summer and fall in the colder climates, and in comparable weather in the warmer climates.

For mild-weather hiking, cotton undergarments, shirt, and pants are best. A hiker sweats while walking, and the evaporation tends to chill him when he stops. Therefore, garments should be relatively light, and loose enough to allow for freedom of movement and easy evaporation.

This is especially true when hiking under intense sun or in desert areas. Under such conditions, wear light-colored clothing, as dark coloration draws more heat. Good colors for intense heat and sunlight are the suntans and mild tints of green and blue. Also, to avoid sunstroke or heat exhaustion, travel in desert areas during the evening and morning hours, if possible, reserving midday for resting. A white handkerchief placed under the hat rim and draped over the nape of the neck helps to keep the sweltering sun off that area.

On a hike in more temperate regions, carry a light jacket or woolen shirt to wear when pausing to rest, as the evaporation of heavy perspiration causes one to cool off quickly. If light showers are expected, a nylon jacket is fine. Otherwise a light poplin jacket will generally suffice to turn any wind and keep you warm. One of the best jackets for the purpose is the top part of a suit of Dacron-insulated underwear. This garment has unbelievable warmth for its few ounces of weight, launders easily, and is inexpensive. Woolen sweaters are not suitable for hikes through country where brush or foliage occur—they snag too easily.

For mild-weather hiking, socks are the one item that should be made of wool. Light wool socks are more comfortable for most people than cotton socks. This is especially true once they are wet. Wool-nylon socks are also good.

During the late fall months, when cold nights are the rule and storms are to be expected, the best material for clothing is wool: medium-weight, tightly-woven wool pants and lightweight woolen shirts.

For extremely cold, snowy weather, light woolen underwear and heavy "mackinaw" woolen pants, together with lightweight woolen shirts and light down jackets, are a good combination. Heavier socks of wool, too, are needed if you are wearing pacs. Pacs are the best footgear for snowshoes, though some woodsmen prefer 10-inch felt gaiters worn inside four-buckle rubber arctics.

Regardless of season, pants used for long hikes should not have cuffs such as are standard for dress pants. Outside cuffs catch snow, rain, twigs, sand, and gravel, and become a hard rope around the ankles. Cuffs also hook on sticks and tend to trip the hiker. Hiking pants, like riding jeans, should have only an inside seam. Pants should not be worn inside the boots, they funnel leaves, dirt, and sticks between socks and leather.

For mild weather both the shirt and pants should be of hard, tightly knit but porous material. This prevents the garments from being snagged and torn, and in insect country cuts down on the bites of mosquitoes, black flies, and gnats. Denim shirts and the Levi type of pants are useful in this respect, and make the pest problem a bit more endurable. For insect-pest regions, shirts should be long-sleeved and pants full-length regardless of warm temperatures.

There is one material that insects can't bore through—buckskin. Shirts, pants, and jackets of buckskin are the toughest of garments. Their utility is limited, however, for extended hiking in a variety of weather. Buckskin garments won't "breathe," and this makes evaporation and cooling almost impossible. Once the wearer stops to rest, his skin becomes clammy and cold.

One of the best kinds of headgear for most hiking is a medium-brim felt hat, light in color and western in style. A quality felt hat of this kind offers protection against light rain and snow, falling limbs and swishing branches, and shades the eyes from the direct rays of the sun. During a heavy downpour, the hat will shed most of the rain if the crown is left un-dented. During extremely cold weather, this kind of hat is still useful if worn with a pair of knitted ear-laps. For desert hiking, a wide-brimmed cloth or straw hat is cooler but wilts easily in any appreciable storm.

For cool weather, and for camp chores, snug-fitting buckskin gloves are good. For colder weather, knit jersey gloves are warm, and leather, rabbit-lined gloves will suffice for all but extreme arctic weather, where down mitts are needed.

A neckerchief such as the Boy Scouts wear is helpful for protecting the back of the neck from insects and sunburn. A large bandanna handkerchief will do just as well, and will often double for other purposes, such as bundling up small items and covering the ears in cold weather.

THE LAUNDRY PROBLEM

Laundering clothes in the outdoors presents quite a problem in certain regions and under certain conditions. Some hardy outdoorsmen simply wear what they have on for a trip's duration. The average person, however, becomes an outdoorsman each year for a period of only a few days to a month. Accustomed to changing clothes at home, he usually prefers to continue the habit in the outdoors.

Field trips of more than a day or so each should always be made with at least a partial change of clothing at hand. No "spares" are usually needed for such items as a heavy stag coat, raincoat, boots, or pacs. Changes of underwear, shirt, socks, and pants should always be taken along on the longer treks.

Generally the best time to do your washing outdoors is not on Mondays, but when it is most convenient to bathe or swim. If your pack contains a change of underwear, rinse out the worn garment after the swim, wring it out, and drape it over a rock or bush to dry while you bask in the sun. If the opportunity to bathe and wash doesn't occur when you can pause to dry things out, the washed articles can be bundled in a neckerchief, carried on the outside of the rucksack, and dried after the night's camp is made.

During colder weather, in regions where tents and overnight huts are necessary, laundering can be done inside. Although facilities for washing clothes may be limited, a bucket or washpan, soap, and water are all that are really necessary to do a good job of laundering.

Soak the soiled garment in warm water, not hot, after it has been soaped. Soaking for an hour or even less will loosen the dirt. Then rub the garment between the hands or up and down in the soapy water until it is reasonably clean. Rinse it in clear water and hang it up to dry.

When drying wet clothes, wring out all possible water and hang or drape them so the greatest surface will be exposed to heat, sunlight, or movement of the air. During the warm weather, air and sunlight are all that is needed. During a storm, some form of artificial heat must usually be employed.

During wet weather, the best place to dry clothes is a line just under the tent's ridgepole or a temporary frame set back from the camp stove. Make sure the clothes are not too close to either stove or gas lantern, where they may catch fire and burn up an entire outfit. Wet clothes can be hung outside during freezing weather. After they have frozen stiff, the moisture can be shaken out in the form of frost particles.

CHAPTER 2

The Hiker's Pack

The size of the pack you carry into the outdoors will be determined by your build and physical condition, the intended duration of the hike, the type of terrain, and whether you go alone or with a partner.

Perhaps no two hikers will carry identical packs with the same expenditure of energy. It is difficult to pick a hiker at random and determine just what he can or should pack. There are, however, basic rules and standards to help each individual choose the best pack for himself.

Just as no one who has not practiced on one-day or overnight hikes should attempt a hike of several days' duration, so no one unused to a pack-load should attempt to carry a heavy pack on his first hikes. As the distance and difficulty of your hikes are gradually increased, so can the weight of the pack you carry.

As a guide to determining the size and weight of your pack, consider these facts: A husky fifteen- or sixteen-year-old boy, in good physical shape, can carry a 25-pound pack, in rolling hill country, with no difficulty. Some fellows can carry a heavier pack, for more miles, than grown men. A healthy man of average build can carry a 30- to 35-pound pack, in reasonable terrain. Toughened by backpacking experience, he can handle up to 50 pounds.

KNAPSACKS

For simply hiking into the outdoors for a day's fun, you need to pack little more than a camera, lunch, personal incidentals, and a small, light emergency kit which will be described in detail in a later chapter. This gear may easily be carried in a small knapsack, such as the official Boy Scout model, or in a small rucksack capable of handling more bulk and weight. Most knapsacks or rucksacks will average from 14 to 15 inches wide, 5 inches thick, and from 15½ to 17 inches high. A larger rucksack is more useful for hikers who may wish to carry back more weight than they take; that is, for such purposes as prospecting, rock-hunting, or gathering small pieces of driftwood along the seashore.

PACK BASKET—TUMPLINE

The woven pack basket is often used for portages on canoe trips, as it handles a variety of irregular-shaped bundles easily; and if the portage is short, the weight can be increased. Guides and seasoned outdoorsmen usually employ a tumpline for carrying bulky gear and heavy objects such as outboard motors, tents, and bed rolls. The tumpline consists of a leather band which goes around the forehead, and two leather straps which are tied to heavy bundles that ride on the user's back. Loads of 100 pounds or more can be lugged with a tumpline—an implement, incidentally, which would kink the neck of a person not used to it.

Modern backpacking equipment owes much to the ancient devices used by the primitive load-bearers of the East. The "A" frame and inverted "A" frame carriers (1), and the "L" frame carrier (2), were forerunners of the modern

PACKBOARDS

The packboard is perhaps the best device for carrying a variety of loads under different circumstances. Packboards have been developed in several basic types. One consists of a vertical framework having the tops of the two side standards closer together than the bottom ends. Another type is the exact reverse, with the tops of the standards spread apart. Still another form of packboard is an integral board-and-sack. Another, of aluminum tubing, has a small horizontal shelf across the bottom to support the load. Each type of packboard has been developed for a special type of load and terrain. It has also been designed for the type of activity of the user. All have been designed with a view toward keeping the center of gravity as constant as possible and preventing horizontal leverage.

3

4

pack frame. The principle of the basket carrier (3) has been adapted in the tumpline used by North Woods' packers today; and the fulcrum or pole carrier (4) taught us the principles of leverage and weight distribution. *Courtesy Himalayan Pak Co.*

As examples of how these factors must be correlated, the carrier of a heavy burden over level terrain needs a packboard which will allow his load to be carried high on the back, about even with the shoulders, where it will in no way interfere with his leg movement, and in such a position that he may walk almost upright. Conversely, the person who must climb steep mountains, using his hands to help pull himself up over rocks and broken terrain, needs a packboard which will permit the load to be carried lower, at the small of his back. Otherwise he would be unbalanced, with a constant tendency to fall on his face. Again, the person who needs free arm and leg movement while wearing a pack, should have a board which distributes the load more evenly from his shoulders to the small of his back. In all cases, the heaviest portions of the load should always be set as

Homemade wooden packboard consists of a frame of two sidebars joined by cross pieces, and a canvas wrap which rests against the back. It will carry gear of a variety of shapes and sizes.

closely against the wearer's body as possible. This adds to the mechanical advantage.

For general outdoor use in all kinds of terrain, a compromise packboard can be made. This type of packboard consists of two elements: (1) a wooden frame resembling a small ladder with three crossbars mortised into two siderails; (2) a canvas wrap which encircles this frame and is laced tightly together at the back. Web straps, fastened to the upper crossbar, pass through an opening in the face of the canvas wrap, over the user's shoulders, then down to his hips where they fasten, usually with buckles, to the lower ends of the frame's siderails.

This simple, all-around packboard has many virtues. It allows a heavy load to be placed well up on the shoulders and back where man's heavy burdens belong under average circumstances. It allows the same load to be reversed and tied upside down on the board, for steep climbing where the hands must be used. This packboard also prevents the load from rubbing against the wearer's back; the taut canvas wrap creates an air space of approximately 1½ inches between load and wearer. This not only provides for ventilation, but evenly distributes the total weight over the greatest possible area. The large loops of the two shoulder straps allow the packboard to be easily put on and taken off, and are quickly slipped off in case of a fall. Finally, the packboard is light in relation to the load.

Years ago, I invented a smaller version of this packboard, which can be carried in the coat pocket on hunting trips and assembled in camp for lugging home the game. The canvas wrap is replaced with one of lighter drill, and the straps are smaller. At camp, the entire frame is either built from the ends of orange crates or shaped from small, dry pine slabs. Mortises are cut into the siderails with an ax, and the crossbars are nailed on. The wrap is then fixed rigidly along the ends by shoving two alder sticks through the seams, and laced with a shoelace tightly around the frame. The shoulder strap is attached with a loop knot to the middle of the top crossbar, run through the wrap opening and tied to the ends of the frame with nylon cord.

The makings of this miniature packboard folded into something little larger than six nails and a bandanna handkerchief; and for years we used it to carry the lunch, rope, camera, and elk bugle on the way out, and 15 pounds of heart and liver coming back to camp. A sack the same size as the board was later added for carrying small articles.

These all-purpose packboards still have to be made by the individual, though some commercial models are beginning to appear. Modified versions are available in the Trapper Nelson packboard; a rugged military model which consists of an integral pressed-wood frame-and-wrap, moulded to fit the wearer's back; and pack frames made of light aluminum tubing.

Aluminum pack frames have several advantages: They are very light for their strength and the load they can carry. Most joints, which are the weakest points in a wooden frame, are eliminated by bending and shaping the metal tubing. Also, they are equipped with a small shelf at the bottom, which prevents the load from sagging or slipping downward. One model of the aluminum pack frame is designed so that a small child can be carried along the trail papoose fashion.

When carrying a pack frame the hiker should lean slightly forward so as to bring the center of gravity over the legs and feet. The lower strap, which rests against the back just above the hips, acts as a fulcrum upon which the load rests, with lift being supplied by the wearer's hips and legs. With the frame evenly loaded, the total weight may be shifted slightly from shoulders to back, and vice versa, by a slight shifting of the walking posture.

Aluminum pack frame (left) is light and strong. Shelf at bottom supports heavy loads and web strap directly behind it rests against wearer's back. Gear can either be wrapped in a waterproof tarp and lashed to the frame or packed in specially fitted rucksack (above). *Courtesy Himalayan Pak Co.*

How a modern aluminum pack frame works: Lift and pull are applied by shoulder straps while base back support (fulcrum) provides upthrust from the wearer's hips and legs. *Courtesy Himalayan Pak Co.*

Placement of weight in a pack is determined by the wearer's activity. A hiker packing a heavy load on level terrain (left) should carry the heaviest part of his gear at about shoulder level (dark portion). Arrows show lift and pull from shoulders and upthrust from hips and legs. A rock climber (right) should pack the heaviest part of his load at the small of his back, bringing the center of gravity as close to his body as possible so the weight does not tip him forward. *Courtesy Himalayan Pak Co.*

GO-LIGHT GEAR

Let's consider an actual example of what might go into a one-man pack, assuming that it is for summer or mild-weather traveling. Further, let's assume that the hiker is experienced on shorter hikes, wants to stay a week, and is conditioned to carry 40 pounds easily.

In this case, the necessary items of gear and food will break down into just over half the weight for gear, and less than half for food.

The basic items will be:

Packboard	3 pounds or less
Ax	2½ pounds
Sleeping bag	4 pounds
Cooking and eating utensils	2 pounds
Down vest	½ pound
Raincoat	½ pound
Underwear, shirt, socks	2 pounds
Camera and film	2½ pounds
Tarp	2 pounds
Emergency kit	½ pound
Whetstone, matches, tooth-	½ pound
brush, first-aid kit, etc.	½ pound
Miscellaneous	2 pounds
Total	**22 pounds**

In addition, the hiker may want to carry a fishing rod, rifle, handgun, or binoculars.

The ax should have a single-bit, 1½-pound head, and a leather sheath. It won't exceed 2½ pounds.

SLEEPING BAGS

There are several types of sleeping bags which will stay within this weight limit and still be comfortable for mild to cool weather. One is the inside portion of the down mummy bag used by the Air Force in World War II. Another is a mummy bag lined with an olive-drab army blanket. Several of the light down robes, used a generation ago, will not exceed this weight, and are very useful.

One of the most interesting lightweight sleeping bags I've ever seen was given to me by an old lion hunter in Arizona. It is made of paper with a thin layer of fiber insulation. The bag itself is lined with a cotton flannel sheet. This bag, too, is warm for its light weight, and very useful in semidesert country where moisture isn't a problem but nights are cool.

COOKING UTENSILS

The cooking kit and eating utensils may be assembled in a variety of ways and still stay under the weight limit. Only a few pots and dishes are necessary. Two light, nested, aluminum pots will take care of all cooking except frying. One is usually used to heat water, the other to cook stew, vegetables, etc. With the water heated, the other pot may be used to cook dried fruit, since beverages will be of the instant kind and mixed in the cup.

Since every ounce of weight is vital on a hiking trip, and since no food can be wasted, most hikers carefully cook only as much as they can eat, and eat the main course right from the pot.

The weight of the cooking pots can be cut down by taking three nested tin cans of suitable size. Remove their tops, hammer down their edges so they won't cut, and use short pieces of thin wire for bails. Bails are left off until the pots are used.

A frying pan is heavy, has an awkward handle, and is useful only if the backpacker obtains fish or small game. Bacon can be cooked in the bottom of a pot. The frying-pan problem can be solved in one of two ways. One is to buy a small frying pan, cut a length off the handle, and rivet a small aluminum loop around the remaining portion. In use, a length of stick is whittled to correct size and shoved tightly into this loop, providing the pan with a long, cool handle.

Others solve the problem by cutting a gallon fruit

can at a 2-inch height, leaving a 2-inch strip of metal all the way up one side to the top. All edges are bent over and hammered into a smooth rim, and the upright strip is bent into a handle. This frying pan will fit under two or three other pots in the pack.

The eating utensils may be reduced to an aluminum plate, aluminum cup, spoon, and fork. A belt knife or even a pocketknife does all the necessary cutting and spreading. The weight of the spoon and fork can be further reduced by using the small plastic forks and spoons available for picnics. A usable spoon, or even a fork, can be whittled out of a piece of flat wood.

CLOTHING

Raincoats have been vastly improved within the last few years with the invention of polyethylene. The old-style, heavy, rubber-fabric raincoat can now be left at home, and a plastic one weighing only a few ounces substituted, if you will be reasonably careful of snags. Perhaps the most usable type is the parka-raincoat, which has a hood to cover the head and neck.

One of the nicest garments for cool evenings and mornings is the down vest. It weighs only a few ounces, is a marvelous windbreaker, and is very warm for its weight. The top part of insulated Dacron underwear, as mentioned before, is also a warm, light garment. Such items fill the bill better than the heavy woolen jackets or shirts once used for the purpose.

For a week's jaunt, an extra denim shirt is necessary, and also may be used as a jacket for warmth. Two pair of spare socks will suffice. The change of underwear should be of the same kind as the ones worn.

CAMERA

Most outdoorsmen now carry cameras. A big share of any trip's enjoyment is the "braggin" pictures one returns with and reviews many times. Unless one is a professional photographer, a 35-mm camera and a spare roll of 36-exposure film will do the picture-taking job.

TARPS

Except for an ax, a tarp is the most important part of the gear. The old standard in tarps for backpacking was an 8-foot square of waterproof 8-ounce canvas, sometimes with triangular-shaped ends (for forming the sides of a lean-to), and grommets along all sides. This served the purpose well, and is indeed today one of the best-known tarp materials where automobile, boat, plane, or horse transportation is available. Such a tarp is tough, snagproof, waterproof, and long-wearing. Its single fault is that it is too heavy for backpacking.

Realizing this, many hikers made their own tarps of muslin or drill. These were waterproofed, and often were made up at home into small one-man tents. These light, cotton materials weren't as snagproof or waterproof as the heavier canvas, but they made up for it in lightness.

Recently a material has been invented for tents and tarpaulins which is half the weight of canvas. This is a nylon base, coated on both sides with vinyl plastic. It is tough, completely waterproof, and stands hard wear very well. Tarps of this material are available in a variety of sizes from mail-order houses.

The best overall size for a hiker's tarp is 8 feet

square. Most tarps of this new material are rectangular in shape. For occasional use, a size approximating 8-feet square will do. For the serious hiker who takes to the woods often, it's better to buy a large size, cut it down to 8 feet square, and re-hem it.

Regardless of material, one should have the local canvas shop put additional eyelets, or grommets, along all sides 18 inches apart. These prove most useful for tying down lean-tos and flys during wind, and for tightly wrapping bundles and gear.

Many old outdoorsmen and veteran hikers will say that even this load is too heavy. Many hikers, could do well in the woods without as much gear. But the purpose in being outdoors is not to see how much one can endure. The purpose is enjoyment, communion with nature, and rebuilding the body and spirit for the remainder of the year.

COLD-WEATHER GEAR

For traveling in snow and below-freezing temperatures, heavier gear is needed. The sleeping bag should be of down. The tarp should either be made into a small, floored tent, or used as a Baker tent or lean-to, with an all-night fire burning in front so that reflected heat will keep the sleeper warm. Deep snow requires snowshoes; level country and dry, frosty snow, skis. Increasing a pack-load to a full limit of 50 pounds, and then using it on webs which sink in at every step, is a job for only the hardy.

The problem of carrying sufficient gear in snowy climes can be solved, however, by using a light toboggan. In steep country, thick underbrush, or varied snow conditions, a man in good physical shape can still drag 75 pounds for many miles with no difficulty.

Under easier conditions, such as along snow-covered stream beds, over frozen lakes, or rolling, open country, 100 pounds is a mild load for a strong man.

The principle of the toboggan is that it distributes the load over a broad surface of snow, and its hard, polished undersurface reduces friction to a minimum. The center of gravity remains very low, preventing tip-overs in sloping country. For the winter traveler wishing to stay in the wilds for several days, the toboggan is an excellent way to transport his gear.

FOOD FOR THE TRAIL

The old Hudson Bay standard for food in the wilderness was 3 pounds per man per day. The traditional staples were the three B's—beans, bacon, and bannock. Tea was the favorite trail drink, as it was light, easily made, and provided more heat than coffee. Bannock was made on the spot from flour. Salt was included, of course. Together with what meat he could find, this simple diet kept the woodsman well fed. All trail food was chosen not only for its nutritional value but for its relative lack of water content and resistance to spoilage.

These should be the factors considered in selecting today's trail foods. Thanks to dehydration, we now can have a far greater variety of palatable foods.

The four basic foods are:

1. Milk and milk products
2. Bread and the cereal group
3. Fruit and vegetables
4. Meat and meat products

Keeping these requirements in mind, here is a sug-

gested list of food for the 40-pound pack-load, for one
man for a full week's stay:

Bacon (in slab)	1 pound
Powdered eggs	½ pound
Cereals (rolled oats, wheat hearts, prepared cereal, etc.)	1½ pounds
Instant tea or coffee	½ pound
(Substitute chocolate or bouillon cubes)	
Sugar	1 pound
Prepared pancake mix	1 pound
Salt, pepper, seasoning	½ pound
Cured ham	1½ pounds
Dried fruit (peaches, apples, prunes, etc.)	1½ pounds
Cooking foil	
Chocolate bars	½ pound
Dry beans	1 pound
Powdered milk	1 pound
Raisins	½ pound
Dehydrated vegetables	1 pound
Dried soups (in envelopes)	½ pound
Rice	½ pound
Pilot biscuit, hardtack, or crackers	1 pound
Chipped beef	½ pound
Macaroni	½ pound
Cheese	½ pound
Total	16½ pounds

Such a list includes the four basic food groups, and
when cooked properly will provide more than the
average man can eat. And fish or game can be added
for variety. In areas of mountain creeks, a bunch of
fresh watercress, picked from cold water, adds tang to

a meal. This list may, of course, be altered here and there according to the tastes of the individual.

In arranging meals, perishables should be consumed first. The ham, for example, might be used the first two days, with any remaining portion used in a pot of beans and ham for supper the third night. Combinations can also be made, such as a few raisins cooked with rice and sugared. Sugar, browned in a pan and mixed with boiling water, makes a fine hotcake syrup. Even a pocketful of threshed wheat, or pinole (described later), to chew on while walking is nourishing and pleasant.

With any grub list the hiker may make up, it's a good idea to try out at least a few of the dishes at home. Most people can stir hot water in soup-mix, soak beans overnight, or brew up a potful of dried fruit and water. But for any dishes you are uncertain about, such as pancakes in a tiny skillet, practice at least once at home where failure won't mean going hungry.

Foodstuffs for trail use should be packaged against both moisture and spillage. One of the best arrangements for such items as sugar, salt, beans, rice, and cereals is a double bag. The inner bag is a plastic container known as a refrigerator bag. The 1-quart size will hold a pint, or about half a pound of kernel goods, and still leave room to fasten the top with a doubled elastic band. This inner bag then goes inside a muslin bag sewed to size on the home sewing machine.

If you have the time, sew a loop seam and drawstring in the top of the muslin bag for tight closure. A simpler way is to use ordinary mailing tags. These have a tough string which you can tie around the top of the bag and label the contents on the tag.

PACKING THE LOAD

To assemble the pack, all foodstuffs, clothing, and gear are arranged on one corner of a folded tarp in a grouping approximately the size of the outside dimensions of the packboard. The entire bundle, except for the ax, is then wrapped in the tarp just as a Christmas package is wrapped—ends of tarp folded in and remainder wrapped around and around.

The wrapped pack is then laid on the back of the packboard and lashed firmly. Usually the bedroll rides on top, and relatively high. If the lower end of the pack can be made a trifle smaller than the middle, this prevents the entire load from sagging when it's lashed down. The ax is shoved head upward through the lashings so there is no possibility of losing it.

To shoulder such a pack alone, grasp the right strap in both hands (if you are right-handed) near its junction with the board. In a single hoisting movement, swing the load upward and to the right. At the end of this movement, and under the upward momentum, swing the right arm under the strap as far as possible toward the shoulder. The strap and weight usually come down with the strap over the upper arm. In another upward hoisting motion with the body, and with the strap loosening under momentum again, place the strap fully over the right shoulder with the left hand. Next, lean forward and bend to the left, letting the pack not only rest on the back, but gently roll to a position where the left strap may easily be placed over the shoulder with the left hand. It's largely a matter of hoisting up quickly and placing the straps while momentum creates a mild slackness in the straps. Care should be used not to twist the body too much, to guard against a slipped disc or other spinal injury.

When resting, experienced hikers pick out any sort of elevation, such as a blowdown, large rock, or tree limb, on which to set the packboard. Loading again becomes just a matter of bending forward and slipping the arms through the straps.

CHAPTER 3

Water Travel

The first craft that primitive man ever rode down a stream was probably a log. One may assume that, finding a particular log wasn't big enough to support his weight on water, he joined together two logs with roots or vines, thus constructing the first raft. Indeed, some of the earliest rafts of history were fashioned in this way. One consisted of three logs, the central log being longest, held apart with crossbars lashed to the logs. The Fiji Islanders built their war canoes on this catamaran principle derived from early rafts. Another step in the development of the raft came naturally when early man, in his need for lumber, tied trees together and floated them downstream. And when he learned to use dowels and sharp-edged tools, raft-making became far simpler.

Simple log rafts are still very useful in timbered country for crossing streams, moving around the shoreline of lakes, or even crossing when occasion demands. They are useful in moving one's equipment down a river when traveling along the bank in wilderness country presents too many obstacles, or when there is too much weight for backpacking.

A log raft is easily made where conifer timber grows

47

adjacent to a stream or lake. The only materials needed are dry timber, an ax, and some type of fastening such as spikes, baling wire, or rope.

WATER DISPLACEMENT

Before cutting into a stand of dry timber, however, the raft-maker should know something about the principle of water displacement. It will save him the annoyance of a day spent cutting timber, only to find that his finished raft sinks when he steps on it.

Briefly, water supports any type of craft if the volume of water displaced by that craft is equivalent in weight to the craft itself. To build a raft, then, it is necessary to have sufficient logs to displace enough water to support the weight of the raft and anyone riding on it.

Since the raft will be made of logs of varied shapes and sizes that taper from butt to tip, it would appear next to impossible for a man lacking a slide rule and a knowledge of engineering to estimate the amount of logs he'll need. Such is not the case. Anyone, by remembering a simple formula and by keeping all figures approximate, can estimate the proper weight to within a few pounds.

Let's take a practical example: Suppose that you come upon a high mountain lake, in lodgepole-pine country, where trout are jumping near the shoreline. You decide to make a simple raft in order to pole offshore and cast to them.

Just off to one side, we'll say, there is a stand of dry pines, some of which average 8 inches thick. The raft, let's suppose, will be 12 feet long, since timber of that length is handy and only one man will be using it.

A 12-foot log, averaging 8 inches in diameter, is about all one person can drag to the water's edge.

If the log averages 8 inches thick midway of its length, it will have a radius of 4 inches. The formula for obtaining the volume, or cubic feet, of any cylinder, is to multiply the radius by itself, times *pi* (3.1416, or roughly $3\frac{1}{7}$), times the length. All figures, for our purpose, should be expressed in feet.

The 4-inch radius, or $\frac{1}{3}$ of a foot, times itself, times $3\frac{1}{7}$, times 12, will equal 4.2 cubic feet, to the nearest tenth. The log, then, will displace 4.2 cubic feet of water. One cubic foot of water weighs 62.4 pounds. Multiplying 4.2 times 62.4, we get 262.08 pounds—the weight of water the log will displace.

This 8-inch pine log will weigh, if perfectly dry, 25 pounds per cubic foot, or 105 pounds. Subtracted from the weight of water displaced (262 pounds), leaves 157 pounds—the weight that the log will support in the water.

At this point some adjustments will have to be made. You will not want the raft to sink to the very top of the logs, as this would wet any load carried on it. Further, allowing the logs to ride well out of the water would not result in a direct proportion in log-height to total weight-lift, since the weight of the logs would remain constant, and have to be subtracted, regardless of the lessened weight. Again, if the timber happened to be partly wet, or after it had become water-logged from use, its own weight would increase well beyond 25 pounds per cubic foot. Also, if the upper sections of the 8-inch trees were to be used, as well they might, this would cut down on the total buoyancy. Maybe some would average only 6 inches. Lastly, since it would take you the better part of a day to build, you decide that you will make it a semipermanent conveyance; and that next month you will bring a partner or two along to enjoy the fishing. The total weight then would be 400 pounds or over on the completed raft.

For a complete safety and utility margin, then, the 157 pounds of buoyancy per log might well be cut way down to, say, 60 pounds. Assuming this figure, it would take about seven logs to support the total weight and allow the raft to ride well out of the water, as well as giving it enough width to prevent tipping.

BUILDING THE RAFT

To make the logs into a raft, roll or drag them to the water's edge. The logs should be alternated—that is, every other one turned end for end—so that both ends of the finished raft are about the same size.

Join the logs together by spiking a crossbar of 4-inch pine near either end. Added rigidity can be achieved if all the underlogs are slightly notched on top, where the crossbars will be set. You will get added length from short spikes if the top part of each crossbar is slightly notched where the spike will be driven. Avoid notching the crossbars too deeply, as this weakens the timbers. Notching the logs eliminates the need for a diagonal brace. All logs should be set as closely together as possible, to prevent a foot getting wedged—something that can be disastrous in fast water—and to prevent water from splashing on the duffel. Limbs should be cut off close to the log, and the logs rotated to get the closest fit.

Eight-inch spikes, set one to each junction, will hold a raft together for average use. For use in wild

Two methods of constructing a raft: If only baling wire or rope is available, crossbars are lashed to logs, and diagonal brace is lashed to crossbars to keep raft rigid. If spikes are handy, logs can be notched for crossbars, which are themselves notched to allow for deeper penetration of the spike (left).

water, or for heavier loads, each junction may be lashed with baling wire, and the ends bent down so as not to catch gear or person. Where weight is at a premium, sufficient baling wire to do the entire job will weigh less than the necessary spikes. When backpacking into an area where you expect to raft across streams, a coil of such wire sufficient to do the job may be carried on the packboard. Figure two loops

A sail can be rigged on a raft to take advantage of pre-vailing winds. Uprights are spiked to the crossbar and guyed with ropes on either side. Top crosspiece, lashed to uprights, prevents them from spreading. A tarp makes a suitable sail, and it can be spiked or tied through grommets at the four corners.

at each junction, or 6 feet of wire—85 feet of wire for the entire raft. If the crossbars are lashed with baling wire, a diagonal brace should be added to hold the raft perfectly rigid.

If considerable duffel is to be moved, a small platform may be built in the raft's center. The load should first be enclosed in a waterproof tarp and wrapped so that splashed water will drain off, not into, the gear. Then the load should be lashed solidly to the raft in case you run into fast water or a sudden storm.

PROPELLING A RAFT

Rafts of this type are ordinarily poled rather than rowed or paddled. A light pole of dry timber, long enough to reach the lake or stream bottom at its deepest point, is all that's needed. Stand toward the rear of the raft, poke the thick end of the pole into the bottom, then push downward and back. As the raft is forced away from you, continue pushing by alternating your hands upward along the pole's length. If you are traveling with a partner, one can pole on either side of the raft.

If a pole of sufficient length isn't available, a paddle may be made from a dry log, and spiked to a short pole handle. Cut the log in half and then split a slab of wood off the flat side of one half. Often it is easier to cut away the sides, leaving a plank at the middle. This is accomplished by scoring both sides with the ax at 3-inch intervals, then slicing off the side chips until a plank remains. In either case, the plank is roughly shaped, and spiked or wired to the handle. By alternately paddling a few strokes on each side, you can propel a raft in a slow, zig-zag fashion.

A breeze blowing in the right direction will move a raft slowly, and will move it faster if a sail is used. A simple sail can be erected on two upright poles fastened to the forward crossbar, guyed with ropes, and held rigidly apart by a cross member attached at either end. The sail may be a tarp tied at each of its four corners.

When floating gear on a raft down streams or large rivers, learn in advance whether there are any sizeable waterfalls, narrow chutes, or stretches of wild water. Such water can upset a raft. Lives and cargoes have been lost in such places. Where treacherous water is known to be ahead, rafts can be poled to the bank well in advance, cargoes portaged around, and the raft guided through with ropes and retrieved below.

RUBBER LIFE RAFTS

The rubber life rafts developed by the military during World War II, though intended for ocean survival, have been used by civilians for boating and fishing on small inland waters. These rafts carry prodigious weights for their own size. The original military rafts are now largely exhausted, but commercial versions are available. Where such craft can be transported to small inland waters, they are still very useful for sporting purposes.

When using a rubber life raft of any type, certain safety precautions must be observed to prevent mishap. First, because of its shallow draft, wide bottom, and odd shape, a rubber raft is almost uncontrollable in wind. It should not be used far out on lakes where sudden wind is a possibility. Again, for the same reasons, people must remain low in it to maintain any stability. When you stand up in a rubber raft, the entire craft is apt to kick out from under you like a thin wooden chip. Also, the short oars with which it is equipped are too flimsy to get a real hold in the water when fast turning or quick control is needed. Lastly, deterioration of the rubber fabric, due to age, weathering, and poor care, often makes these older rafts virtual death traps on a hot lake. If the raft is pumped too full, and the warmth of the day expands the air in the tubes, a blowout is apt to occur. I watched this happen at Water-Dog Lake in Wyoming. One of the fishermen was using a one-man rubber boat far out on the lake. The big tube of his raft gave way, and the smaller tubes wouldn't support his weight. He happened to be a good swimmer, and that saved his life.

In general, a rubber raft should have several separate air compartments. It should not be overloaded or overinflated and should be used reasonably close to shore.

BOATS FOR WILDERNESS TRAVEL

The most basic forms of the boat are still useful to the outdoorsman. One of these is the scow, which is little more than a rectangular box constructed of planking. It is moved either by poling or rowing, and is often used as a ferry. An improvement over the scow is the punt. This is generally a boat of 14 to 16 feet in length, with square ends, and either straight or sloping sides. Sometimes a skeg is placed at the stern to aid in steering.

Specialized boats for use in marsh country are often long and slim, with pointed bow and square transom, and are often poled. On one type, called a rail boat, a flat, elevated platform is built just ahead of the transom. The poler stands on this and shoves the craft along with a long pole.

One type of waterfowl boat has pointed ends, a high coaming, and is decked over except for a small space in the craft's center. The decking serves to protect the user from splashed water, and may be covered with foliage, grasses, or rushes for camouflage.

A more generally useful craft in inland country is a flat-bottomed skiff. This boat has a pointed bow, square stern, and comes in lengths of 14 feet or larger. It is propelled either with pole or oars.

An all-purpose craft has been developed for use on

inland waterways which combines the features of many other small boats. Such a boat usually has a pointed, upturned bow, a flat, or semirounded bottom, and a square transom. There is an appreciable flare to the sides, and the front of the bow is partially decked over. The boat is propelled by oars or a small outboard motor. It is made either of planking, plywood, aluminum, or bonded fiberglass. Boats of this kind are generally 14 to 16 feet in length. Smaller ones are available which can be carried on the top of a car and used for fishing small inland waters.

Almost every outdoorsman today knows how to handle a small outboard motor and appreciates its great advantages. However, in much of the remaining back country, boats must be rowed or poled. Poling a boat is similar to poling a raft: Sit or stand toward the rear of the boat, poke the pole into the bottom, and push. By alternating sides, you can keep the craft moving in a fairly straight line.

For rowing, oars, usually made of ash, are used, varying in length from 6 to over 7 feet, depending on the width of the boat's beam. Six-foot oars have 2-foot blades, and when set in the locks leave a space of approximately 6 inches between the handles when they are brought together. Longer oars still have this approximate distance between the handles, but have proportionately longer blades.

The safest oarlocks are those that have a small-diameter pin which goes through the oar and locks it in place. The lock itself fits into a metal base firmly attached with screws to the boat's railing. The lock also has a small hole drilled in the lower end of the post. This allows a cotter key or nail to be inserted and bent over, thus fastening the lock to the boat. This arrangement is safe on lakes and prevents losing an oar. However, on streams or during wind, or when the boat must be used near rocky shores, it's better not to lock the oar into the lower element. Often an oar has to be suddenly removed and used as a pole to prevent crashing against rocks or shore.

When traveling down rivers, especially those having areas of rough water, the bow should be pointed upstream. The rower gains several advantages by pointing the bow upstream. First, in fast water, he can row upstream, against the current, and slow his downstream pace. In white water, the rower sees exactly where he is going, and with a stroke of the oars can keep the craft riding parallel to the downstream waves. Also, by slowing the pace with judicious upstream rowing, he can cause the boat to ride gently with the troughs and crests of waves, preventing the shipping of water over the ends of his craft. The technique of keeping a small boat riding with heavy water, not against it, must be practiced to be learned.

Heavy water and high waves are sometimes unexpectedly encountered on small lakes, especially in mountainous country. An abrupt "blow" may come from a sudden change in temperature or pressure of the atmosphere, sending a virtual gale of wind tearing down a canyon. When caught on a lake in such a blow, head immediately for shore. If shore can't be reached in time, turn the boat's bow into the oncoming waves, allowing the wind to blow the boat to shore. The bow tends to split and ride up over the waves rather than receive their full force, as would the broader surface of the sides.

A rowboat should be equipped with a can or pail of at least 2-quart size for bailing out water caused by waves or leakage.

In case of an upset, the safest procedure is to *stay*

with the boat. Winds will eventually blow the craft to shore. River currents will also carry the helpless craft to milder water, and eventually to the bank. In analyzing many boating mishaps, it has been found that those who drowned felt certain they could swim to shore. The lone survivor was usually the person who elected to stay with the boat—often the timid one of the group.

DEVELOPMENT OF THE CANOE

One of the most romantic forms of inland water transportation is the canoe, and like the raft and the boat, canoes have had an interesting development. The birth of the canoe probably came when primitive man, riding his log downstream, conceived the idea that he might be able to ride inside the log instead of on it. The dugout canoe had its beginnings in that historic moment.

The dugout canoe, or pirogue, had to be patiently carved out of a single suitable tree trunk. There were various ways to do this, but the bulk of the wood was removed by burning the log (always stopping the fire before the shell became too thin), and chopping out a cavity with a primitive adze. The shape of the dugout had certain advantages over the log raft, notably the pointed ends and the upturned bow and stern. Simple keels, to aid in steering, were often incorporated in early dugouts. The early dugouts also had their disadvantages. Trees available in some areas were often too small, and dugouts made from them were too narrow and unstable. Often their gunwales were too low.

To improve the dugout canoe, certain modifications were attempted which in part paralleled the development of the log raft. The gunwales of the dugout were raised by the addition of hewn planking along each side—comparable to the addition of logs along each edge of the raft. Finished dugouts were often split down the middle, to give added beam width and stability, and the halves joined together at the bottom with a hewn plank. This, of course, necessitated similar shaped and curved center planking at the upturned bow and stern. The overall result was comparable to the stage of the raft where a flat, solid, reasonably watertight floor was achieved.

The next breakthrough in the development of the canoe came when man conceived the notion that stretching tough pliable skin over a wooden framework could be substituted for solid planking. It is entirely possible that this came about during the patching of solid dugouts. For centuries, animal skins had been used for clothing, tents, and water bottles. In the process of wedging skins into cracks, or over holes in wood, man may have gotten the idea of a skin and framework canoe.

The skin canoes and skin boats themselves have had an interesting development. As late as the white's settlement of America, bullboats were extensively used. These were small crafts made by stretching buffalo hides over willow framework. Some bullboats were cup-shaped and had about as much stability in water as a chip in a swill bucket, but they did serve to ferry or float occupants.

The Eskimo kayak is another form of the skin-over-framework design. The kayak is a long, narrow craft, pointed at either end, which is propelled by a double-ended paddle. The skin covering of the early models included not only the bottom, but all the deck area with the exception of a small round aperture, or cockpit, at the craft's center. The paddler sat in this opening and buttoned a skin apron, worn around his waist, over the aperture, making the entire craft watertight. With such an arrangement, he could capsize, roll over and come upright without shipping water. Indeed, during heavy waves, the user of a kayak often purposely capsized, then came up beyond an oncoming wave, to avoid strain on his light craft.

In the Arctic today, there are two remaining forms of the skin canoe which serve useful purposes. One is the tiny skin boat used mainly to retrieve hair seals shot in open water. This puny craft—about 7 feet long —is pointed at both ends, and is made from the hide of a single *oogruk,* or bearded seal. The framework is made of hand-shaped driftwood or whalebone. The sealskin is placed over the bottom of the canoe's skeleton, then laced with leather thong completely around the gunwales. The entire craft weighs only a few pounds and is hauled on a dog sled by the seal hunter. It is propelled for short distances with a single paddle, or with a paddle tied at each gunwale with thong and used as oars.

The other type of skin canoe, merely a larger version, may measure 28 feet in length. It, too, has a skeleton built of driftwood and whalebone. Six or seven sealskins sewed together into a shell are then laced around the gunwales. The skeleton of this type of craft will last for many years, and is placed upside-down on a whalebone rack during the winter. The covering is stored inside until the spring whaling season. I was told by the Eskimos that, with normal use, the skin of this seaworthy craft will last for three years. In such a craft, a crew of eight Eskimos will go to sea, kill bowhead whales weighing up to 60 tons, and bring the oil, blubber, and bone back to their villages.

The romantic birchbark canoe was an American Indian invention and was one of the most successful of the handcrafted canoes. A craft of light weight and high utility, it was made in great numbers in North America until the stands of suitable paper birch were depleted.

From early times, canoes have had certain advantages over boats for many types of water. They are light and therefore portable. They will handle large loads of duffel and cargo in rapid water. When rough water is encountered, an average-sized canoe can be portaged by one man. Canoes travel fast, with a minimum of effort and water disturbance. They may be taken into wilderness areas where larger, heavier types of watercraft could not be hauled.

MODERN CANOES

The American canoe evolved from the birchbark stage to the canvas and wood canoe popular in grandfather's time. Today, the best canoe for the outdoorsman is the aluminum type. It is light, rugged, and durable. The best size for the average person is a 17-footer. A canoe of this length, with a 36-inch beam and semiflat bottom, is very stable and will support two men and their gear easily in most water. It will have a depth amidships of just over 13 inches, and will weigh, depending on the gauge of the aluminum used, from 60 to 75 pounds. Such a craft will haul 600 to 800 pounds safely.

This relatively light weight puts the aluminum canoe in the same class as the early birchbark canoe, in that one man can portage it without undue difficulty. More, aluminum canoes, unlike the wood and canvas models, will not become waterlogged after being used, and the material never needs refinishing. They will also stand more abuse than the canvas models. And, because of mass production, the price is reasonable. Best of all, they will turn upright after being capsized. For use with an outboard motor, a square-sterned aluminum canoe is available. It is usually used for fishing and traveling on sheltered lakes.

Any heavy gear hauled in a canoe should be placed as near amidships as possible. This makes it easier to handle the craft in fast water or wind, where it must respond immediately to the paddle. All loads should be lashed down in case of an upset. This applies especially to the ax, grub, and supplies most needed for survival. Small packages needed during the day, such as a lunch, may be stored outside the main cargo. It's a good notion, too, to place a light covering of spruce boughs on the canoe's bottom under the cargo. If any water is shipped, it will drain from under the load and can be bailed out. The boughs serve the same purpose as the elevated platform on the raft. The weight distribution should be such that when completely loaded and in the water, the canoe rides with the stern just a trifle lower in the water than the bow.

HOW TO PADDLE A CANOE

Paddles for a canoe, unlike oars for a boat, should be related in size to the man, not the craft. A paddle should be just a bit shorter than the person using it. However, for best results the man in the stern should use a paddle just 5 inches shorter than his height.

Several types of hardwood are used for paddles, but ash is perhaps the best choice.

Unlike the rower of a boat who must use oars from a fixed position, the canoe paddler has an unfixed paddle and can work from several positions in the craft. For this reason, he has a greater variety of strokes available to him.

The basic stroke used in moving the craft forward is easier understood and practiced when two paddlers move the craft. Primarily, this stroke is made on the mechanical principle of a wheel and axis—the blade in the water represents the wheel's outside, and the canoeist is the axis. Any force at the paddle's end therefore tends to rotate the craft away from the direction of the stroke. With a paddler in the bow and stern paddling on either side, each offsets the lateral movement caused by the other's stroke.

For this type of stroke, the paddle blade is dipped deeply into the water and pulled back alongside the craft, the inside of the blade being turned slightly outward toward the end of each stroke. The movement of the arms is similar to the opposing motion of the pistons on a steam locomotive. The hand on the top of the paddle pushes forward as the lower hand goes back and, towards the end of the stroke, up. The stroke should not be made with the knob hand used as a pivot and all movement made with the lower hand; neither should the lower paddle hand remain stationary and all the movement made with the knob hand. Rather, the stroke should be made by a combination of pulling with the lower hand and pushing with the upper.

When only one man paddles a canoe, the finish of this basic stroke has to be altered so as to compensate for the lateral movement of the canoe. This may be done with two basic strokes:

One stroke begins with the blade of the paddle at right angles to the canoe. Once the stroke is begun, however, the blade is turned at a gradually increasing angle, like the feathering of an airplane propeller, with the inside of the blade toward the stern. The stroke is completed with the blade traveling closely against the side of the canoe. The different pitch at the end of the stroke tends to move the stern in an opposite direction, compensating for the opposite lateral movement caused by the first part of the stroke.

The second stroke is similar, but at the end of the stroke, and with the change in pitch not so pronounced, the paddle is moved outward against the water. The pattern of this stroke is similar to a fish hook, with the finish of the stroke being the shank. This outward motion offsets the initial tendency for the craft to move in the opposite direction. Both strokes are basic for the lone canoeist, and if done in a gradual rhythmic flow of movement, will keep the canoe on a straight course.

A single canoeist paddling from the bow executes the basic forward stroke by dipping the paddle into the water against the bow and pulling backward just beyond the body, finishing the stroke with the inside edge of the blade behind the outside edge.

To cause a canoe to back up, the first basic forward stroke mentioned is used in reverse.

To make a canoe move toward the paddle, the blade is reached outward from the craft, dipped in, and drawn toward the paddler.

If the canoeist wants the craft to turn in the direction opposite to his paddle, he dips the paddle in, either at bow or stern, and pushes outward in a generally sweeping motion.

Two paddlers, executing either of these two strokes, can turn the craft either right or left rapidly by making such strokes on opposing sides of the craft. Modifications of these strokes are made by either drawing or pushing the paddles in a diagonal direction, either toward or away from the canoe.

SAILING A CANOE

A temporary sail can be erected in a canoe to catch a favorable wind on a lake. This may be made by attaching a tarp or cloth to two 6-foot staves set upright nearly the canoe's width apart. The bottoms of the staves are braced at the bottom of the canoe by either the feet or packages of duffel, and the uprights are held in the hands, like the two rolls of a scroll.

A mild breeze will scoot the canoe along. If it turns into a stiff wind, the entire arrangement may be quickly lowered to prevent an upset. Attaching such a sail permanently is a mistake, as it may easily cause the canoe to capsize.

PACKING AND PORTAGING

Portaging involves heavy work, but in bad water is the lesser of two evils. While initially packaging and arranging duffel for canoe travel, some thought should be given to the problem of portaging. Gear should be divided according to weight and bulk, so that at the portage it won't have to be rearranged into portable packages. All large packages of gear should be within the weight tolerance of the packboard, pack basket, or tumpline.

Some of the best containers for carrying gear on canoe trips are the watertight portable ice packs used by the military in the tropics during World War II. These come in three sizes: Perhaps the most usable one is 19 inches high, 12 inches wide, and 9 inches thick. These containers are made of rugged fabric and rubber. On both larger sizes there are web shoulder straps and adjusting buckles, with ends molded integral with the container and positioned similarly to those on a packboard. It is thus possible to pick up the loaded container and carry it on one's back. The smaller container doesn't have shoulder straps, but has a web strap that makes it possible to carry the loaded package like a haversack slung over one shoulder.

To carry a canoe, place the two paddles across the center thwarts. Lash their knobs wide apart against the gunwales on one thwart and lash the blades to the other thwart so they slightly overlap each other. During portaging, the blades ride on the carrier's shoulders while he supports the forward portion of the canoe with his hands.

If the portage is long, it may be necessary to pad the shoulders with a rolled-up shirt or jacket. Some canoeists use a wooden yoke which fits over the shoulders and partially around the neck, similar to the old yokes used by western homesteaders for carrying two pails of water. Such yokes support the canoe's weight better, but represent an additional item to take along and portage.

For two men, shouldering a canoe is a simple chore. It is more difficult for one man, but there is a knack to it. Turn the canoe away from you onto its side and stand midway of its length. Bend over the craft and lift it onto one knee. Then, reach over and grasp

Army surplus ice packs are excellent waterproof containers for carrying gear on canoe trips. Shoulder straps permit carrying the container like a pack during portages.

the far end of the thwart and boost it upward in a rolling motion, helped by a lift from the knee, onto your back. Adjust it so that the paddle blades, or the yoke, is in position on your shoulders, and balance the craft with your hands at the gunwales.

To place the canoe into water without damaging it, set the stern into the water first. Then lift the bow until it is clear of any rocks, and gradually feed the canoe into the water. Two men do this easier than one. Each grasps an opposite side of the thwart or gunwale, lifting the canoe clear of the shore. One man must handle it by the bow.

ROUGH-WATER TACTICS

In streams too shallow or too rough to risk possible injury to the craft's bottom, a canoe often must be "lined" through the shallows by attaching a length of rope to each end and manipulating the craft from shore while it is in mid-stream. A coil of 100 feet of $\frac{3}{8}$-inch hemp rope is just right for a 50-foot length at both bow and stern. Nylon rope is better, as it is far stronger for its diameter.

In going upstream, the man with the bow line, which should be longer than the stern line, walks a bit ahead of the canoe. This angles the craft into the current, where it may be pulled forward and controlled by the lines.

When lining a canoe downstream, the bow line is kept shorter. This tends to keep the stern headed out. The canoe may be moved outward against the pull of the lines, or allowed to drift in closer depending upon the need.

There are no set rules for running fast water in stretches where it must be ridden out instead of lining or portaging. Fast water is fast because of the pull of gravity. Normally, where fast water occurs the bottom of the stream is rocky. This is a hazard for both the canoeist and the boatman when running wild water; hence, the deepest channel should be chosen through rapids. Here the current is the fastest, but it is safest since it is deep. Only experience in observing the riffles, eddies, swirls, backwashes, and oily chutes of fast water will enable a person to detect the submerged rocks which create them, and estimate the depth of the water.

The canoeist's best procedure is to stay parallel with the main current. Enough forward speed should be maintained to prevent back currents catching the craft and turning it sidewise. The responsibility for sighting dangerous rocks and currents rests with the bow paddler. The stern paddler anticipates the bow man's change of direction, and supports the action.

Kneeling is the safest position for paddling a canoe, as it keeps the center of gravity low. Do not sit and paddle in any kind of water representing even a mild danger.

REPAIRING THE CRAFT

Everyone who travels on the water should know how to repair minor damage to his craft. The farther you are away from tools and materials for making repairs, the more you need to know. With the older wood and canvas canoes, minor repairs of the fabric covering are made as follows:

1. The canoe is dried out.
2. The edges of the break are carefully lifted away around the immediate puncture.
3. A piece of canvas somewhat larger than the puncture is dipped in marine glue or waterproof cement and pressed into place under the outer shell, and the outer canvas covering is firmly pressed down against it.

A bag of powdered resin and a catalyst are better for the purpose, but necessitate leaving the craft out of the water overnight while the material hardens. This type of resin is very useful for welding broken wood in a canoe.

In cases where the wood has been too badly damaged, it sometimes has to be replaced on the spot with dry timber from the shoreline. Bending wooden parts, after steaming them in a container of hot water, represents a challenge, but it can be done with patience.

Aluminum canoes are repaired in a somewhat different way. If the break is too severe, the only cure is to have the craft welded by a professional. Fortunately, with aluminum canoes little or no metal is wasted or completely ruined when minor damage occurs. The edges of a break or puncture can be hammered into shape again, using a stone and a piece of wood in the same way that car fenders are repaired. The leak can then be filled with resin and left to set. If no resin is available, use chewing gum, old-fashioned pine gum, or a strip of adhesive tape. If spruce or pine gum is used, it works better when warmed with a bit of bacon fat.

Wooden boats often spring leaks en route and have to be repaired. Many times leaks at junctions can be repaired by removing fasteners and replacing the screws with longer ones. Leaks between seams may be plugged with caulking compound, or by pounding lamp wicking, or even cotton cloth which has been soaked in liquid cement, into the openings. A screwdriver or pocketknife is often the only tool needed. If the leak is bad, it is wise to dock the boat, let it dry thoroughly, and fill the crack with a mixture of the powdered resin and catalyst.

A new material called "poxy resin" will weld almost anything. It is particularly useful for repairing fiberglass craft. A repair kit containing all the necessary items for repairing fiberglass craft, including sheets of plastic cloth, costs only two to five dollars and is obtainable at most sporting goods stores and marinas. If the puncture is small, a gob of the resin mixture is applied directly over the hole. After thoroughly drying, it is sanded down and the repair is complete. For repairing larger holes, the craft must be completely dried out, and the damaged area sanded. A piece of the fiberglass cloth larger than the puncture is welded on with the resin, allowed to dry overnight, and sanded down. Fiberglass cloth has great tensile strength, and such a repair is usually quite permanent.

CHAPTER 4

Finding Your Way

One of the hazards most feared by those going into the outdoors is getting lost. As is usual with any hazard, those who know least about it, its preventatives and its solutions, are the ones who fear it most. Actually, the risk of getting permanently lost in the outdoors and undergoing severe hardships and possible tragedy is a minor one. There are far more risks involved in our daily use of electricity, pressure-cookers, automobiles, power saws, or construction scaffolding than in hiking into the wilderness. Yet we accept these other calculated risks every day, since the proportion of benefit far outweighs the likelihood of misfortune. We should have the same attitude toward our journeys into nature.

One of the first things to do before setting off on a hike into wilderness country is to leave word with the family or a neighbor just where you expect to go, and approximately how long you expect to remain. This is rescue insurance, in advance. Should you not return when expected, or within a reasonable time thereafter, others can begin looking for you. Many lost persons have been found while conserving their energies and waiting for a searching party. But you

71

should expect this kind of favor only if you have an abiding willingness to help rescue others, *any* time the need arises.

MAPS

The next precaution to take is to learn everything possible about the area. For this purpose, maps are your best source of information, unless the area is close to human habitation, in which case local information also helps. Any large-scale map of the state or province in which the area is located is good to begin with. Even the detailed highway maps in a road atlas are adequate. A map of this size will indicate mountains, peaks, rivers, large creeks, lakes, airports, roads, and the nearest towns or villages. Once the area you intend to explore has been located on this map, a more detailed map of the particular area should be obtained. This map should be of sufficiently large scale to show changes of elevation, all current or abandoned settlements or landmarks, all topographical features, townships (areas 6 miles square), degrees and minutes of latitude and longitude, and meridian lines. These meridian lines are survey lines and run in a true north-south direction.

Virtually every inch of North America has now been mapped, either by land or aerial survey. For the purposes of the average outdoorsman, detailed maps scaling four to six miles per inch will be sufficiently large. Maps of this scale are available from several sources, including the Department of Interior's Geological Survey, the Forest Service (maps of the National Forests in forty-one states), private map-makers catering to specialized interests such as mining and political surveys, and airports.

I have three detailed maps before me. One is the map of an entire state, obtained from a company making maps for prospectors. This one measures 29 by 36 inches, and shows all roads, creeks, and rivers, all sizeable lakes, county lines, township boundaries, National Forests, and all recorded mineral claims and locations. The marked boundaries of mineral locations, incidentally, are often helpful in getting one's bearings.

The second map is a detailed map of the Bridger Wilderness Area in Wyoming. This map is scaled to approximately six miles to the inch, and was obtained through a regional Forest Service office. It shows meridians, townships, all peaks and higher mountains, all creeks, lakes (numbering nearly 1000), roads and jumping-off spots around the Area's periphery, and the single horse trail traversing the region.

The third map is a detailed map of the Port Moller area in Alaska's Aleutian Islands, issued by the Geological Survey Division of the U.S. Department of the Interior. This map is scaled to 1:250,000, or four miles to the inch. It shows latitude to the quarter-degree, all water including two coast lines, settlements of any size, lakes, and islands. Of perhaps greatest value, this map shows all elevations from sea level with contour lines at intervals of 200, 250, 500, and 1000 feet.

For the serious outdoor traveler headed for remote wilderness country, the best maps are those issued by the U.S. Geological Survey, Federal Center, Colorado, or Washington 25, D.C. These cover all parts of continental United States and Alaska. Comparable topographic maps are available for Canada, and may be obtained from The Surveys and Engineering Branch, Department of Mines and Resources, Ottawa, Canada.

THE COMPASS AND HOW TO USE IT

Anyone going into strange country needs a compass. To many people, a compass is a little watchlike gadget which points north and shows them how to get out of the woods without getting lost. But a compass is only a precise instrument which indicates its own relationship to a given direction, as the earth relates in space to celestial bodies.

Here is an analogy that will give you a fair notion of how a compass acts: Imagine a railroad track which extends across the continent, headed in the general direction of a line between the sun at noon and the North Star. Assume that one end stops somewhere in northern Canada, and the other extends into the Pacific Ocean. Imagine further that there are similar parallel but slightly curving lines adjacent to this track, on both sides, which end in the same places. Lastly, imagine that you place a yardstick between the tracks of the railroad, paralleling them.

The tracks are comparable to the magnetic lines of force running through the earth, and ending in a "pole" in northern Canada; and an opposite pole out in the Pacific Ocean. The yardstick is the compass needle. From this homely comparison, it will be readily seen that a compass needle doesn't point north, or, in fact, at anything. It is merely a magnetized needle which, in the earth's magnetic field, will run parallel to the lines of magnetic force. If the compass, then, were taken to a spot in northern Canada just over the northern pole of this great magnet, the needle would point straight down. And if taken out into the Pacific Ocean over the opposite pole, the compass needle would point upward. Place a compass needle west of the earth's magnetic lines of force, and the needle will point east as well as north. Similarly, if the compass were taken to the east coast, east of the magnetic lines in the earth, the needle would point west as well as north, or some degree of northwest.

Carrying this to an extreme, if a compass were taken east of the north magnetic pole it would point west. West of the magnetic pole, the needle would point eastward. Only over a varying magnetic line running through the United States from central Lake Superior-Kentucky-North Carolina and off the eastern coast of Florida will a compass needle point true north.

The deviation, or declination, is shown for all parts of the United States on a chart obtainable from the United States Printing Office, Washington, D.C. Ask for "Map Of The Compass Declination In The United States." It is a valuable addition to a detailed map, and it is necessary when going into unfamiliar country as the declination will vary from that at home.

With these simple tools—compass, map, and declination chart—it is a simple matter in strange country to find true north. Lay the map on a flat surface such as a camp table. Place the compass on the map so that compass north lies precisely over one of the north-south meridians marked on the map. These meridians run true north and south. With the compass held solidly on the map, rotate the map itself until the needle points to the degree of compass variation shown for that area on the chart. Now both the map and the compass will be oriented to true north.

FINDING NORTH STAR

Another way to determine true north at a wilder-

Method of determining true north at night when North Star and Big Dipper are in alignment. Map placed beneath the string will orient the hiker to his surroundings.

ness camp at night is to find the Big Dipper and the North Star of the Ursa Major constellation. When the seventh star, at the dipper's handle, is either vertically above or below the North Star, the star itself is in a true north position.

This direction may be marked at camp by lining up one straight side of a tree at a marked height with the top of a stake driven into the ground and lined up with the star. In daylight, a fishing line or cord may be tied tightly between the two points, if desired, making a simple woods' compass. The map, laid precisely under the taut string, will show surrounding land features in their true direction.

SHADOW STICK

A unique method for determining directions in the woods was discovered by Bob Owendoff of Falls Church, Virginia. The method is so simple and reliable that the Army expects to adopt it.

All you need is a straight stick about 3 or 4 feet long. Set the stick in the ground in an open area where sun will strike it and cast a shadow. Mark the tip of the shadow with a stone. After a few minutes, when the shadow has moved over the ground, place another stone at the tip of the shadow. Draw a straight line through both stones.

This line runs east and west. The first stone is at the west end of the line. Now, if you draw the shortest line from the base of the stick to the east-west line, you will have found north (in the Northern Hemisphere).

You can also tell time with the shadow stick. Just draw a line parallel to the east-west line through the base of the stick. Then add a semicircle between the two parallels and centered on the stick. The shadow is a moving hour hand. Noon is the north line, 6 P.M. the east end of the semicircle.

ROUTE SKETCHING

An excellent method for finding one's way in the strange country is to sketch a map of the route of travel. This map should be begun at the point of departure into strange country. It should be drawn on some kind of tough paper which will withstand repeated folding, and should be enclosed in a waterproof envelope. Once the jumping-off place has been left, all vital information should be recorded. The best technique for doing this is to sketch the route as it unfolds, according to a reasonable scale of reduction, and place each bit of important data and all of the larger natural landmarks in proper position as you progress.

In practice it works like this: At the point of departure from familiar country, the initial thing to do is to draw a known boundary and note its true compass direction. This boundary may be an old road, a nearby river or creek, a deep canyon, or a row of mountains.

This landmark should be drawn to a scale that will permit the map to be completed on the available paper. For example, a map of average outdoor country covering a five-mile area can be sketched on a sheet 10 inches square, with a scale of half a mile to the inch. For rough or hazardous country, this scale can be increased to a quarter-mile per inch or larger.

One need not be an artist to sketch a simple map. Heavy lines may represent rivers, geographical boundaries, or roads. Continuing chain-links may represent mountains. High peaks may be indicated with an inverted letter V, and lakes may be drawn with a series of concentric circles. A vertical line topped with an inverted V makes a good "tree." If necessary, all may be more clearly identified with small lettering. Or, if space is limited, a legend may be made in the margin, such as: T = tree; L = lake; M = mountain; X = camp; B = bog, etc.

N

W · E

AREA TO BE EXPLORED

RETURN, 192°, 10 MILES
36°, 2½ MILES

LEGEND
L = lake
R = old tote road
∧ = peak
🌲 = tall tree on bluff
〰 = ridge
∘∘∘ = blazes
X = "Pivot" or place of beginning

L

RETURN, 107°
28½, 2½ MILES

RETURN, 216°
36°, 4 MILES
9½ MILES

X

R

∘∘∘∘∘∘∘∘∘∘ RIDGE IS 160°, ½ MILE FROM X

S

Example of a field-drawn map that will help a hiker find his way out of strange country. From point of departure, X, he has recorded compass readings on three prominent landmarks, a tree atop a distant hill, a lake, and a peak. To return from area to be explored, he will overcompensate on his course from the tree so he comes out on road R. If he undercompensates, he will hit blazed row of trees.

The next step consists of placing on the map all the more prominent landmarks within the limits of vision, recording their position on the compass from the point of departure and their estimated distance. Choose such landmarks as a large tree at the top of a distant hill, a distant peak, the end of a lake within sight, or the sharp bend of a river.

Up till now, the map will read something like this: Old logging road, with general course running north-north-east. The point of departure at the road's end. A peak, 36 degrees from this point, estimated as 4 miles away. Lake end, 287 degrees, 2 miles. Limestone promontory with tall fir tree, 2 degrees, 10 miles. Long wooded ridge, paralleling logging road, 260 degrees, 1/2 mile.

Incidentally, it is far more exact to record all compass directions in terms of degrees, not directions. Beginners learn to "box" a compass to the extent of sixteen directions. This isn't enough for the outdoorsman on extended trips into strange country. The variation of but a degree or two, when multiplied by an appreciable distance, can result in a sizeable error.

The map so far, simple as it is, can be extremely valuable to the hiker. For example, the peak recorded on the map can be used to find the way back by taking a compass reading exactly opposite from the recorded 36 degrees, or 216 degrees. This will point the way back to the end of the logging road. Similarly, a compass reading from the tall fir tree, at 182 degrees, will also point toward the end of the logging road.

Unfortunately, you cannot always head for a distant objective and reach it by hiking a straight line. Often you must detour a bit to avoid a swamp, a mountain cliff, areas of bad muskeg, or a lake.

When a zig-zag route is followed to an objective, in order to return a compensation must be made. If, for example, you veer off 10 degrees going, you must compensate 10 degrees in the opposite direction in order to return to your starting point. This is a matter not only of direction but of time. If you walk off course, say, for an hour, then you must compensate in returning for that distance. To do this, you must keep your wits about you and remember for how long, or for approximately how many miles, you have veered off course in order to offset this error on the return trip.

This cannot be done with accuracy. Often you will be tired when returning and mistakenly think you have traveled far enough in one direction to offset your shift in course. Also, the very nature of outdoor terrain makes it necessary to alter your course constantly. It is a good notion, for this reason, to locate the camp or point of departure along a creek, lake, old road, drain canal, ridge of hills, or similar boundary. Thus, if you miss your target, you can find it by going up or down the river or ridge.

The best way of doing this is to overcompensate on the return route. For example, suppose the camp is located near the eastern end of an old logging road, and that the direction of return is straight southward. Setting a course slightly west of south would bring you out on the road a bit west of camp. Knowing that you have overcompensated to the west, you can then proceed confidently east on the road until you find your camp.

Unless you are aware of your bearings, the tendency on a long hike is to go in a circle. It has been demonstrated that, while blindfolded, a person will travel in some degree of a circle. The tendency is more pronounced the farther he goes.

This can be quickly proven at home. In a field, select an object, say, 200 yards away. Then, with the eyes closed, walk toward it as far as is feasible without bumping into anything. On opening your eyes, you will find that you have traveled in a circle, or an arc of a circle, despite all effort to avoid it. Why this

By lining up three landmarks, A, B, and C, a hiker can stay on course without constantly consulting his compass. When he passes rock B, it becomes rear landmark and he spots a third beyond C.

happens is debatable. Some claim that it is because the normal stride of one leg is longer than that of the other leg. Whatever the reason, the result is the same.

One way to avoid circling, on clear days, is to walk keeping the sun at your back, or at any consistent angle. Naturally, the position of the sun will gradually change, but for short periods of time this won't cause too great an error, if you make periodic checks with the compass for the true reading.

The best way to stay on course is to pick out two landmarks in a line at different distances in front of you. Behind you, at the starting point, pick another landmark. Walk directly on a line toward the two forward landmarks, keeping all three in a straight line. When you reach the first landmark in front of you, the farthest landmark then becomes the first, and you select another distant landmark up ahead for the second. As you pass each landmark, it in turn becomes the rear one. By keeping all three landmarks in a straight line, you can maintain a fairly straight course for a considerable distance. This avoids constantly checking with the compass every few rods, and keeps your attention directed toward your objective.

In order to help you return to your camp or starting point, it is a good idea to mark the general camp area in some way so that it may be located at an appreciable distance. If camp happens to be in conifer country, or near any tall tree, a good way of marking the location plainly is to shinny up a tree and tie a white dish cloth or spare shirt to the top. Such a flag can be seen for great distances, especially when using binoculars.

BLAZING A TRAIL

A trail can be blazed from camp either on trees or brush. In some areas the defacing of living timber is prohibited so you must blaze the brush. (Blazing means to cut a strip of bark from a tree every so often along the route of travel to mark the trail for your return.) A blaze 6 inches long is sufficient, and if the strip of bark is left hanging it helps later to denote the age of the blaze.

When blazing brush, the tips are cut and bent over in the direction of the route. Brush should be blazed as near to your height as possible for easy visibility. It should also be done on twigs large enough not to be mistaken for the work of browsing moose.

Hardwood trees, or trees growing in arid climates, will retain blazes longer than trees growing in humid country. Also, larger trees will show blazes longer than small trees. Small, fast-growing trees will grow around the blazes, sealing them partially over. The foliage in Canadian and Alaskan bush country, because of the rank, humid growth, won't retain blazes too long. I have traveled along Canadian trails blazed by Tahltan Indians where only faint scars remained here and there on the scrub aspen or silver poplar. On the other hand, I have ridden over the trails made by Sheep Eater Indians in Idaho's rugged interior where their blazes on the big ponderosa pines were as plainly visible as the drawings they left in surrounding caves. These were made before the white man's settlement.

Too much blazing defeats the purpose and becomes confusing. This is especially true if two travelers happen to be in the same area and both blaze. In any case, blazes should be uniform in size and similar in characteristic. Then the maker can identify them as his own.

USING NATURE'S SIGNS

A seldom-used method of getting one's bearings is to learn the direction of the prevailing winds in the particular area. This may be done in clear weather by paying attention to breezes. When they appear, dry dust is sifted downward and will follow their direction. When the first clouds appear, their general direction will indicate the wind's direction. Heavy storm will normally come with the direction of prevailing winds.

One should not be misled by thermal breezes, the daily movement of air in mountains. Normally, warming air will rise, cooling air descend. This means that faint breezes will follow ridges upward in the morning and follow them downward at night. The changing weather will alter the course of winds, but if you observe the general pattern for several days, you can usually decide from what compass direction the prevailing winds come. This knowledge can be useful in foggy, stormy weather when neither the sun is visible during the day nor the stars at night.

For example, deciduous trees will shed their leaves in greatest bulk in the direction opposite from that of the prevailing winds—the winds blow them there. Again, if snow is on the ground, the pattern of its drifting will indicate the wind's course. On the windward side of large trees, the snow will tend to pack into a shelf. On the opposite side, because of eddying backcurrents, it will build up into a ridge. The trees themselves will often indicate the direction of the prevailing winds; branches, and even the trunk, may be bent in the opposite direction.

Trees may be used in other ways as compasses. On solitary trees, moss is apt to be thickest on the bark on the north side. This is not a dependable guide, however, when trees are growing in clumps and there is ample shade. Again, the bark of large trees will be thicker on the north side, as will the individual growth rings. Both may be measured by chopping into opposite sides of the tree and making a comparison.

Wild plants and flowers, too, may often be used as compasses. Where blossoms and stems form on a plant in an open area, they normally turn in the direction of the sunlight, just as plants in home windows, and garden flowers such as dahlias, will seek sunlight. This means that the preponderance of the flowers and stems will usually occur on the south and east sides of the plant. Where flowers have fallen, the remaining stems of many plants will still hold a readable message for the observing person.

GETTING LOST

While it is true that very few people become permanently lost and meet with disaster because of it, there are few outdoorsmen who have *never* become confused in the woods. The person who maintains that he's never been confused in the woods has never spent much time there, or else he is kidding you. This temporary confusion is not serious in itself, but it is all too often the point at which many people allow the situation to become critical.

The biggest danger in getting lost is the normal tendency to panic. The cure can be as certain. The person who has the self-control to defeat his own panic won't stay lost very long.

The first thing to do on becoming lost is to accept the fact calmly and stop traveling. Regard the situation as but a temporary nuisance, like fixing a flat tire. Next, try to locate an identifiable landmark. If you have followed the rules and have a compass and maps both detailed and field-made, this is simple. The compass will show directions. The field-made map will indicate approximately how far you are from camp. The detailed map will show other identifiable landmarks within striking distance.

In looking for landmarks, one should climb to the highest elevation possible within the immediate area. Lakes, streams, distant mountains, open areas, and valleys or canyons all show up well when seen from high above. If storm or sudden fog has blotted out the surroundings so this cannot be accomplished, the wise thing to do is to stop, conserve your strength, and wait until the weather clears and landmarks be come visible again. Often this requires staying out overnight or, in some cases, an extra day or so. This will be uncomfortable, but not necessarily harmful or fatal. The human body has enormous stores of energy and sustenance, some that are rarely tapped. Men have survived after a complete fast of thirty days or more. So the scarcity of food need not prove fatal, as long as water is available.

The secrets of survival are to conserve and ration your strength; make yourself as comfortable as possible; augment the body's energies with any form of food carried along; add to the supply of food, if possible, with edible wild plants, wild fruit, fish, or any small game; and lastly, build a fire and keep it going both day and night, piling on green boughs to make it smoke and smolder during the daylight hours. This will keep you warm and provide a signal day and night. There are few remaining places where a big smoldering fire cannot be spotted by someone. State Fish and Game Departments have regular patrol flights over the more remote fishing and hunting areas in their territory. In National Forests, a continuously smoking fire is certain to be detected by the Forest

CODE LETTER	MEANS
L	Require fuel and oil.
LL	All is well.
△	Safe to land here.
⌐K	Aircraft badly damaged.
▷	Indicate direction to proceed.
▷	Will attempt to take off.
→	Am proceeding in this direction.
N	No, or negative.
Y	Yes, or affirmative.
⌐L	Not understood.
W	Require engineer.
▢	Require compass and map.
‖	Require signal lamp.
I	Serious injuries. Require doctor.
II	Require medical supplies.
X	Unable to proceed.
F	Require food and water.
⋙	Require firearms and ammunition.

Service rangers, either from a lookout station or plane.

Civilian rescue groups, such as sheriff's posses, now operate in most of the more rugged areas. They use jeeps, saddle horses, snow tractors, aircraft, and boats. In addition, state and provincial air rescue groups now operate widely over the continent.

The best way to signal an airplane is to form the letters SOS on the ground. In open areas of snow, dark-colored saplings or poles can be laid on the white snow in the shape of these letters. On sandy beaches, especially if the sand is white, the letters may be spelled out with rows of rocks. Charred wood from a fire also makes a good contrast against light surfaces. In clear air, domestic chickens can be seen from a plane at 2000 feet. Contrasting letters 6 to 10 feet in size can be seen by most low-flying planes.

There has been developed in recent years a system of signaling known as the Ground-Air Emergency Code. The code consists mainly of large symbols stamped out in the snow or formed on the ground. The code symbols and their meaning are shown in the accompanying table.

A flare has been developed recently for use by lost persons signaling for help. It is called the Penguin Aerial Flare and consists of a small tubelike device which is held in the hand and shoots flare cartridges. A flare is threaded into the device and set off. It leaves the tube with a report comparable to that of a .22 blank cartridge and rises to a height of over 100 feet. As it rises, it leaves a bright red trail, and at the height of the rise bursts into a bright red ball of flame and gives off a loud report. It will burn for from three to five seconds.

CHAPTER 5

Forecasting the Weather

Outdoor trips can be delayed or completely ruined by adverse weather. Because of this, a basic knowledge of weather, and some ability in forecasting it, is vital to the outdoorsman. Though man is constantly learning more about the secrets of weather, much is still unknown. A standing joke is the wide disparity between the weather man's daily predictions, and the weather we actually get. This is largely due to the unstable nature of the many factors influencing the weather.

THE ATMOSPHERE

A knowledge of fundamental weather forecasting begins with an understanding of the earth's atmosphere and its relationship to the earth's surface. Briefly, the earth is completely surrounded by a band, or layer, of air into which a constantly varying amount of water is being evaporated. This evaporation of water into the air comes from the ocean areas—the greater part of the earth's surface—and inland waterways, as well as from the moist earth itself. This water vapor, seemingly in defiance of the law of gravity, accumulates in the air; condenses when the right combination of temperature, elevation, and saturation occurs; then drops as rain or snow. This is nature's way of irrigating the land areas of the earth.

The actual pattern by which this occurs begins to become evident when we understand that the layer of atmosphere is not constant as to pressure. The "normal" pressure of the atmosphere is equivalent to the weight of approximately 30 inches of mercury at sea level. At higher elevations, where there is less remaining air above, it is less. Indeed, a mercury column, showing to what height the air pressure would push mercury in a vacuum, was the earliest barometer, an instrument for measuring atmospheric pressures. Smaller barometers, based on the action of atmospheric pressures on a flat metal box which has been partially vacuumized, are available to the serious outdoorsman to whom weather changes are most vital.

Due to changes in temperature and elevation, and largely because of the earth's rotation on its axis, the pressures throughout the atmospheric band vary. Areas of low pressures are known as "lows" and areas of higher pressures are called "highs." The vapor in the air, being in the aggregate heavier than air, moves toward areas of low pressure, and fills in what are known as the "troughs." When sufficient moisture has accumulated, it forms clouds, condenses, and becomes rain or snow.

Winds are caused by unequal atmospheric pressure, and as a large area of moisture fills in a low-pressure area, winds form and become an integral part of the "low." It might be said then that "highs" indicate fair weather until the high pressures of the area are dispelled and that "lows" indicate building storms and wind, until the low-pressure area is moved, by masses of air movement, out of that region. "Low" areas may cover several states, or parts of states. The winds accompanying a low, in the Western Hemisphere, habitually blow around the low cell in a counterclockwise pattern.

As these clouds and winds form, they vary in intensity and place, because of differences in temperature and humidity, where they "bump into" areas of different pressures, and so forth. For one thing, clouds are generally higher by day than by night. They are higher in the tropics than at the earth's poles. And where the average height of clouds may range in summer from 10,000 to 12,000 feet, their average height in winter may be only one-third that height. All clouds are charged to some extent with electricity, which is most pronounced during thunderstorms. In a basic way, high clouds don't shed their moisture; low cloud formations do. Light-colored clouds are not apt to shed moisture; dark, dirty-colored clouds are.

CLOUD FORMATIONS

For the outdoorsman, simple weather forecasting may well begin by observing forming clouds and interpreting the winds that accompany them. Correlated with changes in temperature and matched to the season of the year and area, this information is enough to predict weather for the immediate future—at least far enough ahead to plan sensibly for outdoor activity.

Clouds are of four basic types: cirrus, cumulus, stratus, and nimbus. Broadly speaking, cirrus clouds are those feathery puffs of clouds high in the atmosphere, with slender fingers running out in all directions. A halo around the sun is simply light filtering through cirrus clouds. Cumulus clouds are big, white, rounded masses of individual clouds with a soft and fluffy appearance, and which often appear in fair weather in a blue sky. Stratus clouds are generally long horizontal banks or bands of clouds which form near the earth's surface, massing together so as to nearly cover the sky. Nimbus clouds are low masses having no definite contour, and from which rain or snow is usually falling.

These primary formations often overlap and modify as they descend, and become combination patterns. Such formations are known as cirro-cumulus, strato-cumulus, cumulo-nimbus, etc.

With only this meager knowledge, it is possible to predict simple weather probabilities and changes:

Suppose it has been clear and calm, but a breeze

Cirrus clouds are thin, white, feathery puffs which usually indicate fair weather. In abundance, however, they mean rain in twenty-four hours.

Cumulus clouds, fluffy horizontal masses in a blue sky, generally mean fair weather. They normally increase during the day but disappear at night.

Cumulus clouds building vertically in large banks are warning signs of possible brief showers, usually in the afternoon or evening.

gradually comes up, which settles into a steady and increasing wind. If the wind holds steady from the normal direction of storm for that area and season, it means a "low" is forming somewhere in that direction; that the actual storm is to the right of the person facing the wind, and that it might be smart to get the tent set up and the gear inside before dark.

Suppose a fresh breeze springs up during a prolonged rain. The rain has been from the southwest (normal for that area and time of year), but the new breeze is from the north and continues to come. This probably means that the low-pressure area may have bumped into an adjacent high-pressure area moving in from the north. The "high" is pushing the "low" out. It is likely to clear, and the weather turn cooler.

Perhaps it has been hot and sultry all day. By afternoon, banks of low, dirty-colored clouds form on the horizon and build fast. This may mean a localized "low," rapidly building because of the heat. If the cloud banks continue forming, a stiff wind may suddenly blow up ahead of them, and there may be a thunderstorm. If distant rumbling can be heard, or if distant lightning flashes can be seen before the wind arrives, the storm is liable to break any moment.

WEATHER SIGNS

It is useful to learn to recognize and interpret outdoor "signs" of weather changes. These signs are all about. Many are universal; others are localized in significance. Such signs occur in the atmosphere and heavenly bodies, in the foliage, and in the behavior patterns of birds, insects, and the different species of wildlife.

Stratus clouds are long grayish bands near the earth's surface. Their increase means rain is in the offing.

Nimbostratus, a form of nimbus clouds, are dark-gray masses close to the earth's surface from which rain or snow is falling or will fall. *All photos courtesy of U.S. Department of Commerce, Weather Bureau.*

As examples of atmospheric signs which may be used to predict weather changes, the following have been observed by enough outdoorsmen to make them fairly reliable:

A pronounced halo around the sun or moon in summer means probable rain within a day or so. A bright silvery moon in late summer or fall indicates frost.

In winter, when "sun dogs" (rainbow-colored arcs on either side of a halo) appear around the sun, either in early morning or late evening, it is a sign of much colder weather in the near future.

The old rhyme, "Rainbow in morning, sailor take warning; rainbow at night, sailor's delight," has much basis in fact.

A heavy dew on grass and weeds in early morning is an indication of clear weather for the remainder of the day. If the grass is dry in early morning, and the air has a hot, hushed and dry feeling, a storm is probably on the way.

The colors of the sky give some indication as to forthcoming weather changes. A bright blue color, changing from pale blue at the horizon to a deep indigo-blue at the zenith means clear weather. A hazier, grayer blue means dust in the air from winds, and possibly approaching storm. A "mackerel sky"— bits of high clouds speckled somewhat like the markings of a mackerel, and the total formation lying in a long elliptical shape—means winds aloft and approaching storm.

When smoke coming from a campfire hugs the ground as it rolls away, it means a storm is coming. Smoke that rises straight aloft from a fire means continuing clear weather.

For campers or hikers along the coastal areas, the

incidence of tides has a bearing on the weather. A falling tide lowers the atmospheric pressure; and with humid air, rain is more likely at low tide than at high tide.

High visibility over ocean water indicates coming rain since a normal haze over salt water is moved out by shifting air movements.

In many areas, better television reception is obtained when a thick cloud cover is overhead—the waves "bounce" downward from it. Similarly, a lowering cloud ceiling will cause sound waves to resonate. When distant sounds are loud and hollow-sounding, a rainstorm is on the way.

Odors afield become stronger under the influence of a low-pressure area. A high-pressure area pins them down—hence, when odors are strong storm is on the way or to be expected.

Foliage grows according to the prevailing winds, with its leaves lying in a natural position. Overturned leaves mean a shift in wind direction.

A sultry hot night, during a normally cool season of year, means approaching storm.

Low, blue-black storm clouds which rapidly build on the horizon in the direction from which prevailing rainstorms come, mean excessive rain and possible thundershowers. Preceded by sultry heat, and sudden gusts of cool air moving ahead, they mean hail.

WILDLIFE BEHAVIOR

The behavior of wildlife, if interpreted correctly, will provide clues to weather changes; indeed, wildlife are among our best weather prophets.

If elk, deer, or similar species behave peculiarly despite no contact with the sights, smells, or sounds associated with man, it usually means coming storm. With a big storm only hours away, elk will often bolt or stampede for no detectable reason.

During late fall, if elk suddenly begin migrating out of the high country, and apparently lose some of their fear of the presence of man, it means that heavy snowstorms are on the way—snows that would lock them in the high ranges. Elk will often move twenty-four hours ahead of such violent snowstorms.

Wild geese, similarly, move ahead of frigid weather southward to warmer climates as the bitter temperatures proceed. A temperature of 28 degrees will normally move geese from the lakes of the North country, which would freeze them in. If long wedges of migrating geese or whistling swans appear headed southward, you can bet that frigid weather is not far behind.

Grouse that stay all winter in timber country will bury themselves completely under the snow surface, their only air provided by a small hole. However, when their triangular tracks begin appearing on the snow, you may be sure the weather is about to clear of storm.

Waterfowl fly higher during clear weather, lower during stormy weather. When birds begin appearing, or start singing or flitting about after prolonged storm, it means that clear weather is not far away.

Prior to a summer thunderstorm, Chinese pheasants will usually crow repeatedly in areas just ahead of the coming storm.

In wooded country during the fall season, owls will often hoot intermittently throughout the night. This, in my own experience, has always meant storm of some sort within a period of three days.

The black bear is something of a long-range weather

forecaster. If he hibernates deep, and gathers a considerable amount of twigs for his bed, it usually means a cold winter with shallow snow. If a bear hibernates close to the surface, it normally means heavy winter snow.

If, in the spring, a black bear emerges from hibernation, then goes back to his den, it usually means that rain or a spell of hot weather has interrupted his sleep, but more cold weather is yet to come.

All of these weather signs will be affected to some degree by seasonal weather patterns and the particular region in which you live. However, when region, season, and weather history are taken into consideration, these signs will prove to be valuable indicators for short-term weather predictions.

DANGEROUS WEATHER

It is one thing to be able to predict bad weather to a reasonable degree, and yet another to be able to meet bad weather as it occurs in the outdoors. This means, in short, that the outdoorsman must be able to ride out bad weather with patience and philosophy and keep his equipment and himself dry during storm. He must also know how to meet dangerous weather.

Dangerous weather, for the outdoorsman, consists largely of thunderstorms, excessive windstorms such as cyclones and tornadoes, and to a lesser degree, unseasonal or violent snowstorms.

Thunderstorms are bred by heat, and reach a high degree of savagery on high mountain-tops, which are known as "weather breeders." They often come on the heels of hot, sultry weather when there is a hushed calm to the air. An experienced outdoorsman can almost "feel" a thunderstorm coming.

The natural reaction to being caught in a thunderstorm, is to get under something for protection. In wooded country, there may be no cover except trees, and the result is often fatal. High trees draw lightning. A single tall tree in an open area is worst of all, and most apt to be hit. Certain species of trees are more vulnerable to lightning than others; for example, it is said that oaks are hit more often than beeches.

The best place to be during lightning storms is close to the ground. One should not move; a moving animal or person is more apt to be struck than a stationary one. If caught in a thick wooded area, one can often do no better than to get under the protection of the shortest, thickest trees, and huddle till the electrical violence passes.

If you are caught in an open meadow, the safest procedure is to lie flat on your stomach. Rain usually accompanies lightning storms, but it is better to get soaked on the back than to be struck by lightning. If you can reach a brushy area before the storm gets too near, a good place to huddle is under the lowest, thickest foliage. A thick stand of any kind of foliage is far less apt to attract lightning than a single tree or bush.

During a lightning storm, you should not hold any implement containing steel. An ax, for example, with a metal bit and wet handle soaked with the salt from human perspiration, makes a fine invitation for electricity.

Violent wind can often be dangerous. It can blow you against trees or rocks, or topple rocks, dry trees, or limbs onto you. As in thunderstorms, safe places are close to the ground, in ditches or similar depressions in the earth, in a cave if available, under a rocky ledge (not one having loose rocks) or beneath an overhanging dirt bank. Regardless of the terrain, there will be *some* place accessible that is low and protected.

Cyclones and tornadoes are among the most violent of wind storms. Cyclones are tropic-bred. They are large storms, covering great areas. The inward-whirling movement of air characteristic of cyclones is thought to be induced in part by the cold air of polar regions meeting the rising hot, humid air. Cyclones are always accompanied by torrential rains and winds of high velocity.

Some warning of the approach of a cyclone is given by the sky. The sunrises and sunsets are bloody red. The air is sultry and oppressive. Cirrus clouds change to cirro-stratus, the barometer drops fast, the sky rapidly becomes overcast, and nimbus clouds occur. Soon, wind, water, and clouds are lashed to a fury, and the cyclone is on.

The only safe place in a cyclone is a storm cellar with the lid on. If you cannot get out of the storm area, stay close to the ground, behind solid embankments or rocky bluffs, or cling to something completely stationary.

A tornado is a small, localized whirling of air, like the cyclone in that both rotate counterclockwise in the Northern Hemisphere. Tornadoes are found only in the United States. They cross the land surface at from twenty to forty miles per hour, generally from west-south-west to east-north-east. The wind velocity, at the same time, may reach up to 400 miles per hour. Tornadoes are characterized by a dipping, twisting funnel, dropping down from low cumulo-nimbus squall clouds:

Like thunderstorms, tornadoes are bred from sultry weather conditions. The worst months for tornadoes are May through July, with the mid-winter months the least susceptible to these violent, funneling winds.

As with cyclones, the best place to be, if you are in the path of a tornado, is in a cellar with the lid on. However, due to the slow land speed, and their general direction being known, you can usually avoid an approaching tornado by traveling rapidly at right angles to its path.

A heavy fall of snow, especially if unexpected or if accompanied by wind, can be mildly dangerous to the outdoorsman. Generally speaking, such a storm can be predicted far enough in advance for a person to reach camp or adequate shelter before it gets too bad. In any case, a heavy snowstorm should be accepted with patience. If you stay in one place, keep a fire going, and conserve your strength, you'll be safe. With clearing weather, you can find your way to camp, or out of the country, without becoming lost.

CHAPTER 6

A Shelter
for the Night

Unless one is fortunate enough to stay in a wilderness cabin, the best outdoor shelter is a good tent, properly set up. The experience of generations has gone into tent making, and models are now available to suit every purpose. Whenever possible, the person going into the outdoors should take full advantage of the variety and high quality of modern tents.

Where the question of weight rules out packing a tent, the next best shelter is a tarp. The 8-by-8 foot tarp mentioned earlier for use with a packboard can be fashioned into various types of shelters. Often this can be done with nothing except simple framing material found on the spot.

If you are caught in a rainstorm while hiking with a packboard, you can in less than a minute shed the packboard, unroll the tarp, and slip under it with your duffel until the shower passes.

TARP SHELTERS

For a more permanent shelter, you can utilize material at hand as a temporary framework over which

104

A tarp is one of the most versatile of shelters. Pitched over a ridgepole lashed to a tree, and the sides pegged down, an 8-foot tarp will keep a sleeper dry in heavy storm.

the tarp can be spread. For instance, in timber country you can lay the end of a long sapling or pole on a fallen log, the other end on the ground. Then spread the tarp over this sapling in the shape of a letter A, leaving a space of about 1½ feet between the log and the upper end of the tarp. The sides of the tarp, of course, are pulled down tight and staked with cords from the grommets to wooden stakes or any available brush. The high end should be uphill. There is room under this shelter for you, your gear, and sleeping bag. It may be cramped, depending on the height of the log, but you will sleep dry.

A more roomy and comfortable A-tent arrangement can be made by fastening one end of the sapling to a blowdown or handy tree, and supporting the other end with two short shear poles. A shelter of this type can be 3 feet high and over 5 feet wide inside—room enough for sleeping and for storing gear. If a raincoat is in the duffel, you can hang it over the end, in case the wind direction changes.

In erecting any kind of shelter, attention should be given to the lay of the land with respect to drainage. It should be placed on high ground, in an area where considerable rain won't drain under it, and in a position so your head is as high or higher than your feet. If at all possible, it should be placed with its side toward the direction of the rain. Where this is impossible, the raincoat covers the open end.

You can quickly make another effective shelter by tying the end of a sapling to a tree trunk at about a 6-foot height. The other end of the sapling rests on the ground. Place the tarp over this ridgepole and tie one corner to its upper end near the tree, the opposite corner to the lower end. If the length of the pole, from tree to ground, is just over 11 feet, the tarp will just reach. If you want a space between the tree and the edge of the shelter for getting inside conveniently, then the ridgepole may be longer, and the upper end of the tarp tied farther back. The loose corners of the tarp are spread apart, and the edges of the tarp are tied down to stakes. The steepness of this shelter will allow rain to run off. Since a tree builds up the earth higher around its base, your head should be nearest the tree. Also, you have more room in that position for your head and shoulders, and you won't have to sleep with canvas in your face.

If two shear poles are substituted for the tree, even more room is afforded at the front of the shelter, and you can keep a fire burning at the entrance. When using these shear poles as a support for the front end of the ridgepole, the tops of both poles should be

Ridgepole can be supported by two shear poles and the tarp pitched in this manner. Back of tarp should face toward the wind.

slanted toward the rear of the shelter—otherwise the shelter will tip over forward. In this arrangement, it is best to have the back end face into the wind. A fire placed in front of such a shelter will reflect heat on a sleeper and can be used for cooking. If the fire is kept small, it may be built close enough to the shelter's front for you to sit on the end of your sleeping bag and cook, loaf about, or simply wait out a storm.

An even better form of tarp shelter may be made in the form of a lean-to. If two trees can be found close enough together, a ridgepole can be tied between them. If only one tree is available, shear poles can be set under one end of the ridgepole and the other end tied to the tree. In an area without any

With ridgepole lashed to two trees, tarp can be pitched as a lean-to. In chilly weather, heat from a fire built in front will be reflected onto bed at rear.

standing timber, shear poles can be used to support both ends of the ridgepole. To keep the finished shelter from toppling over sidewise, tie a guy rope to each shear pole where it joins the ridgepole and stake it at each side.

Once the ridgepole is set up solidly, lay several poles just over 8 feet long so they extend from the ridgepole to the ground. If the bottom ends are sharpened with an ax and stuck into the earth, the tops won't need too much anchoring, except for the two outside poles, which must be tied firmly to the ridgepole. The tarp is then spread over this framework and tied to the bottom of the outside poles.

Those outdoorsmen who often use lean-tos of this type usually sew a tapered flap to opposite sides of the tarp. These flaps become the sides of the lean-to forming a three-sided shelter, or half of an A-tent. With this type of shelter, the sleeping bag is laid lengthwise along the rear. A fire in front of the lean-to, if kept burning all night, warms the sleeper by heat reflected downward from the tarp slope, similar in principle to the reflector oven. The shallowest part of the lean-to, nearest the sleeper, is the warmest.

In swamp or muskeg country where the only available framework for a shelter may be underbrush, low bushes, or willows; or in desert country where the only "timber" is sagebrush, the tarp shelter is equally effective.

A clump of low willows can be used to support a tarp. Clear away all stalks and other brush from the side away from the wind. Then spread one side of the tarp over the clump, tie the eyelet cords to individual stalks, and lay the opposite side on the ground, stretched taut, and peg it down with willow stakes cut from the brush. The result isn't shapely, but it's a shelter.

Similarly, in sagebrush country, one side of the tarp may be spread over several closely-set sages, tied, and the opposite edge staked to the earth. The rear end can be made windproof by stuffing it with sagebrush tips built into a brushy "wall."

In low, swampy areas which are traversed mainly by boat, and where suitable framework is not available, you can use a boat or canoe to make a tarp lean-to. Turn the boat or canoe on its side and anchor it. Lay one edge of the tarp on the upper edge of the boat, and hold it down with heavy objects—oars, anchor, or anything handy. Stake the opposite edge of the tarp to the ground, and you have a waterproof shelter.

In the Arctic, the Eskimos who hunt during the winter always carry a short crosscut saw and squarebladed shovel on their dog sled. When staying out overnight, they cut blocks of packed snow with the saw, and build a small rectangular-shaped enclosure. They cover the top of the enclosure with a tarp, using snow and ice to hold the edges down. A small oil or kerosene stove provides some heat. The temperature outside may be 30 below zero. I spent one night in such a shelter near Cape Lisbourne in the Arctic Circle, together with two Eskimo guides. It was cramped and cold, but it was far better than no shelter.

In jack-pine country, one can even use a tarp to make a wigwam type of shelter. Tie three poles near their tops and spread them to form a tripod. Then lay a number of poles in the V at the top of the tripod to form a cone-like frame. Stretch the tarp over the framework, covering sufficient surface to make a weatherproof area on the ground beneath.

LEAN-TOS AND OTHER FRAME SHELTERS

Many of the shelters previously described can be built without using a tarp, if none is available. It will take longer, require more material, and the shelter won't be quite as waterproof, but it will be usable.

The lean-to is perhaps the best. The sloping poles are laid along the ridgepole in the same manner except that more are necessary to prevent the final covering from falling through. A thick covering of boughs then is laid over the sloping roof members. The best kind are green balsam, spruce, fir, or pine. These are not placed haphazardly in a pile, but laid individually in the manner that a house is shingled.

Place sloping poles close together along a ridgepole to make a bough lean-to. Starting at bottom, lay boughs with butts upward, overlapping them like shingles.

beginning at the bottom, with the butts pointing upward. The next row is laid similarly, with the tips overlapping a portion of the first row. Successive rows of boughs are laid in this manner up to the ridgepole. It is wise to lay several additional poles across the roof, to hold down the boughs firmly in case of wind. The sides of the lean-to may be built of saplings angled against the roof, their butts sharpened and driven into the ground. More boughs are then woven in and out between these sloping uprights until a suitable side wall is built. This type of lean-to will act as a windbreak, especially if dirt is piled along its outside edges, and it will shed an appreciable amount

Sections of bark can be used instead of evergreen boughs as covering for a lean-to. Bark is laid convex side up in overlapping rows.

of rain. Built in winter and covered with 3 to 5 inches of snow, it will make a very snug shelter.

In birch or aspen country, where plenty of large trees are available, sections of bark will make a fine covering for the roof of the lean-to. To remove the bark from a tree, girdle the trunk at 3-foot heights. Then vertically split the section of bark between on opposite sides. By pushing the toe of an ax blade between bark and tree, the bark may be pried away in a semicylindrical shape.

Rows of this cupped bark are laid, convex side up, along the length of the lean-to. Smaller sections of bark are then placed over the joints of the first row—much as curved tile is laid on a roof. Two or three rows of bark placed this way will make a waterproof roof.

Evergreen boughs can be used to build other types of shelters. One is an A-shelter, made with a ridgepole lashed between two trees, or lashed to one tree and supported by shear poles at the other end. Long green boughs placed butts down, with their tops leaning against the ridgepole, form the sides. In areas where long boughs are not available, short saplings may be used for the sides and shorter boughs woven through them.

Another bough shelter consists of a frame of three poles—a ridgepole set with one end on the ground, and the other end lashed to two shear poles which are sharpened at their butts and driven into the ground. The shears should lean slightly toward the ridgepole. The sides are then formed of boughs.

Evergreen boughs form the sides of this A-shelter. The butts are sharpened and driven into the ground.

This bough shelter consists of a frame of a ridgepole lashed to shear poles. Boughs are placed similarly to those in A-shelter.

One of the simplest shelters to make in cedar or juniper country is a tree shelter. Choose a thick cedar or juniper tree and cut off all the boughs on the side opposite the wind. Next, stand several saplings against the tree's overhanging branches, leaning them toward the trunk. The boughs cut away are then woven into the side walls so that the result resembles the entrance to a wigwam.

DESERT AND SEACOAST SHELTERS

Along seacoasts or in swampy areas where not too much timber is available, but where there is an abundance of grass or brush, a brush blind can be built using thin saplings as rafters and side studs. Others of smaller diameter are woven back and forth between these, forming a rough mesh. Through this mesh, long grass may be woven to make a good windbreak or shelter for temporary storm. A raincoat over the top helps to waterproof it.

In desert areas containing tumbleweed, heavy winds will blow stretches of the dry weeds across the plains, until they are caught by an obstruction such as a fenceline or a patch of sagebrush. Under the wind's

Saplings leaned against tree branch in shape of a wigwam can be woven with evergreen boughs to form a simple shelter.

pressure, tumbleweeds will matt together, and often a great heap of these weeds can be hollowed out and fashioned into a windbreak or shelter.

Another desert shelter can be made only of sagebrush. In order for sagebrush to hold together, the walls of any shelter must be thick. The best shape is that of a large letter U, with the walls gradually shaped inward until the whole affair is canopied over, quite like the entrance of an Eskimo igloo. The result looks like an overgrown outdoor adobe baking oven similar to the ones New Mexico Indians still use.

Along many large rivers, seacoasts, or desert arroyos, where clay or sandy soil is predominant, and water has cut channels over the centuries, abrupt and sizeable cutbanks are often left. Often these vertical banks have depressions cut into their sides which may be enlarged into a space big enough to permit a sleeper to lie down. With a night fire out front, they make snug shelters. However, flash floods in desert arroyos often pour down an unbelievable amount of mud and water. One must stay above the ocean tides along any seashore, of course, and there is always the possibility of a sudden rise in the water level of a river. When you bed-down in a cutbank, be sure you choose a safe spot; otherwise you may be washed away during the night.

ROCK SHELTERS

Rock shelters are often useful along rocky seacoasts and above timberline in mountainous country. The rock cairns built by waterfowl hunters are perhaps the best type. Like weed shelters, they are built in the form of a big letter U. The curved end of the shelter helps keep the built-up rock walls from tumbling. A fire at the opposite end helps keep you warm inside. With driftwood used as rafters, and a raincoat as roofing, a rock shelter becomes a snug, waterproof home.

Timberline in the conifer regions of most of the continent occurs at around the 10,000-foot elevation. Elevations above this are usually rocky in nature owing to soils having been weathered away and washed down. If you are hiking above timberline, it is wise whenever possible to descend into fringing timber before night overtakes you. But if you must spend the night up in the rocks, the first thing to do is to find the side of a bluff opposite to the prevailing wind. The leeward side of a bluff will have eddying currents of wind, but these are far more endurable than the blasts on the windward side. Look for shelving rock with a near-vertical or overhanging face. The back of such a place forms one wall and perhaps a partial roof. The ends of the shelter may be built up of flat rocks from talus slides. Heat from a fire in front will be reflected by the vertical wall or overhanging rock onto the sleeper. Smoke will be a problem, owing to the eddying wind currents, and the kindling perhaps only grass and bits of wood collected from the scrubby growth where the timberline tapers off.

CAVE SHELTERS

When you can find them, caves provide good ready-made shelters. Look for them when traveling in mountainous country. In many desert areas containing lava flow, caves are formed by the molten lava cooling around air pockets. Some caves formed this way are enormous; one even became a National Monument—The Craters Of The Moon. There are small ones spread throughout much of the lava desert of the West.

Some caution must be exercised in exploring caves. Caves are dark, so be sure to carry a good flashlight or lantern. Many caves are moist and drip water, making footing slick and hazardous. As one can easily get lost in the larger caves, never explore beyond the point where exit is certain. A 100-yard spool of fishing line tied near the entrance and uncoiled as you investigate will permit you to find your way back.

Small caves may be inhabited by bats, mice, packrats, or bobcats. Their presence may be indicated by smell, dung, or tracks in the dust of the cave floor. In using a cave for a shelter, stay near the mouth, just far enough inside beyond the overhang to prevent rain from coming in. Most caves smell better there. A fire at the cave's mouth will prevent any varmint from entering, or rodents from getting too close. I know of two men who used a rocky cave for a shelter, and during the night the big gray rats which also called it home nearly grazed up their sleeping bags.

SELECTING A CAMPSITE

In wooded country several factors influence the choice of a campsite: a suitable water supply; an area of ground level enough to pitch a tent or build a shelter and free from rain or snow drainage; the availability of wood for making a fire and shelter; and the incidence of mosquitoes or other insects.

A point of land that juts out into a lake or stream is a good place to pitch camp. Such a point is generally level enough for a tent or shelter. It allows a view in at least two directions. Water is handy. An open point of land catches available breezes and helps keep insects away. The danger of fire, caused by gusts of wind coming up, is minimized. And drainage is away from the campsite in three directions.

In desert travel, one usually carries his own water supply in a canteen. The main things to look for are some source of fuel for a fire, material for making a windbreak, and a spot for the sleeping bag free of desert cacti and other spined vegetation. Often this will be on the sheltered side of some low knoll, in a patch of high sagebrush. If you have brought along a tarp, and there is little danger of storm, lay it on the ground under the sleeping bag and fold half the tarp over the bed. Desert nights are cool, and dew will usually form towards morning. The tarp prevents any moisture from coming up from below, and keeps the dew off on top.

After the spring runoffs, good camping areas can be found on high gravel bars along riverways. The spring floods often carry huge piles of driftwood downstream, where they lodge in shallow water. After the heat of summer, the wood dries out and makes suitable firewood. If the shelter can be made against such a large pile, it not only furnishes fuel but acts as a windbreak. A little remodeling of the pile is often all that is necessary to have a suitable backdrop; and with a fire out front, such a spot can be very comfortable. Care should be taken to see that the spot is high enough above the prevailing waterline to be entirely safe from any sudden rise in water.

Old gravel bars, laid down centuries ago when a river was cutting its channel, are also good campsites. These overlook the river and normally have sufficient quicksand mixed with the gravel on the surface to be smoothed into a place for the bed. Pieces of old driftwood are usually found in such areas.

In high mountain country, the best place for a campsite is a small open space of level ground near a thick copse of timber and, if possible, near water. A lush growth of conifers or other foliage is usually a sign of the beginnings of a mountain spring.

When camping in snow, a thick copse of timber, as near a running creek as possible, provides a good windbreak and wood for fuel. If the creek is frozen or drifted over, it often can be found by digging. Often a spring in such an area will be warm enough at its origin so it does not freeze, and can be found by going a distance upstream. A boggy area, not covered with snow, sometimes indicates a spring. If no running water is present, snow can be melted, although snow water lacks the minerals to make it palatable and tastes flat. One of the reasons why tea became such a popular trail drink, especially during the winter, is that snow water had to be used; and tea not only warmed the person but made the water taste better.

Choosing a campsite in swampland presents difficulties. Usually the highest possible elevation—a small ridge or a neck of land between bodies of water—will be the driest place for a camp. Dampness in the sleeping area often has to be offset by piling boughs, leaves, or grass into a heap and placing the bed on top.

Where sufficient time and fuel are available, the sleeping area can sometimes be dried out a bit by building a fire over it and letting it burn for an hour or so. This burns down any roots and brush stumps and heats the ground beneath. Scrape the fire and coals away, sprinkle a layer of fresh earth over the blackened ashes, lay fresh boughs or grass over this, and place the bed on top. If you are without a bed of any sort, this arrangement will often keep you warm all night solely by the heat left in the ground from the fire. But make sure the fire has been extinguished or covered with earth before bedding-down, especially if dry fuel has been used. A fire blazing up beneath you in the middle of the night is not conducive to good sleep.

ANIMAL PESTS

Animal pests are a nuisance one has to contend with in the outdoors. In wilderness country, bears are especially bothersome. When you leave camp temporarily, be sure to hang your food where they can't reach it. One method is to enclose the food in a sack and suspend it from a tree limb at least 12 feet high and too small to support the weight of a bear. Attach a long rope to the sack, throw it over the limb, and tie the rope in an inaccessible place.

Grizzlies, far less numerous and wary, won't often come into a camp where there is activity or where the smell of smoke lingers. When they decide to, nothing except a high-powered rifle can stop them.

Rodents are a worse nuisance. Mice, chipmunks, and ground squirrels will eat foodstuffs and chew on fabrics. Food and valuable gear should be stored out of their reach, especially for the periods you are away from camp.

Porcupines are especially bad in timbered country. They crave salt and will gnaw the handles of axes and canoe paddles, as well as the leather of riding saddles and the rigging of packsaddles for the salt in the remaining perspiration. All such items should be placed high enough so that porcupines can't reach them.

Skunks are another very real hazard. It is a good policy to discard garbage far from the sleeping area— at least 50 to a 150 yards away. Skunks will usually find this by smell during the night, but if the main food supply is covered, they will usually be content with the garbage.

At a permanent campsite, where black bears have discovered a garbage pile and continuously return to it, you can rig an alarm system in the tent area so that a bruin announces his presence. One way is to lay a row of empty tin cans in openings between trees. Another is to run a fishing line around trees near the tent, pull it taut, and place the reel by the bed. A sudden banging of cans or the whirring of the reel during the night will alert you to the intruder. By yelling and throwing something in his direction you will usually scare him away. Experienced old pest-bears have to be killed or the camp moved.

CHAPTER 7

Firemaking

Fire, man's greatest discovery, has been a great civilizing influence; but, conversely, a warm campfire in the evening can also become the connecting link between modern man and his primal ancestry. However, no one has a moral right to use fire in the outdoors who will not assume responsibility for its hazards. A full understanding of the dangers of fire is necessary both to your safety and to your full enjoyment of the outdoors.

HAZARDS OF FIRE

The principal hazard of fire is that it will get out of control. There are many ways a campfire can do this. Sparks will fly from too large a fire or from wood which still holds moisture in its cells. A small fire often catches branches or brush which are too close for safety to the fire itself. As fire burns, it heats the surroundings and dries them out—often to the degree that otherwise green or wet material will burn. Ordinarily this occurs most unexpectedly. When the fire dies down, someone piles on a new supply of fuel —perhaps too much—and when the fresh fuel flames up, surrounding materials are ignited.

This is especially true near conifer trees. A fire under a green pine, for instance, will heat the boughs to the point where they easily catch fire. The green needles burn quickly; a flame shoots up the side of a tree, and the makings of a forest fire are there in seconds, for the fire will then jump from treetop to treetop where it can't be reached.

Wind is another cause of fires getting out of control. Often a fire will be safe until a sudden gust of wind, or a change in the wind's direction, either blows sparks into dry tinder or blows the flame itself into adjacent inflammable material. Many people don't realize that fire makes its own wind, and the larger the fire, the greater the draft in the immediate area. Wind is nothing more than air moved by a change in atmospheric pressure. There is a difference between relatively cool air, and the abrupt, red-hot air heated by a fire. This difference in pressures causes a sudden draft, or wind, causing a large fire built on a calm day to break into a roar.

Another, more insidious hazard of fire is its ability to creep along ground apparently barren of fuel. This is noticeably true in conifer woods where, as a result of blowdowns having accumulated over the ages, the top layer of ground is largely punk. Sometimes, after a fire has been thoroughly doused with water, live embers at the outer periphery will eat beneath the surface for some distance, come to the top, and catch onto dry needles.

Fire that gets out of control—often hours after apparently having been extinguished—does unbelievable damage. A burned conifer forest will take a hundred years to grow back again. I recently rode through a western forest that was almost completely consumed by fire forty years ago. One or two of the old charred stumps had a diameter of 18 inches. The new growth of pines averaged only 6 to 8 inches in diameter. Even when a fire consumes only part of the timber, the remaining trees are slowed down in growth from one-third to one-half. Scarred trees allow wood rot and insects to penetrate, further destroying their utility.

If you are aware of the dangers implicit in the use of fire in the outdoors, you can take the necessary precautions to prevent your campfire from ever getting out of control.

First of all, plan the camp so the fire will be on rocks, gravel, sand, or bare earth whenever possible. If only a grass or sod floor is available, clear off all grass down to damp earth in a 10-foot area and place the fire in the center of this circle. If you are in an area where doing this will leave an eyesore on the landscape, the turf may be shoveled away in blocks, piled up, and later replaced. To do this, simply cut down through the grass to a depth of 3 inches in a grid pattern to produce blocks of turf a foot square. After the first one is started, these are easily sliced off beneath the grass.

It is never safe to build a fire beneath a tree or against it. Neither is it safe to build a fire in a pile of dry driftwood along a stream bed—the wood needed should be removed from the pile. In desert country or rangeland, it is never safe to build a fire in a grassy area or in a high wind.

FIREPLACES

Once a spot for the fire has been chosen and cleared, it increases the safety factor, and also the convenience when cooking, to make some kind of fireplace.

One of the simplest is three rocks placed in the

form of a triangle. The fire is built in the center. Place the rocks with their flat surfaces up, then work them down into the ground so that the three top surfaces are even. This can be accurately determined by setting a pan of water on the rocks and noting on which side it spills.

A fireplace of rocks in the form of a stubby letter U has several advantages. The open end can be placed toward the wind, providing a draft for the fire. Fuel can be shoved in through this open end. Large cooking pots will rest on the sides, supported by hot coals built up nearly even with the top. Smaller pots may be hung over the fireplace on a dingle stick, rack, or tripod.

A dingle stick is a length of green sapling sharpened at the butt. It is shoved into the earth and angled over a rock support or a forked stick so that its tip hovers over the fire. A pot is hung on this end by the bail. The height is regulated by varying the distance of the supporting rock from the fire or by setting the forked-stick support higher or lower. Often Canadian guides merely bend a green alder or willow sapling toward the ground and tie the pot's bail to it with a wire fishing leader. The weight of the filled pot keeps the sapling bent, and a small fire can then be built under the pot.

A rack may be erected over the fireplace by shoving two forked sticks into the ground, one at either side, and laying a length of sapling into these forks. The ends of this horizontal bar may be tied to the forks for added support. Green saplings should be used, especially for the bar, otherwise it is apt to burn in two. A wire coat hanger, bent into a long loop with a hook at the bottom end makes a good potholder. So does a forked branch notched at the bottom end. The fork hangs on the bar; the notched end holds the pot.

A tripod of green saplings can be used to support pots over a rock fireplace as well as over other types of cooking fires. Three green saplings approximately 4 feet long form the tripod. Their butt ends are sharpened and shoved into the ground, straddling the fire. The tops are brought together and lashed in place. Wire is best, but cord or rope may be used if the fire is kept low.

With a bit more effort, a cooking crane can be made which will support heavy kettles and allow you to regulate the distance of the pot from the fire. The crane is begun by driving a 4- or 5-foot post into the ground by the side of the fireplace. Next, an arm is tied to this post with wire or rope so that it will be secure but still loose enough to swing when pushed. The outer end of the arm is tied to the top of the post with a rope. A pot, hooked to the end of the arm, can be swung over the fire or off to the side to regulate cooking heat.

Another type of fireplace, which is handy for a more permanent camp, is built of two rows of rocks set a foot or more apart with the fire between. Fewer rocks are necessary if a shallow pit is dug where the fire is made. Allow the fire to burn down to coals and rest the larger frying pans either across the rocks or directly on the coals. Dutch ovens are set on the coals, which are heaped upon the flanged lids. The heat can easily be regulated by shifting the coals along the space between the rocks. The Sheep Eater Indians often used this type of fireplace, and a few of the old rock rows are still visible in the West.

Where transportation permits, any of these cooking arrangements is improved by the addition of some kind of grid or length of flat metal. A piece of sheet iron placed across the sides of a rock fireplace provides a flat cooking surface that not only prevents spilling things but helps distribute the heat. A metal grid with legs is handy when it can be transported. It is set up directly over a bed of coals, with the four legs shoved into the ground, or else laid, with the legs folded under, across the top of a rock fireplace. A fine light grid may be made by bending light metal rods into a loop around each corner of the grate from an old electric oven, and cutting them at approximately 18-inch lengths. These legs will fold flat during transit.

One of the simplest fireplaces consists of two green logs 6 to 8 inches in diameter and about 3 feet long. These are laid on either side of the fire after it has burned down almost to coals. The green logs won't burn, and they permit the necessary draft to enter from either end. The cooking pots are simply set on the logs. Flatten the tops of the logs slightly with an ax, to prevent the pots from slipping. The size of the bed of cooking coals can be easily regulated by distributing them in the opening between the logs. Or the main fire can be kept going at one end, and the cooking coals raked toward the opposite end. The heat can be further regulated by moving the pots along the logs.

Often the outdoorsman must build a fire on wet ground, especially when camping in muskeg country in the North or in swampy areas in the South. The best method is to elevate the fire on a platform of poles and branches. Such a platform will soon dry out sufficiently to allow the fire to burn well. A fire built on wet ground is usually smoky and hard to keep going. The fire heats the ground, which in turn gives off steam that tends to put out the fire.

BUILDING A COOKING FIRE

Seasoned outdoorsmen all say to use hardwood for a cooking fire. This is fine in hardwood country. In other areas, one must use softwoods, pine splits, aspen branches, willows, mahogany clumps, damp driftwood, and even sagebrush. Many an early-day camper cooked up a fine mess of coffee and bacon over a fire burning nothing more aristocratic than buffalo chips.

Fuel for a cooking fire should be obtained, if possible, from standing timber. Even during the driest weather when the earth is parched, wood lying on the ground will have soaked up dampness. A fire made of such fuel will be smoky, slow-going, and hard to regulate.

It is important to remember that fire catches most easily onto wood that has been shaped so that it has the greatest amount of surface area in proportion to its bulk. For example, fire from a match won't ignite a pine split 2 inches in diameter. But if the stick is split into six slats, and one of these is shaved into paper-thin shavings, a match would quickly set fire to the shavings, and the burning shavings would ignite the slats. The point to remember is that the initial fuel should be *thin*, with considerable air available to every surface.

One good way of starting a fire, using pine splits, is to split several lengths into sticks an inch in diameter. These are shaved into "fuzz sticks." It is not easy to be able to whittle a series of shavings along the length of a stick without breaking any of them off, but with a little practice it can be done. Three or four of these fuzz sticks are laid on the ground, each crossing over the top of the other. More of the inch-thick sticks are then stood around this pile like the poles of a wigwam.

This arrangement allows air to circulate freely all around the shavings and wood. A match touched to the lower fuzz stick, on the windy side, will start the fire quickly and easily. All fires, incidentally, should be lit from the windy side.

Another method is to poke the fuzz sticks into the ground, leaning them together like the bundles of a wheat shock, and place larger sticks around them. A fine arrangement is to crosshatch several shaved sticks, like a small log pigpen, and lay larger wood on top. Any of these arrangements will allow free circulation of enough air to supply oxygen to the thin starting-fuel.

Waxed paper is a very useful fire-starter. Some purists would frown on it, but generally while they are shaving up a batch of "whittlin's," the other fellow's fire is under way. In damp weather, the waxed paper from a sandwich lunch will start a fire and keep it going until the heat dries larger twigs.

Another good fire-starter is a small wax candle. The tiny ones used to decorate birthday cakes will burn long enough to ignite even damp shavings. Carry a few in your coat pocket. Larger candles will serve the same purpose, will start even wetter wood, and can be used also for temporary camp lights.

A fine fire-starter can easily be made at home by rolling a foot-long section of newspaper into a solid stick and tying it with thread. Dip the roll of newspaper into a pan of melted paraffin wax until the hot wax saturates the entire roll. When the roll is dry, cut off half-inch lengths with a sharp knive. These can be carried in your pocket, and will quickly ignite a fire.

The woods themselves provide many suitable fire-starters. Regardless of the severity or duration of a storm, heartwood from dead, standing timber will remain dry. A little chopping will yield chips and small pieces sufficient to get a blaze going. When the fire becomes large enough, damp wood can be dried over it.

Often a storm will hit standing timber only on one side. Chopping into the sheltered side of a wet tree will produce dry wood just under the bark. Or after a light storm, the cambium layer at the inner surface of tree bark will still be dry, and this also makes a fine fire-starter. The shredded bark of dry cedar, unless actually hit by rain, will make a good fire-starter, even in a heavy rainstorm.

Another good starter found in conifer country is pitch. This is found in old, dry conifer stumps and exposed roots of timber long dead. Such pitch in a resin-impregnated stump or root is yellowish in color, and shows yellow and gummy when shaved with a knife.

A few shavings of pitch will start a fire as though coal-oil had been poured over the kindlings. Experienced outdoorsmen who have set up a permanent camp, look for such pitch roots as fire-starters. Even when plenty of dry wood is available, a few shavings of pitch wood will start a fire on a cool morning when otherwise one would be shivering and waiting for slower kindling to burn.

Generally speaking, a cooking fire should be small. Allow the fire to burn down to a bed of coals, if the available wood permits, and cook over it in its receding stage.

The fire for comfort should also be kept small. This minimizes danger and conserves both fuel and energy. Usually the fire used for cooking is later fed with available splits, tips of branches, or whatever is handy. This keeps one warm until bedtime. It should be a standing rule never to go to bed while a roaring fire is going.

Sometimes you will want your fire to last all night.

The best way to do this is to lay two round logs 2 inches apart over the coals. By morning, the logs will have burned partly through; or if small, completely through, but the ashes will have fallen over the remaining coals, sealing them from air. Or the burned log ends will have charred over, with live fire underneath. By blowing hard next morning, either into the ashes or against the log ends, the smoldering fire can be coaxed into flames. A few shavings or tinder placed on the coals will help. It also helps to build the initial fire in a shallow pit. Its sides help seal off any air from the coals.

KEEP YOUR MATCHES DRY

The most important necessity for firemaking in any area is dry matches. The best type for outdoor use are long wooden matches. The paper matches put up in book form, like those used by cigarette smokers, are next to useless in the woods. Even when dry, they have been properly dubbed "go-fur" matches—you light one, it goes out, and you go for another. After being wet, paper matches can't be lit.

The short wooden matches about 1½ inches long, called "safety" matches, are better but not ideal. They must be struck on the abrasive surface of their boxes, and this prevents their being carried loose in a pocket or match safe.

Standard wooden matches, 2½ inches long, can be lit by scratching them with a fingernail, by raking them across the pants, or by rubbing them on a hard, dry surface. These are the kind to carry on camping trips.

For extended trips especially, matches should be carried in some kind of waterproof match container.

Several are available. One is simply a plastic tube, long enough to accommodate a dozen wooden matches, which closes with a screw-on cap over a waterproof washer. Another is similar, but has a small compass in the top, making a useful combination.

A good match container can be made of two fired shotgun shells—a 12 gauge and a 20 gauge. The smaller shell is filled with matches, shoved into the larger shell, and sealed tight at the junction with melted paraffin or a couple of turns of scotch tape.

An even simpler container, but slightly more bulky, is a small, round bottle having a screw-on metal cap. A glass bottle is susceptible to breakage, but a small one carried in a coat pocket rarely breaks.

Of course, one is apt to leave even a match container at home. For this reason, it is a good policy to carry at least three paraffined matches in some article of gear. A hunter can remove the buttplate of his rifle, bore a $5/16$-inch hole $2\frac{1}{2}$ inches deep into the wood of the stock; poke in three matches which have been dipped in melted paraffin; and replace the buttplate.

Another trick is to bore a small hole into the top standard of the wooden packboard frame. The matches are inserted, and the aperture closed tightly, either by a small cork, rubber stopper, or wooden dowel. This plug is then cut off flush with the standard, and the matches become a part of the packboard. When you need them, the plug is removed with a knife tip.

Fishermen, who get wet more often than others, can carry three treated matches wrapped in a tiny plastic refrigerator bag or strip of vinyl sealed with scotch tape. The puny package is then slipped into the envelope carrying the fishing license. Most license envelopes are somewhat waterproof themselves, and this doubles the protection. Matches so treated and wrapped will survive a complete inundation in a river or creek and come out dry.

Other places to carry a few extra matches are in a money belt or in the pocket of a knife-sharpening kit. During hunting season, three matches may be placed inside an empty cartridge of .30 caliber or larger shell, and sealed with a small wooden plug.

FIRE WITHOUT MATCHES

In cases of emergency, when you might be caught in the woods without matches, there are four primitive methods of starting a fire.

FIRE DRILL

The first is fire by friction. The practical application of this principle is the fire drill. The idea is to make a bow that will revolve a spindle in a shallow notch in a board fast enough to create a spark.

The bow can be made from a curved branch of a length to permit at least a 30-inch of thong to be tied between its ends. It should be hefty enough to prevent undue springiness. A curved alder, aspen, or willow approximately an inch in diameter is suitable.

The bow string can be made from the leather laces of one's boots, a braided fishline, or nylon cord. A leather string a half-inch wide can be cut from a circular piece of leather by cutting from the edge in ever smaller circles until the center has been reached.

For the spindle and fire board, certain woods are better than others. Dry quaking aspen, dry willow, and dry cottonwood are among the best. The board is cut from a chunk of wood, reduced to about half-inch thick, 5 to 6 inches wide, and any length over a foot. One edge is squared like a board—flat on both sides, square on the edge. A half inch inside this edge, several cone-shaped holes are gouged halfway through the board. A V-notch is then cut from the board's edge to each hole. The apex of the V should extend nearly to the hole's center.

The spindle may be fashioned from a slab of the same wood, or a length of dry willow or aspen a foot long may be used. The spindle is not left round, but shaved into a six-sided stick, or hexagon. The hexagon shape prevents the string from slipping. One end is tapered, and the tip is sharpened somewhat like a pencil, though blunter. The other end is rounded off.

A 3-by-4 inch chunk of wood an inch thick over which the hand will fit is used for a knob to hold the spindle. On one side a small round hole is made, which will fit over the spindle.

A pile of dry tinder such as cedar bark, broken up, shredded, and rolled in the hands until it is a dry dust, is placed under one of the notches in the fire board. The bow is assembled by tying the thong to one end, wrapping it twice around the spindle, pulling it taut, and wrapping it around the other end of the bow. It's best to wrap this end rather than tie it. The wrapping is held in the palm, and the thumb is placed between thong and bow. This way, the tension on the thong may be increased by pressing the thumb toward the palm.

The round end of the spindle is placed under the knob, the tapered end into a notched hole in the board. By sawing back and forth on the bow like an inspired cellist, the spindle can be revolved. The idea is to start lightly, then increase the pressure. Long strokes are best, and with the increased pressure, these strokes should be speeded up.

If all goes well, smoke will appear at the notch. When it boils up, drop the bow, tap the smoking dust in the notch onto the tinder, and blow long and gently against it. The tiny spark created may thus be fanned into flame.

FLINT AND STEEL

Another primitive method of starting a fire is to strike flint sharply against steel. The steel must be an old file, the back of a pocketknife, or another object having a sharp corner or edge. The punk must be some material like the cotton wicking found in an old kerosene lamp. Finally, dry tinder such as mulched cedar bark is needed. All this assumes that you have a piece of flint.

With the dry tinder handy, the wicking is held in the hand on top of the flint. The steel is struck obliquely against the flint, so that any spark produced will land on the wicking. When that occurs, the wicking is placed quickly into the punk, held in the cupped hands, and blown against gently until the live spark catches onto the tinder.

MAGNIFYING GLASS

You can utilize the sun's rays to start a fire, if you have a magnifying glass. I have a reading glass 3 inches in diameter with a focal length of 7 inches with which I can start a fire every time. The only other necessities are a handful of punk and some

In an emergency, a fire can be started with some type of magnifying glass—the lens from a telescope or binoculars, a convex watch crystal, or even a flashlight lens. Here the author uses a large magnifying glass to focus the sun's rays on dry tinder. Shavings will be laid on once fire is started.

shavings. The best punk is the dry, rotten wood of a fallen and aged pine tree. Shredded cedar bark is also good. A handful, rolled into a ball and "bunched" on the ground, is ideal. The dry shavings are laid on this, once the blaze is started.

To make the fire, hold the magnifying glass at right angles to the sun, and move it back and forth until the rays are brought to a tiny pin-point of light on the tinder. Smoke will rise within seconds. The light should be kept steady on the point until the punk bursts into flame. Blowing lightly on the punk encourages this. When the live spark has burst into flame, the dry tinder and shavings are carefully laid on top.

FIREARM AND CARTRIDGE

Another method of starting a fire is with a firearm and a live cartridge. Remove the bullet from the cartridge by tapping it judiciously all around with a rock or the back edge of a knife while holding it firmly on another rock. Tapping loosens the crimp and expands the brass at the seating area until the bullet may be twisted out with the fingers.

With the bullet removed, the powder is fired into such inflammable material as cotton wadding or charred cloth. The resultant spark is then fanned into flame by blowing on it. It helps to put part of the live powder from the cartridge case with the punk. A small wad of cloth can be placed in the cartridge mouth and fired through the bore.

In some rather extensive field experimentation, both with revolvers and rifles, I have found that this method of starting a fire is most difficult to accomplish. Modern, progressive-burning powders, lacking the resistance of a heavy bullet to build pressures and facilitate combustion, tend to "blow" out of the bore as unburned kernels of powder, instead of igniting either the forward portion of the charge or the tinder.

EXTINGUISHING THE FIRE

It is just as important to know how to put out a fire as to know how to build one.

In general, it is always best to allow the fire to die down before attempting to put it out. It is easier if the fuel has been largely consumed; and the fire is more apt to be completely extinguished.

Next, the remaining wood may be slightly scattered, but *not* beyond the cleared area. This helps remaining fuel to burn up more quickly, and makes the bed of fire more shallow for soaking with water.

The final step is to drown the fire completely with water. Water should be poured onto a wood fire until it quits steaming. Careful attention should be given to the edges of the fire area. Occasionally the water is all dumped on the major part of the fire, with this thin border neglected. Afterward, fire creeps into adjacent dry grass or foliage.

In areas where sufficient water isn't available, such as in desert camps, the fire may be extinguished by allowing it to die completely, then burying it deeply with earth in which there is no foliage. If the earth is dug up in a circle just outside the fire area, the ditch formed acts as a safeguard against the possibility of fire creeping beyond.

CHAPTER 8

The Water Problem

Next to air, the most important immediate need of the human body is water. The body is composed of 67 per cent water, with the moisture level being continuously depleted and replenished. Normally, the body will lose moisture by perspiration, and as waste through the kidneys. The latter will run on an average of $2\frac{1}{2}$ to 3 pints per day, though slightly less during periods of excessive perspiration. It takes a minimum of at least $1\frac{1}{2}$ pints of water per day to keep the human organism functioning. Dehydration usually takes place, if all water intake is stopped, after approximately three days, four days at the very maximum. These are facts every outdoorsman should remember in planning his trips into the outdoors. Man can survive on little food for long periods of time if he doesn't exert himself, and if he has water. Lacking water, his chances of survival greatly diminish.

In wooded mountainous country, the water problem tends to solve itself. High mountains act as watersheds for melting snow and rain, forming springs, streams, and lakes. Born fresh from the earth, these sources of water are normally pure; thus the higher you go into wilderness country, the less likelihood of your finding the water contaminated.

This is especially true of mountain springs, creek beginnings, and alpine lakes. Contamination normally comes with the increasing incidence of people and industrial and human wastes. Most outdoor travelers in the mountainous West, as an example, have no hesitancy in taking a drink from any mountain spring or creek they come across, but they would be reluctant to drink from the river created by these same springs and creeks farther down.

This is no assurance that a mountain creek or even a spring is not contaminated. There is no visible way in which contamination can be determined. The only sure way is to have a chemical analysis made of the water.

The old notion that a creek, traveling through gravel, will purify itself, may or may not be true. Water traveling through rocks and gravel, however, does tend to dissipate any contamination originating higher up by sheer volume or increased dilution.

In many of the more widely traveled areas of the outdoors, such as the National Forests, contaminated water is usually marked. Signs stating "Good Drinking Water," or "Unfit For Drinking," should be heeded. In remote areas, one's nose becomes a partial guide. Water that has a peculiar odor should not be drunk until tested.

As an example of this, there is an area in British Columbia where the creeks and lakes smell peculiarly sulfurous. In the early days of the Alaska Highway, the small cafes in the region used to serve pop with meals because the water in that region comes from springs containing Epsom salts, and to drink it results in violent diarrhea.

PURIFYING WATER

There are several ways to purify questionable water. The oldest method is to boil it vigorously for at least five minutes. This kills any germs, but gives the water a flat taste, which can be offset somewhat by pouring the water back and forth between two containers.

An easier way to purify water is to treat it with chlorine or iodine. Chlorine tablets for this purpose are available at any drug store, with the required number of pills per gallon designated on the bottle. Household laundry products containing chlorine, such as Purex and Chlorox, will accomplish the same purpose. A small bottle of such a bleach taken along to treat questionable water isn't too much bother, considering the risks involved with impure water. The correct dosage for household bleach is eight drops per gallon of water. If the water is colored or turbid, use twelve drops per gallon. Tincture of iodine will also purify water. The ratio for iodine is sixteen drops per gallon.

When using any of these chemicals, the treated water should be allowed to stand for at least half an hour before drinking it. For this you may use any kind of container—even a birchbark kettle, described in Chapter 15. Water can even be boiled in such a bark kettle by heating rocks in a fire and dropping them into the water. If metal foil is available, a light "pot" may be made of the material, in which small amounts of water can be boiled by holding the pot directly above the fire. To make such a pot, find a green forked branch whose ends can be bent and tied in a knot or fastened with a string. A single branch-tip can sometimes be bent and tied into the shape of a small landing net or tennis racquet. Into this push a doubled sheet of aluminum foil, forming a pot at the bottom, and allowing an inch of foil to extend over the top all around which is folded down over the wooden loop. You can then pour water into this pot and hold it over the fire to boil.

Melted snow must sometimes be used for cooking water during the winter or in alpine areas above timberline. When using snow, dig down beneath the surface and get the whitest snow available. This occurs during the heaviest part of a storm, when the air is purest; and the whiter the snow the freer it is of dirt, conifer needles, etc. To purify snow water, either boil it for several minutes or treat it with one of the above chemicals. Many campers defeat the flat taste of snow water by making tea of it. Boiling the water for making tea purifies it in the same operation.

Ice and snow are both used for water by Eskimo hunters in the Arctic. They haul along several blocks of freshwater ice on the dog sled when hunting on the frozen ocean during winter. They melt the ice over a small oil or gasoline stove, prepare tea, and drink it scalding hot. Before tea was available to these hardy hunters, they used snow or ice water to cook meat, then drank the broth of the boiled meat.

LOCATING WATER IN THE MOUNTAINS

In unfamiliar mountain country, water can be located by several methods. One of the best is to use topographical and aerial maps. With maps of this type, it's just a matter of ascertaining your current location, getting a compass bearing on a stream, and going to it.

If no map is available, the overall contour and elevation of the terrain will indicate where to look for water. Water seeks lower elevations, of course, and this means that canyons, low valleys, and gorge bottoms are the most likely spots to find water in mountainous country. Climb to the highest immediate elevation and scout the lower areas. Binoculars help in pin-pointing areas, but creeks, small lakes, and any sizeable streams can often be seen by the eye alone. As water is a fine reflector, a curve in a watercourse is apt to catch the sunlight and reveal itself.

Foliage is another sign of water. Green, lush vegetation, or a more luxuriant growth than normal, suggests moisture and possibly a watercourse. A row of high willows or large bushes in any canyon bottom often indicates water.

Mountainsides are also good places to scout for water, and especially any areas of pale-green foliage occurring in a tiny pocket along a mountainside. Springs and bogs on a sidehill are normally accompanied by a lighter tint in foliage coloration.

Water also can be found at high altitudes just below remaining glacial snow. Pockets in the earth's surface in the general drainage area below the snow, are apt to be water-filled.

Dry creek beds in mountainous country which show evidence of early-spring runoff will almost certainly have outcroppings of water farther down their courses.

In heavily timbered country, the thriftiest stands

of trees will normally follow the areas of good surface moisture.

Game trails will help an observing person to locate water. In their natural pattern of woods movement, such species as deer, elk, and moose will normally intercept at least sufficient water to satisfy their thirst within the day's travel. Moose are especially helpful. They may be found high up on wooded plateaus during the heat of midday; but their tracks will show that they head for water both early in the day and toward dusk. In fact, the very presence of a moose normally indicates that water—often considerable quantities of it—is within walking distance. Upland birds such as the ruffed grouse also stay in the vicinity of water. The spoor of this bird usually means that a spring or creek is fairly close.

If you find a spring, scoop out the earth and rocks into a pocket, where the water bubbles up. By using the material scooped out to build a circular bank at the lower side, the pocket may be made large enough to dip up a full pail without muddying the water or getting any dirt into the bucket. Tiny springs will replenish themselves between dippings.

If the spring comes out of rocks, or trickles away downhill, you can make a small trough and "pipe" the water into a more accessible flow, under which you can set the pail.

A suitable trough of sufficient length can easily be made from a section of a straight pole, split lengthwise with an ax into halves. Gouge a V-notch along the center of one half with the toe of the ax, used as a chisel.

If a board is available, such as the slat from an orange crate, this can be made into a similar trough

A trough to pipe water from a mountain spring can be made of the split half of a straight pole with a V-notch gouged along its center. Rocks support the trough, which angles slightly downhill.

by splitting it in two lengthwise, then nailing the two pieces together at right angles to make a V-trough.

A strip of aspen bark cut wide enough to form a small crescent can be placed concave side upward to do the same job.

If a flat slab of rock can be found, it, too, can be made to create a small waterfall for the bucket.

When making a trough, pile earth and rocks underneath to form a solid trestle to where the water falls from the end.

WATER IN THE DESERT

The water problem is always most severe in arid country where sources of a new supply are often far away. When the water supply is short, there are many things you can do to stretch the available amount. You can ration the amount of water on hand. You can prolong your body supply of moisture greatly by refraining from hard exertion. Every effort should be made to keep from perspiring, as nothing will deplete the body's store of moisture faster than perspiring heavily on a hot day. When moving about, keep a constant lookout for any wild fruit or berries which may be eaten to relieve thirst. Most wild berries are edible, and are high in water content. On the other hand, do not eat anything containing much salt, as this increases thirst.

In desert areas, certain cacti contain small quantities of water in their barrels. The barrel cactus is one of the best. Often the wild desert sheep in cactus country will butt these plants, break the stubby barrel, and eat the moisture-filled pulp inside. Similarly, if you chop into a barrel cactus and eat the pulp, you can get enough moisture to keep you going.

The lowly cactus known as the prickly pear also has in the pulp under the spines a considerable amount of moisture. This can be chewed, the moisture sucked out, and the dry pulp spit out. In many desert areas, jackrabbits derive most of their water supply from prickly pears.

When the water supply is very low, you can get some relief for a dry mouth by holding a small, smooth pebble at the side of your tongue. This does not, of course, add any moisture to the body, but does stimulate the salivary glands to produce more moisture in the mouth.

The bloom of most wild flowers, including desert flowers, is edible. If eaten at daylight, small amounts of dew may be present, and this helps if the emergency is extended.

To get an idea of the very minimum amount of moisture the human body can survive on, consider the Australian aborigine who survives in the salty, uninhabitable outback. He eats rodents, bugs, ants, and insects—their bodies contain moisture. He follows any rain cloud in the sky, even for miles, until it gives up its moisture, then licks it up from the earth. He digs in land depressions where previous rains have gathered until his fingers get down to wet earth; then sucks the moisture from it and spits out the sand. He eats the roots of shrubs for the meager moisture they contain.

Or consider the Arctic explorer at the other end of the earth who was caught on an ice floe, and survived for days with no fresh water except the condensation of his breath on his hair, mustache, and parka collar.

If, after a partial degree of dehydration, you find a water supply, you should exert all your will power not to drink too fast and too much. Drinking too much water after dehydration is comparable to drinking too fast after overheating from strenuous exertion; you are certain to get nauseated and sick. A good way to take water after intense thirst is to soak any available piece of cloth, such as a strip cut from a shirttail, place it in the mouth and suck it, gradually increasing the amount.

With sensible planning, you need never get into any emergency this extreme. It is good insurance to know, however, that if you do, *anything* containing water or moisture will prolong the time before dehydration takes place. This includes any birds that can be killed, birds' eggs, rodents, roots, flowers, insects, or even earth down at the moisture-level that may be dug into and sucked dry.

If the thought of eating crickets, mice, and grasshoppers repulses you, remember that under circumstances of starvation or extreme thirst, things look differently. A man starved for three days will eat almost anything. A man suffering extreme thirst will drink anything. Wasn't it John the Baptist who not only survived in the wilderness on nothing except wild honey and locusts, but actually flourished on the diet?

CHAPTER 9

Meat for the Pot

Fresh meat is hard to carry on wilderness treks, and next to impossible to keep during the summer and fall months during which the majority of outdoor trips are taken. For this reason, the grub supply may have to be supplemented by wild game once you are on the trail. Usually this consists of such small game as rabbits, squirrels, and those species of upland gamebirds native to the area. Today's backcountry explorer finds such game as useful as did his forebears, and for extended jaunts has come to depend on it to a considerable extent for his meat supply.

In advance of any trek into an area where game is expected to be taken, learn the current regulations to make sure that such game may be legally in season during the time of the intended trip. Also, find out if the species likely to be found may be legally taken with rifled firearms. In some areas, for example, grouse may be taken only with shotguns.

FIREARMS

The best weapon for taking small game is a firearm. Through the decades, many types of firearms have been especially developed for meat hunting. One of the earliest was Marble's Game-Getter, a lightweight combination shotgun and .22 rifle with a skeleton stock. A selector made it possible to shoot either barrel. The gun was useful on small game at close ranges.

Another was Harrington & Richardson's Handy Gun, a .410 shotgun with a short barrel and no stock, just a pistol grip. Later, this gun was designated as a sawed-off shotgun by the Federal Government and was discontinued. Anyone owning this gun today must register it.

Other similar shotgun-rifle combinations have been manufactured. The Savage Arms Company, as an example, currently markets an over-under gun with .22 long rifle and .410 shotgun barrels. Recently, several types of survival guns have appeared which are designed for military personnel who are stranded in wilderness areas. Among the most successful of these is the Armalite AR-7 Explorer, an eight-shot automatic rifle chambered for the .22 long-rifle cartridge, which weighs under 3 pounds and can be broken down so the barrel and action fit inside the molded fiberglass stock. The rifle will then float. Skillfully used, it is one of the best weapons for bringing in meat for the camp. For extended wilderness stays, even where all gear must be backpacked, it would be wise to leave other duffel at home in order to include it. Up to a range of 50 to 75 yards, the rifle will shoot accurately enough to bag small game.

A less expensive but slightly bulkier gun for meat hunting is a bolt-action single-shot .22 rifle which may be handily taken down. An old one I have used for years measures just 26 inches when taken down into two pieces, and weighs under 3 pounds. Strapped to the back of a loaded packboard, it is easily carried.

An even lighter weapon for bagging grouse, rabbits, and squirrels (where permitted) is a lightweight .22 pistol. My old H & R 922, bought in the 1930 depression days for a few dollars, weighs only 23 ounces, and has bagged innumerable grouse and cottontails. Smith & Wesson's Airweight Kit Gun weighs only 14¼ ounces. It, too, handles the inexpensive .22 rimfire cartridges, which are greaseless and may be carried in bulk in a pocket.

The best way to shoot small game with a pistol is to approach as closely as possible; then sit down slowly and hold the gun in both hands. Shooting should be deliberate, as at a paper target.

An accessory that helps to steady the handgun is a leather thong used as a neck lanyard. The ends of the thong are tied so as to get approximately a 27-inch loop. In the end opposite the knot, a loop large enough to slip over the grip is made by tying a single overhand knot. The lanyard is placed around the neck, the loop slipped over the grip, the gun held in both hands, and the lanyard drawn taut. When used in the sitting position, the lanyard steadies the aim to an unbelievable extent. Used in this manner, a handgun will account for small game up to 25 yards. For this range, the .22 long-rifle cartridge is usually sufficient. Only hollow-point shells should ever be used on small game. The newer .22 WMR cartridge is better for the purpose, but requires a heavier handgun, and is far more noisy.

Small game such as cottontails, snowshoe rabbits, and the fool-hen species of grouse such as the Franklin and pine hen, may all be stalked to within this range. I have repeatedly photographed snowshoe rabbits and grouse as close as 8 feet. It's better to spend time slowly stalking the game for one good shot, than to fire at random and scare it away.

Franklin grouse and pine hens are especially easy to bowl over with a rock. Ruffed grouse, except in wilderness country, are far more wary. So are adult sage grouse, squirrels, and cottontail rabbits, though an occasional young one of all these may be hit with a rock.

A Wyoming outfitter once told me that he had often caught fool hens, which are the most stupid species of grouse, with a length of fishing line tied to a long, slim willow or jack pine. He tied the line to the pole's end, then formed a loop at the line's other end. By moving slowly and carefully he could often approach a fool hen, lower the loop over its head, and with one quick jerk have grouse for supper.

HUNTING WITH A SLING

The ancient sling, such as Biblical David used against Goliath, is an effective emergency weapon. Used with stones about the size of a hen's egg, it has ample power for knocking down small game and grouse at several rods. It takes a little practice to learn to use a sling properly and develop the accuracy necessary for hitting small game.

A sling is made of two leather thongs and a "pocket." The tough leather laces used for heavy boots are fine for the purpose, and may be used in an emergency. The leather pocket is made from soft leather such as buckskin, or, when vitally needed, from the tongue of a shoe or boot. This pocket is cut

Pocket for hunting sling is made from triangular piece of leather with small, diamond-shaped hole cut in the center. Thongs are tied to each corner through slits.

in a diamond shape, approximately 5 inches long by 3 wide. It helps to cut a tiny diamond-shaped hole in the exact center of the pocket, to permit the stone to nestle more firmly into the leather. At each corner of the longer dimension a slit is cut far enough inside the pocket's edge so that the remaining leather won't tear out under a strain. A leather thong is then tied into each of these cuts, using a slip knot or three half-hitches. A 2-foot sling is a good size for the beginner. Both thongs are cut 26 inches long, and a loop formed at the end of one with a bowline knot, for use around a finger.

To use a sling, place a round, smooth stone into the pocket and hold it with the left hand (for a right-handed thrower). Thread the looped thong over the middle finger of the right hand and hold it there by crooking the finger. Then grasp the other thong between the thumb and index finger at a point so that the two thongs are the same length between hand and pocket. Next, lower the pocket gently so that the stone holds the thongs taut, with the stone resting alongside the leg. In a sweeping motion, whirl the sling rapidly around the head at arm's length. Centrifugal force holds the stone in the pocket. At about the fourth whirl, as the rock comes from behind in a right sweep, let go of the loose thong-end, whipping the stone forward with considerable force. Like pistol shooting, becoming proficient with a sling requires ammunition of consistent size and lots of practice.

Hunting sling is whirled around the head to get momentum, then thong-end held between thumb and index finger is released as rock comes forward in a right sweep. The stone is whipped forward and away with great force—but it takes practice to develop accuracy.

THE SLINGSHOT

A far more accurate though less powerful emergency weapon is the old-fashioned slingshot. In grandfather's day, any farm boy worth his salt not only owned a slingshot, but was quite deadly with it.

The rubber bands were strips 5⁄8″ wide cut from an old bicycle or auto tube. After they were tied to the arms of a crotch stick, they measured 8 to 9 inches long. The pocket was cut from the tongue of an old shoe.

Finding a suitable crotch was painstaking work. A good crotch had to fork evenly in the middle, and the forks themselves had to be at least 4 inches long. The butt, or handle, had to be 4 inches long and up to 3⁄4-inch in diameter. The branches of plum or apple trees yielded the best crotches.

To assemble the slingshot, one end of each rubber band was fastened to a slit cut in the pocket. Usually one boy threaded the rubber band through the slit, bending it back over itself, while another boy wound string around the join, finishing with a square knot. The other end of each rubber band was folded lengthwise, laid against a circular notch cut around each of the crotch's forks a quarter inch from the tips, and similarly wound and tied with string. The notch held the rubber band from slipping off the end of the fork.

Ammunition for a slingshot was any round pebbles a boy could find, approximately the size of a marble. With such an outfit, he could bag birds, ground squirrels, cottontail rabbits, and similar-sized quarry.

With a modern commercial slingshot, and the uniform ammunition available, a high degree of accuracy can be attained with practice. For practice, pebbles or lead fishing sinkers may be used. For hunting small game, special ammunition is available at a reasonable price. Most manufacturers of slingshots sell extra rubber bands.

STEEL TRAPS

Cottontails, snowshoe rabbits, and jackrabbits are especially easy to trap where they occur in appreciable numbers. And the easiest way of trapping them is with a steel trap. A single-spring steel trap, size #1, weighs under a pound. It comes equipped with a short length of chain with an integral spike at the end, which may be driven into a log or tree to anchor the trap. In addition to this, it is wise to bend onto the chain ring a 3-foot length of ordinary baling wire with which to anchor the trap to a stake or bush.

Trapping an animal is an art employing deception. The trap must be so placed that the animal in its normal course of travel will pass over the trap without suspecting its presence, step on the pan, and set it off. This normally requires concealing the trap; and for animals with a keen sense of smell, it means that all traces of human odor must also be removed.

Rabbits, however, pay little attention to human odor, and not much more to visual signs left by people; hence trapping them is easy. The trap is usually concealed in a runway, trail, or entrance to a burrow. To set a runway trap, a spot must be found where rabbits move about considerably. This is often a trail through underbrush or along a stream bank. In heavy desert sagebrush, jackrabbits make numerous trails between high sages. A study of the tracks will indicate both the quantity of game and those places where the bunnies travel most. The place for the trap is where tracks are thickest.

Setting trap in ground: 1. Trap is set in shallow, scooped-out spot in trail where tracks are numerous. 2. At areas X in figure 1, dirt is carefully sifted between jaws and trigger-pan until a cone-shaped elevation is made just higher than the pan. Be sure no dirt gets under pan, as this will prevent tripping. When dirt cone is just higher than pan, light twigs and tiny sticks (like toothpicks) are laid across dirt-cone top. Leaves are laid on these, and the set is lightly brushed so covering looks natural.

First, hollow out a place in the dirt deep enough to lay the set trap without its jaws protruding above the surface. Next, sift small quantities of the scooped-out dirt into the trap, between open jaws and pan, to build up a tiny inverted cone. When the top of the cone is above the level of the pan, lay tiny needle-like twigs across its top, forming a trap pad. This keeps the covering of leaves from sinking in and tripping the pan. Lastly, scatter leaves thinly over the entire trap, and cover the leaves with a thin layer of dust. By brushing the entire surface lightly with a leafy branch, the set may be made to look like a natural part of the forest. The chain is anchored to a bush, tree, or log, and similarly concealed.

When snow is on the ground, the trap is set and placed in the bottom of a small scooped-out place in the snow. The bottom of this hollow should be flat so the set trap won't tilt. Next, lay a block of snow, or a piece of snow crust slightly larger than the hollowed-out area, over the trap. With a knife shave the entire top portion of this snow block, little by little, until only a thin shell of snow remains. This prevents the trap from freezing and makes a bridge of snow over the trap thin enough so the foot of a rabbit or other animal will break through and trip the pan. The anchoring chain is similarly concealed under the snow. Sprinkling the surface with snow, or brushing it with a twig, removes all evidence of the set.

Setting trap in snow: 1. Trap is set inside small, scooped-out hole in snow. 2. A slab of snow is found, or shaped, large enough to fit across the opening. 3. With slab in place, surface is shaved with edge of knife carefully so that it becomes very thin (as thin as the strength of the packed snow will permit) over the trap's pan. Trap should be set deep enough into hole so that there is air space enough for jaws to trip without hitting snow covering.

Such a snow-set is used in the Arctic for white foxes, which are far more wary than rabbits. On a trip inland from the coast, an Eskimo hunter will poke a piece of driftwood into the snow on top of a small knoll. On the next trip, he will return to the spot and observe whether a fox has left tracks and urinated on the stick. If so, he makes a snow-set close by. Owing to the scarcity of trees in the area, the fox will return to the stick for the same purpose and be caught in the trap.

When baiting a trap, place the food in a position so that the animal must get under it to eat. The trap is set beneath. For rabbits, suspend bits of lettuce, a carrot, or a piece of cabbage on a piece of string from a foot to 18 inches above the trap. During winter or after heavy snowfall, a bunch of grass dug beneath the snow and hung in this way makes a good bait. As with any set, a baited trap should be placed where evidence of the game is greatest. Its success is largely determined by the amount of game and the scarcity of the food supply.

BOX TRAP

A baited box trap will catch squirrels, cottontails, and other small game—if you have sufficient patience. The box is set precariously on the end of a small stick which rests on some hard surface, like a flat rock or tiny chip, and a string is attached to the bottom end. The string, concealed by leaves or dirt, leads away to a place of concealment. With the trap set, bait is spread far enough under the box so that the quarry will have to get under the box to get it. When and if this occurs, the person in concealment at the

Baited box trap

other end of the line jerks the stick out; the box falls; and he is left with the task of catching the game a second time—inside the box.

SNARES

Metal snares may be bought from several companies advertising in the trapping magazines. They are made of flexible wire and feature a device which locks the loop after it has been drawn tight.

In my own early days in a rural area, we used to unravel chicken wire and use it for making snares. At that time, hordes of jackrabbits, white hares, and cottontails would nibble at the haystacks and girdle the bark from the trees of the young orchard. We'd bend a tiny loop in the end of 3 feet of straightened chicken wire, form a lasso, and drape it near the bottom of a ditch, along a fenceline, or in a trail in the snow by a young apple tree. Nearly every morning we'd have a strangled jackrabbit, which we skinned and fed to the chickens.

In an emergency, even nylon monofilament line or fishing line may be used similarly. The 10-yard coil of line recommended for the emergency kit will be strong enough for cottontail rabbits, or a coil of light flexible wire may be taken along especially for the purpose.

Well-traveled trails, patches in the snow, and entrances to holes and burrows are all good places to set a snare. The loop should be approximately twice the diameter of the animal and hung so that it drapes over the path with its center the height of the animal's head. The running end of the snare is led off to some form of anchorage and tied.

The pull of a struggling rabbit will tighten the wire loop, and subsequent twisting will lock it in place. When using nylon or thread line, the same result can be achieved by using a hangman's knot to form the loop. With a nylon monofilament snare, don't use the hangman's knot for the main loop, but rather use it for the small loop through which the running end of the line is threaded to form the lasso loop.

The best anchorage for a snare is a twitch-up, made by bending a flexible sapling and holding it under a forked or notched stick driven into the ground. The snare is tied to the end of this bent sapling, and the loop draped over the trail. When the animal is snared, its struggles free the sapling from beneath the forked stick, and the animal is jerked into the air. This prevents its chewing through a line snare.

In placing a snare over a trail, the more naturally it can be hung from adjacent brush, the more chances it has to succeed. Often these chances can be improved along some narrow spot in the path by casually moving a log into such a position that a natural-looking entering V is created in the foliage. Most game prefer to follow the easiest route and will enter such an unobtrusive passageway. As rabbits, racoons, and other small game move considerably at night, and a snare is less visible after dark, it is likely that the game will be caught after sunset. All care should be used with both traps and snares to see that they are continuously tended, and that caught game doesn't suffer. On leaving an area, all traps and snares, without exception, should be picked up.

SKINNING SMALL GAME

To prepare small game for the pot it must be skinned, dressed, cooled, washed, and cut into serving pieces. A young jackrabbit is the easiest small game animal to skin. The job can be done in thirty seconds with no tools—not even a knife.

If you are right-handed, grasp one hind leg between the foot and the hock joint in the left hand. Then completely circle the leg just above the hock joint with the thumb and index finger of the right hand. The hands, in this position, will be close together. Bring them up before the chest, and pull hard. This breaks the skin of the leg at the hock, in a complete circle, and allows it to be stripped down against the rabbit's thigh. The skin of the opposite leg is pulled up against the body in the same way.

Next, insert a finger into the broken skin at one hip, poke it across the rabbit's back at the root of the tail, and bring the finger out the opposite opening in the skin. Grasp the skin thus held by the finger, and pull hard. This pulls all hide away from the back, strips the hide off the tail, and breaks the skin completely across the rabbit's rear end.

Then turn the rabbit over and grasp the underside of the skin all the way across, at the edge of where it has been broken, and again pull. This strips all skin away from the hind part of the rabbit, except a small patch over the genitals.

Skinning jackrabbit without tools: 1. Grasp hind leg in both hands as shown. Pull apart with twisting motion. Skin will break at dotted line all around leg. 2. Skin is then torn along dotted lines to base of tail, by running finger *under* girdled skin at figure 1, and lifting up. Work toward tail from each side. 3. Pull "cased" skin downward toward head. At points X, where "elbows" of front legs appear, insert finger. Grasp leg in one hand, skin in other. Pull apart. Skin on forelegs will break at dotted lines above foot. Pull skin on down to head, and away from ears as with front legs. For animals with tougher skin, such as squirrels, cuts with knife are made at all dotted lines.

With that done, grasp both hind legs in one hand, and pull on the skin, toward the head, with the other. A continuous pull will peel the skin over the shoulders. At this stage, both front legs will be partially skinned, with the hide folding downward toward the feet and showing an elbow of skinned flesh. Poke a finger between the hide and bone at each elbow, grasp the hide with one hand and the leg with the other, and pull apart. This will peel the leg all the way to the foot, where the skin will break off. Each front foot comes out with a "mitten" of fur left on.

Another pull brings the hide down over the head. As at each elbow, a finger may be pushed between skin and rabbit at the base of the ear. A pull between cartilage and skin strips all hide from the ear. A final pull strips all remaining hide from the head, and the job is done.

Many persons are afraid of handling wild rabbits for fear of contracting tularemia. Any rabbit showing signs of logyness or disease should never be touched, although wearing a pair of rubber gloves during skinning is still a good precaution.

Other small game animals are skinned in the same way. When the animal's skin is too tough to break at the legs and rear, cut it with a knife at these points. This means that the skin must be girdled at the two hind hocks, a cut made from these to the tail, and the skin girdled above each front foot.

DRESSING SMALL GAME

In dressing any small game, unless the entire hide is wanted for taxidermy, the animal is only skinned to the base of the skull. The head is then twisted away or cut off and left with the discarded hide.

To dress a rabbit or squirrel, place the skinned animal on its back on a flat rock surface, and with a sharp pocketknife make an abdominal cut from the tail to the throat. Also cut through the pelvic bone, separating the hips; and cut through the rib cage, opening it for cleaning. When splitting the pelvis, care should be used not to cut into the genitals and anus. These are girdled in the process, left attached to the internal organs, and pulled with them through the pelvic opening. Finally, wash out any remaining blood or intestinal fluids.

The best time to skin and dress small game is immediately after it has been killed. If the animal has been killed close to camp, cleaning and skinning it immediately is no problem. Where game must be carried for an hour or so before reaching camp, it should be dressed immediately but the skin left on to protect the meat from dirt. The abdominal cut is made as before. Then, grasping the hind legs, whirl the carcass around the head, quite like a sling, giving a jerk at the termination of about the second swing. The viscera will pull free and be thrown clear.

A grouse or other gamebird is cleaned in a similar manner. Girdle the leg skin with a knife above the hocks; pull off the skin; girdle the tail and anus; cut an abdominal incision from tail to rib cage; and pull the insides free. Finally, sever the neck and pull the windpipe from the body cavity in the same operation; cut off the legs and wings at the hocks and elbows.

If birds must be carried for some time before reaching camp, they should be cleaned without removing the feathers. A simple way is to cut fully across the abdominal wall just ahead of the pelvic bones, so the intestines droop out. Then, holding the bird by the

Dressing small game such as rabbits and squirrels, after skinning. As shown in this belly view, make incision all the way from anal vent to throat. Split pelvis and rib-cage, shown by double dotted lines. Girdle around genitals and anus, leaving these attached to viscera. Pelvis and chest is best cut by placing strong knife blade *under* bones, and lifting upward. With incision complete from tail to throat, insides may be pulled free with fingers, or flung out by throwing carcass around head and jerking. Remaining blood is wiped out, or washed with clean water.

wings, make a practice shot for the sling. Remnants may be finished off with the knife and fingers.

Any game, large or small, should be cooled thoroughly before cooking. Body heat gives a nauseating flavor to meat, which, if eaten, induces diarrhea. Grouse may be eaten the same day, once they are thoroughly cooled. Rabbits and squirrels should be hung for one to four days before cooking. With any tough animal, this also breaks down the muscle fibers and helps to tenderize the meat.

A good way of cooling small game, and removing any traces of blood at the same time, is to soak the meat in a pan of salt water. Small game may be soaked a full day in cold salt water without damage, then hung where air will circulate or placed in a camp cooler.

COOKING SMALL GAME

Anyone who takes to the hills should know the fundamentals of cooking and a few basic recipes. Small game can be prepared in camp in various ways, from the primitive to the elaborate, depending on time, equipment, ingredients, and the skill of the cook.

The simplest method of cooking a grouse, squirrel, or rabbit is to roast it at the end of a stick held over the fire. This takes time and patience, and the meat must be constantly turned to prevent scorching. It helps if strips of bacon are attached to the game to baste it. Otherwise, the meat has a tendency to dry out on the outside and remain raw within.

Another method is to roast the game spitted on a wire stretched taut between two stakes driven into the ground on opposite sides of the fire. The position of the game over the fire may be regulated by sliding it back and forth, and it may be turned at times with a stick and propped with a forked branch so that all sides cook evenly.

A simple way of preparing small game is to boil the meat, after it has been cut up, in a cooking pot. The addition of a single vegetable, such as a carrot, onion, or potato, improves the dish considerably and turns the recipe in the direction of a full-fledged stew.

Frying is basically a poor form of cooking, as it coats food with hard-to-digest fats. However, frying is a quick way for the outdoorsman to prepare food, and as he is usually active and in good health, his digestion will not suffer. Also, modern cooking oils have increased the digestibility of fried food, and if only a part of the meal is fried, the normal person should have no difficulty.

To fry small game or birds, simply cut into serving pieces and place in a skillet containing butter, bacon fat, or cooking oil hot enough to sizzle. The pieces of meat should be as uniform in size as possible. They should be left in the hot fat only a couple of minutes to sear, then turned over and seared on the opposite side. This seals the surfaces and retains the inside juices.

With both sides seared, the skillet should be covered with a lid and cooked over less heat to prevent burning the meat. The tighter the lid the better, as this helps save the moisture steaming up, causing it to baste the meat as it cooks. Ten to fifteen minutes is enough for grouse and rabbit.

The best utensil for frying is a heavy Dutch oven. It keeps the heat constant, will cook after the fire lowers, and has a seal sufficiently tight to save most of the moisture.

Here's one of the choicest recipes for grouse, if a Dutch oven is available: Split the bird into halves with an ax, through the sternum, and sauté in ⅛th pound of sizzling butter. Sear quickly on both sides, then cook slowly until the halves are golden brown. Salt and pepper to taste. One grouse per person makes a fine serving.

After learning the simplest methods of roasting, frying, and boiling camp meat, you will want to graduate to more difficult and better tasting recipes. Here are some tested recipes for small game:

FRIED SQUIRREL

Soak the cut-up pieces in salt water overnight, and drain. If the squirrel is tough (hide will come off the same way), parboil pieces for 10 minutes. This means simply to boil for 10 minutes, throw the water away and save the squirrel. Roll pieces in flour. Fry in butter, bacon fat, or cooking oil until tender.

FRIED RABBIT

Prepare as for squirrel, except add 2 tablespoons vinegar to the soaking water, parboil in salt water, and save the broth. After rabbit pieces are fried until tender, add 2 tablespoons flour to the skillet, stirring until it browns. Add broth, stirring constantly until brown sauce boils. Sauce may be poured over pieces, or used as gravy for slices of bread. Similar brown sauce may be made for fried squirrel.

FRIED GROUSE

Soak overnight in salt water. Dredge pieces in flour containing salt and pepper. Dip into slightly beaten egg. Fry in deep fat, in Dutch oven, for 7 minutes.

Fricasseed Grouse

Rub soaked and drained pieces with salt and pepper. Brown in hot fat in Dutch oven. Add 2 cups of water, cover, and simmer slowly until grouse is tender. Remove pieces. Thicken remainder with a little flour and cook until smooth, after adding bay leaf and celery seasoning. Serve over meat or bread slices.

Squirrel Stew

Put serving pieces in saucepan together with ½-cup vinegar, 1 teaspoonful mixed spices, 1 diced onion, and 6 celery leaves. Cover with water. Let stand 3 hours. Drain and place in Dutch oven. Brown pieces. Salt and pepper. Add 2 diced onions and 2 diced carrots. Cover with water. Put on cover and cook slowly until tender. Thicken broth with flour to consistency of thick cream, and serve with watercress salad.

Rabbit Pie

Cover serving pieces with boiling water. Add onion, bacon, salt, and pepper. Cover Dutch oven and simmer until meat is tender. Thicken broth with flour in ratio of 2 tablespoonfuls to each cup of liquid, and pour over rabbit. Make thick dough of ready-mix biscuit flour. Pat into sheet ¼-inch thick. Cut slits for steam to escape. Place over contents in Dutch oven and cook in hot coals for 30 minutes.

Grouse with Dumplings

Put serving pieces in saucepan. Cover with boiling water. Add salt and pepper and simmer until meat is tender. Prepare dumpling dough with 2 cups flour, 4 teaspoonfuls baking powder, 2 tablespoonfuls shortening, 1 teaspoonful salt, and canned milk to thicken.

Mix flour, salt, and baking powder. Add shortening to mixture by cutting it in with 2 knives. Add canned milk until a thick batter results. Drop batter, a teaspoonful at a time, into the boiling broth with grouse. Cover Dutch oven and boil 12 minutes. Serve at once.

GO-LIGHT STEW

Cube the meat into 1-inch cubes. Cube 1 raw potato into similar size. Cut 1 onion into sections, and slice 1 carrot into ½-inch slices. Mix and season with salt, pepper, and savory salt. Wrap the contents into two thicknesses of foil, bend edges over to make a good seal, and cook in hot coals for 20 to 30 minutes. Foil isn't large or strong enough to cook more than one serving at a time. The above proportions serve one.

CHILI

Soak 1½ cups of red chili beans overnight. The beans may be quick-soaked by boiling them in 2 quarts of water for 5 minutes, then letting them stand in a covered Dutch oven for 1 hour. Keep the water they soak in.

Cut 1 pound, or as much as you have, of any game meat into tiny cubes and brown them in bacon fat or butter. Add 1 large sliced onion, 1 chopped green pepper, 1 small can tomatoes, 1½ teaspoons salt, ⅛th teaspoon each of cayene pepper and paprika, 1 bay leaf, and from 1 to 2 tablespoons chili powder. Pour this sauce into beans, simmer for 2 hours or until beans are tender, and serve.

PREPARING BIG GAME

The enjoyment of the outdoors is often connected

with the sport of hunting big game, and many of the best camp dishes are made of those portions of a game animal which can't be successfully packed out of the hills but in order to be utilized at all must be served at camp.

Deer, elk, and moose liver is good to eat; antelope and caribou liver isn't so good; and bear liver should not be eaten. The best way to prepare liver is to soak it in cold salt water overnight, cut into strips half-inch thick, and fry in butter or bacon grease with sliced onions. It should be served piping hot.

The heart of deer, elk, antelope, moose, and caribou (except during the rutting season) all make fine eating. Heart may be sliced half-inch thick, dredged in flour, and slow-fried until done; or baked with dressing in a Dutch oven. A good dressing is made of 2 cups stale bread cubes, half a teaspoonful chopped watercress if available, 2 tablespoonfuls melted butter, salt, pepper, dried sage, 3 tablespoonfuls diced celery, 1 teaspoonful chopped onion, 2 teaspoonfuls poultry seasoning, and water or broth enough to make the dressing pack well. The heart is stuffed with this dressing, and a ring of it is laid around the meat in the Dutch oven. The oven should be prepared with 2 tablespoonfuls melted butter and 1 cup water, to prevent sticking. Cook until tender; baste occasionally.

The choicest cut of an elk or moose, the tenderloin, is often wasted, owing to the difficulty of cutting up the huge quarters and transporting them. Tenderloin of elk or moose should be immediately cut out in a continuous strip, cooled overnight, and eaten at camp. A fine way of preparing it is to cut the tenderloin into pieces 1-inch thick, across the grain, and sauté in butter in the Dutch oven. Add salt and pepper to taste after cooking.

Another fine cut of elk or moose ordinarily left with the offal in the field is the tongue. After the head of a big-game animal is severed, the tongue may be removed by a minimum of cutting from the neck end and through the mouth.

Tongue should be boiled in salt water for two to three hours until the outer skin loosens and it becomes tender. Next, the skin is peeled off and the meat sliced thin like sandwich meat. Nothing is better for lunch-meat than cold sliced tongue.

HUNTER'S STEW

One of the most famous of all camp meats is hunter's stew. This, too, may be built around a discarded cut of big-game meat. There is no better meat for a stew than that section of the neck of an elk, just behind the ears, cut in small chunks half the size of a fist. Pieces of bone may or may not be included. The meat pieces are cooled at camp overnight in salt water. Next, the pieces are put in a large kettle or Dutch oven, and slow-boiled for two to three hours over the campfire. The broth from the boiling meat is occasionally skimmed. The kettle should remain covered.

With the meat nearly done, vegetables are added. The best vegetables are carrots, onions, cabbage, beans, and potatoes. However, any vegetables available at camp, and in any combination, may be used for a hunter's stew. They should be added according to the length of time it takes to cook them. That is, any dried or quick-soaked beans or peas should be added first, then carrots, cabbage, onions, and potatoes. The main idea is to have all ingredients tender at about the same time.

Lastly, a can of condensed tomato soup should be

added. If tomato soup isn't available, a small can of stewed tomatoes, may be substituted. Add salt, pepper, and savory salt just before serving.

The virtues of a hunter's stew are that the longer you cook it the better it gets, and it may be reheated several times until it is all used.

Most big-game animals have to be trimmed considerably before packing the quarters out on pack stock. The odds and ends of meat trimmings make good "bullburgers," especially if mixed with 20 per cent fat pork or bacon. If no grinder is available, the meat may be cut into small bits, as in making camp chili.

A delicacy greatly enjoyed by the Indians of the Far North is roasted moose nose. This is the large gristly portion just beyond the animal's septum. They prepare it simply by putting the entire portion into a fire and roasting it in the coals. This burns off the hair and cooks it at the same time. When done, the hide is peeled off and the nose is salted and eaten.

The best meat I have *ever* eaten at camp was barbecued ram ribs. This was prepared by standing the ribs on green stakes before a fire bed 3 feet long. The loin portion of each was thinned down so that the thickness of each slab was uniform. Wild sheep meat is normally fat enough so that, during the barbecuing, the fat bastes the entire slab of meat. The sections were reversed occasionally so that both sides were cooked evenly. Cooking time was two hours. A portion was an entire rib, cut full length and eaten like corn on the cob, each person salting his own.

CHAPTER 10

Fish for the Pan

In addition to natural baits that may be found on the spot, or artificial lures that may be carried in the duffel, an outdoorsman can catch fish for the pan with emergency lures made in the outdoors with nothing except meager equipment, lots of imagination, and a modest degree of skill. Everyone going into wilderness country should, in case of emergency, have some knowledge of how to make such lures.

SHIRT-TAIL FLIES

A logical place to start is with artificial flies, because both trout and bass are widely spread throughout North America and both take artificial flies. Moreover, artificial flies will take other species of fish as well, and the material for making them can be found *anywhere*. The necessary hooks, thread, and line weigh next to nothing and are handily taken along. It's a broad statement to make, but give me a hook, a yard of thread, and some nylon leader material and I can make an artificial fly, regardless of the situation, which will take trout.

My interest in emergency flies began many years

176

ago in the Cassiars of British Columbia, where Doc Ernie Wygant and I were fishing for Arctic grayling at the inlet of Cry Lake. No matter what fly we put on, those beauties would nail it. As an experiment, Doc took twelve flies out of his book and laid them on the canoe seat. These flies ranged in size and variety from a #16 Red Ant to a hulking #6 wet nymph. We tied on those twelve flies, alternately, one fly for one cast, then we'd change. We even took turns casting. We caught twelve of the grayling feeding in the current of the inlet in twelve casts, with twelve separate flies.

"Doc," I said, "I believe if anyone was caught up here in an emergency, he could catch those fish on anything."

This gave me an idea. I was wearing a blue woolen shirt at the time. I took my hunting knife and cut off a worm-like strip from the tail of the shirt, threaded it onto a bare fly hook, and cast. On the second cast I hooked a grayling! Since then, experimenting with creations which could be used for survival situations, I have made and tested trout flies of almost anything you can name.

The accompanying photo shows examples of flies I have tied with odd scraps of material:

1. A fly made from a single grouse feather, plus a strip of aluminum foil used to wrap camera film. The tail is of fibers from the grouse feather. Aluminum was wrapped on as a body. Hackle is remainder of feather.

2. This streamer fly was made of nothing more than a string of cloth cut from my red shirttail and hairs cut with a hunting knife from my chest.

3. This fly is similar to No. 1, except it was made from one domestic hen feather. A few fibers were tied

Emergency flies fashioned on the spot from materials found in the outdoors. All have been tested by the author and have proved to be excellent trout-takers. See accompanying text for tying details.

on for the tail. Other fibers off the butt end were bunched together, rolled around the hook into a rough body, and wound with thread. Hackle was made from the tip end of the soft feather.

4. This fly was created out of nothing more sophisticated than a piece of a cloth shoelace, a length of white twine, and some deer hair picked up at the campsite. The lace, wound on, formed the body. The twine made the body ribs. The deer hairs were tied on as a streamer.

5. This fly was tied of several elk hairs and a strand of burlap unraveled from a potato sack. The strand was wound onto a 4X-shank hook. The hairs were tied on at the front end as a streamer. In the water this material looked extremely natural. The burlap after wetting, gave the fly a lifelike, translucent body like that of a real insect. In the water, the brownish elk hair had just the right coloration to resemble wings, and could be made to pulse back and forth

just like the wings of a dying bug. The finished creation looked so good, I promptly gave it a name—Ormond's Bull-'N-Burlap Fly—and started fishing with it. The trout on the Yellowstone River really nailed it!

Enthused with the results, I created similar Buck-'N-Burlap flies out of burlap and deer hair, and Bear-N-Burlap flies with the streamer hairs of three separate species of bruins—all with the idea of using materials found in widely scattered areas.

Under extreme necessity, all these flies and dozens more like them can be tied out of nothing more than materials at hand, with no vise, bobbin, varnish, or wax. You need only a hook, a yard of sewing thread, and something that looks like fur or feathers. Hooks may be stuck into the tip end of a sharpened sapling in place of a vise, or simply held in the hand. Without varnish and wax, a camp-made fly will soon unravel and wear out. By then it will have served its purpose.

EMERGENCY LURES

Other types of emergency lures can be made for other types of fishing. As an example, a neighbor boy had so much success with wobblers he had made out of pop-bottle caps that he considered making them commercially. He hammered the caps flat into various shapes, threaded a barrel-swivel into a hole at each end, and attached a trailing hook to the lower swivel. He removed the cork from the underside, leaving brass on one side and the painted lettering on the other.

I have seen fish caught with a spinner made from the bowl of a plastic spoon, a wobbler made from a

How to make a plastic-spoon wobbler: Obtain a red or yellow plastic spoon (1) and cut off the handle by carefully notching it at the points shown (2). Drill a hole at each end by twisting the point of a knife blade back and forth (3), but be careful not to shatter the plastic. Attach a snap swivel at the front, if one is available, and either a single or a treble hook at the rear (4). If you lack a snap swivel, tie the line directly to the spoon.

How to make a trolling spoon from a beer-can opener: Take an ordinary beer-can opener (1) and pound it flat with an ax or hammer. Also hammer it along center X's to make it slightly concave (2). Then pound it into a mild crescent shape (3) to give it a fluttering action in the water and attach monofilament loops for line and hook. If a file is available, opener can be tapered at end to give a minnow-like shape (4).

metal beer-can opener, and a multiple-blade trolling spinner made from a tin can. It is the pride of old-timers to be able to whittle a wooden plug from a clothespin, attach a hook, paint it with fingernail enamel, and catch bass with it.

For anyone who must travel light in wilderness country, it is wise to include in the minimum tackle the makings of emergency lures—hooks, a few swivels, a spool of thread, and a coil of nylon leader.

How to make a multiple-blade trolling spinner: (1) Cut a tin can along dotted lines; lay it flat on a wooden surface (2) and cut out blades in graduating sizes from 1 to 2 inches (3). Pound blades in center with a rock until they are lightly concave, and punch holes. (4) Cut ellipse-shaped clevices from tin. These, when folded in half, must fit through holes in blade. (5) Shape wooden beads, which help blades to rotate freely, from small branches and burn out centers with a hot wire. (6) Assemble blades, clevices, and beads on lengths of fine wire 5 to 8 inches long. Tie loops for line and hook.

How to make a clothespin bass plug: (1) Start with an old-
fashioned wooden clothespin. (2) Flatten top of knob and
burn a small dent at partition center with hot wire to keep
hook from slipping. Tie hook between prongs with monofilament, bringing it from top and bottom and knotting it
along the side. Then loop it around the neck (3) and tie
on top of plug. Burn eyes into head. Plug should be
charred along top to simulate shading, and "scales" can
be added by chipping lightly with a knife blade (4).

EMERGENCY TACKLE

Emergency lures not only can be made on the spot
but fished with a minimum of tackle. Spoons and
wobblers may be used with nothing except a length
of line attached. The line may be loosely coiled near
the water's edge; a length held in the hand and swung
around the head like a sling; the lure thrown into a
river pool or into a lake, and hand-lined in rapidly
enough to make it wobble.

Another method is to wrap the line around the
bottom edge of a coffee can and hold the can by the
other edge. I know an old river hermit who swears
he invented spincasting by this trick. He even nailed
a short handle to the bottom of a pound coffee can
and tied the end of his line to the handle. Next, he
wound the line around the can and affixed his bait
and sinker to the end. Then, holding the handle in his
left hand, he threw the lure with his right. The line

of course, would peel off the can like monofilament off a spinning reel, to be wound on again as he retrieved.

If you have a reel and line but your rod has been broken, you can make a temporary rod of a long willow, alder, or even a tiny, dry jack pine. The reel can be wound onto the butt end with fishing line, cord, or a shoelace. Guides may be cut off the damaged rod and wound on in the same fashion. If no guides are available, you can make them from a couple of paper clips, pot bails, or even tiny twigs that angle abruptly. Tie one at the rod tip and the other midway on the rod.

Again, with only a line, hook, and some natural bait located on the spot, you can still get fish for the pan by setting a bait overnight. The lure may be tossed into a river or lake and the other end of the line tied to a springy bush. If, during the night, a fish

How to make a coffee-can spinning reel: The handle is a short piece of stick (1) and the spool an ordinary coffee can (2). Drive a nail a quarter of the way into the end of the handle, then remove it and punch a hole in the bottom of the can. Stand handle on the ground and with a rock drive nail through hole in can into hole in handle (3). Tie end of fishing line to handle and wind it around can (4). Holding reel in left hand, throw lure and line with right so line "spins" off can.

gobbles the bait and becomes hooked, the springiness of the bush keeps it from breaking the line.

Snagging game fish is usually against the law in most areas, though often trash fish may be snagged. However, in an emergency, most people would consider snagging a fish to prevent starvation the lesser of two evils. With patience, fish can be snagged in pools and eddies of a stream. Tie several hooks to a line about 6 inches apart, and tie a sinker—a nail or small pebble which can be half-hitched several times—to the end of the line. Then toss or lower the rig into a pool and leave it on the bottom until you see a fish cross above it. An upward jerk usually snags him.

A trick to get a lure well out into a stream when no rod is available is to put the lure on a wooden chip, let it float with the current from above the desired spot, then jerk the lure off the chip. Another stunt, when no thread is available to tie an emergency fly, is to unravel the seam of a pants' cuff and use the thread.

If you have no fish hook, a usable hook may be made from a length of tough stick such as a thorn. Taper the stick at both ends and sharpen the ends to points. For average-sized fish, the hook should be about 1½ inches long. Next, cut a groove exactly at the center, so that the leader can be tied snugly around the stick. Push the hook into the mouth of a grasshopper or work it carefully into the length of a worm so just a point protrudes. When a fish bites, allow it to swallow the bait, then jerk the line quickly but not too hard. This pulls the end of the stick into the flesh of the fish's mouth, tilting it so it lodges crosswise in the mouth. Such a hook will hold sufficiently long for a small fish to be landed.

CLEANING FISH

Since gamefish represent an important part of the wilderness diet, and since the farther from civilization one gets the easier fish are to catch, every outdoorsman should know how to clean them and at least a few basic ways of preparing them. The easiest way to clean a small fish is first to slit the abdominal wall from the anal vent to the apex of the angle formed by the cartilage under the gills. This V of hard cartilage will join, by a thin membrane, a larger V—the lower jaw. A second cut should be made, crosswise, through the membrane between these two V's, and forward until the knife severs this lower V cartilage loose from the lower jaw. With this cut made, the lower jaw will be left intact with the fish's head, as will the outer gill plates. The V of cartilage should then be grasped with the fingers of one hand, and the fish's lower jaw with the other. By pulling the cartilage and lower jaw apart, the gills, pectoral fins, and intestines will be stripped free. Occasionally the gills will fail to pull free at their upper edge, where they join the spine. Pinching them at this junction with the thumb and index finger will break them off, after which the stripping motion is continued.

With the insides pulled out, the layer of blood lying against the spine is scraped out with the thumbnail. A small notch is cut and the anus removed, and the fish is washed in cold water to complete the job. The head may be left on or removed. Fish with heavy scales should be scaled before cleaning with a sharp knife, scraping from the tail toward the head. If the fish is fresh, the scales will come off easily. Older fish are more difficult to scale.

NO-UTENSIL COOKING

Perhaps the simplest, quickest way of preparing trout and other small fish is to rub them with salt, skewer each fish on a peeled hardwood stick, and cook them before the hot coals of a fire. Sharpen the bottom end of the stick and shove it into the ground at an angle, so the fish is held at an appropriate distance over the heat.

Another fine way of preparing fish with a minimum of utensils is to roll them in a double thickness of tin or aluminum foil and cook them in the hot coals of a diminishing fire. The whole fish, sections, or filets are first salted and peppered, and a tablespoon of butter, if available, is spread along the full length of the fish. The foil is rolled and placed in the fire so that no joints are on the bottom, or else the butter will run out as it melts. Cooking time is twenty minutes for 10- to 12-inch fish.

Finally, when no cooking utensils are available, a simple way of preparing fish is to "plank" them. First filet the fish, or split them into halves with the skin left on. Then prepare a plank of wood by smoothing one side of a slab cut from a log. Pine isn't a good wood for this, as it gives a strong flavor to the cooked fish. Grease the plank well with butter or bacon fat and place the filet skin side down on the plank and fasten it solidly by nailing or tacking the upper edge of the skin. Prop the plank at a steep angle before the fire and allow the fish to bake. If possible, drape strips of bacon over the fish as it cooks, as this bastes the meat and keeps it from burning.

If no timber is available for a plank, a flat slab of rock may be substituted. This will have to be used a a milder angle, since it will be impossible to fasten the filet to the rock.

Planked fish may be salted either before or after cooking. Careless cooking, or not tending the fire, can easily result in a ruined fish. With some cooks, it's better to throw away the fish and eat the plank.

FRYING FISH

Small, pan-sized fish may be fried whole. The butter or fat should be hot enough to sing when they are placed in the pan. The fish are cooked on one side until partly done, turned over, then slowly cooked until done with a lid on the skillet. Some prefer to salt the fish first, others just before eating. Freshly caught fish will curl up when fried. To avoid this, open the fish its full length and lay the halves, which remain joined along the dorsal side, flat in the pan.

Another fine way to fry small fish is first to roll them in flour which has been salted and peppered. Flouring the fish helps prevent burning them.

Larger fish must be cut into pieces before frying. These pieces may be several inches long, of steak thickness, and are made by cutting across the fish. Salmon and steelhead are especially good when cut this way, and fried or sautéed in butter.

If a Dutch oven is available at camp, one of the finest ways of cooking fish is to fry them whole, in 1/8-pound of butter, for eighteen minutes (in a hot bed of coals) without removing the lid. This will cook them through without the necessity of turning them, and the tight lid of the oven holds in all juices and flavor. One of the best meals my wife and I have ever eaten was a half-dozen golden trout cooked this way by the outfitter, just after we'd got into camp from an all-day horseback ride in a rainstorm.

FILETING

Fileting is another fine way of preparing larger fish. To filet a fish, lay it on its side on a flat surface and girdle it all around with a sharp knife at points just ahead of the tail and just behind the pectoral fins and gill coverings. Then make another cut lengthwise along the backbone, connecting these two cuts. Next, beginning at the back, cut the halves of flesh away from the ribs and spine. The shaving-like cuts are made just over the bones, all the way down to the abdominal incision, and the flesh is lifted away. The result is two halves of meat, leaving the fish's skeleton intact. All fins are cut away from the halves, which may then be cooked as is, or again cut into smaller filets.

During hot weather, fish in some waters have a strong or gamey taste. This taste is most pronounced in the skin and cartilege surrounding the fins. Fileting is a fine way to cook such fish, but it is advisable to skin them first to remove the gamey taste. A fish is skinned after the two girdling cuts and the cut along the spine have been made. A corner of skin is cut away until it can be grasped in the fingers. Then a hard pull will strip off the skin on some species. With others, grip the skin with a pair of pliers and pull hard, while holding the fish down with the other hand.

Fileting, incidentally, is the best way to prepare fresh sturgeon. The flesh is first sliced into sections by cutting across the fish. These sections should be 4 inches long. Each section is then cut into filets by cut-

How to filet a fish: First, girdle fish with a sharp knife just ahead of the tail. Cut down the spine outside the ribs on each side and girdle around behind the gills. Then peel off filet in one piece, leaving entire skeleton of fish intact.

ting lengthwise along these chunks to get rectangular pieces 1-inch wide, 4 inches long, and ⅝-inch thick. These filets are then cut free of any fat, which in a sturgeon is the red, stringy meat, and slow-fried in melted butter. Allow forty-five minutes for the filets to cook through and turn golden in color. There is no better delicacy.

BAKED FISH

Fish may also be baked at camp in a Dutch oven, or by using two "dripping-pans," one inverted over the other. If the fish is not too large, it is baked whole. Salt and pepper before cooking, and lay strips of bacon, if available, over the top to baste as it cooks. Baked fish is excellent with tomato sauce. Ten minutes before the fish is done, pour a can of condensed tomato soup over it and cook until the soup thickens.

Another way of preparing baked fish is to fill the body cavity, and make a ring around the fish, with poultry dressing. A good dressing is the one suggested for grouse: dry bread crumbs to which several spoonfuls of raisins have been added.

Leftover fish which has been fried or baked can be made into chowder; or it can be made into a fishloaf. Here is a good recipe for fishloaf:

FISHLOAF

Two cups flaked fish. 2 well-beaten eggs. 2 tablespoons melted butter or margarine. ½-cup cornmeal. ¼-cup bread or cracker crumbs. ½-cup canned milk. Combine the fish, eggs, butter, cornmeal, and crumbs. Add milk. Season to taste. Mix lightly with two forks. Form into loaf and bake for 20 minutes in a well-greased Dutch oven. Thicken condensed tomato soup into heavy sauce and pour over baked fishloaf.

SMOKED FISH

Often in wilderness country you will be confronted with the problem of having caught a number of large fish which you cannot eat before they spoil. Such a situation is ideal for smoking fish.

The outdoorsman can build several types of smoke-houses with material available on the spot. The Indians in the Far North, for example, often make smokehouses of large strips of birch and aspen bark shaped into a small wigwam. Racks of green alders are erected inside, on which the fish are laid. The smoke-house is erected on a cutbank, and a small fire is built below. The smoke is piped from the fire to the house by means of a trench dug up the side of the cutbank and covered with green bark sections, like shingles, over which dirt has been placed.

One of the simplest temporary smokehouses consists of a rack of green alder saplings 2 to 3 feet high wrapped in a canvas tarp, with a tiny smudge of fire kept going just inside one edge. With this arrangement, the canvas can be kept open enough at the top to provide just enough draft to keep the smoke rising inside. Such a simple house requires almost constant attention to see that the fire doesn't blaze up.

A better smokehouse can be made of two lengths of stovepipe and a large pasteboard carton. The alder frame is made of four uprights. To these, crossbars of alder are tied or nailed, and enough green alder sticks are laid across these crossbars to make a platform. These sticks for the platform should be laid about 1 inch apart. As the fish smokes and cooks, it softens, and will drop through if the sticks are too far apart. Two such shelves will hold a large catch of fish.

The "house" is simply the large carton turned up-sidedown over the framework. A small draft hole in the top of the box is made by cutting three sides of a rectangle, leaving it hinged on one side so the draft can be regulated.

The lengths of stovepipe are used to pipe the smoke from the fire up the cutbank and into the bottom of

Smokehouse of green alders or willows laid across two crossbars which are supported by four stakes. Canvas draped around rack contains smoke from small smudge fire just inside edge.

the smokehouse. The fire itself is built in a small rock cairn several feet down the cutbank. The fire may be covered with green bark strips or foil so that the smoke leads into the pipe. Covering the cairn also keeps the fire from blazing up too much. A small pit can be dug in sandy ground if no rocks are available for making a cairn.

To start the smoking process, clean the fish and soak them overnight in a strong solution of salt water. Wipe them dry and lay them on the shelves of the alder rack. Invert the carton over the framework and build the fire. Once the fire is started, it is fed with green wood, which will smoke continuously.

A more elaborate smoke-house, also of green alders, but having several levels and covered with a cardboard carton. Stovepipe (bottom) funnels smoke from smudge fire built in rock cairn.

Apple wood is one of the best for smoking fish but is seldom available in the woods. Green aspen is nearly as good and is usually found in wilderness country where enough fish for smoking purposes are apt to be caught. Small trees of 4 to 6 inches in diameter are fine. Cut these into lengths which will fit into the cairn or pit and split them into quarters. Such green aspen logs will burn if just enough dry twigs and small branches are periodically added to keep a fire going. It takes a bit more fire to burn smaller, unsplit branches, which are also fine for the purpose. If the fire can be tended only a few hours each day, it can be allowed to go out overnight and started again the following day.

It takes seven hours or more to smoke fish properly, depending on their size. When the fish become brown, wrinkled, and look like old moccasins, they are usually done. They may be tasted occasionally to check on the progress.

CHAPTER 11

Edible Plants

North America's inventory of cultivated plants has traditionally been so extensive that we are unaware of the many nutritive wild plants that can sustain the human organism. There is hardly an area of the entire continent where some of these edible plants are not found, and the outdoorsman should be able to recognize them and know how to use them as emergency foods.

In traveling over the more remote areas, there won't be many occasions when a total dependence on edible plants will be necessary. Exceptions to this generality are such misfortunes as being lost from a camp or source of supplies, being in an airplane crash over wilderness country, or being capsized with a boat on inland waterways. It is comforting to know that in such emergencies food in some form lies all about. It should be of added assurance to realize that an entire race of people, the early American Indians, thrived on the edible plants that nature provides.

In changing from accustomed foods to wild edible plants, some judgment should be used. In the main, it is best to make as gradual a change as the situation will permit. That is, one should not, if possible, change abruptly to a complete diet of wild plants.

When for any reason the supply of domestic food runs low, the remainder should be rationed to last as long as possible, and complementing amounts of wild edible plants and fruits should be added. This can usually be done, except in dire emergencies, by simple forethought and planning.

Mixing the remaining food gradually with the wild plants and berries which nature provides accomplishes several vital purposes. First, the change to strange, less palatable foods is made more easily. Secondly, there is less shock to the digestive system. Some wild foods tend to act as emetics or cathartics; but by gradually introducing them into the system, the body will accommodate them without trouble. Perhaps even more important, if by mistake one happens to eat a toxic plant, a small amount is far less apt to cause trouble than a full portion.

If you accidentally eat a wild food that is toxic, the best remedy is to get it out of your system as fast as possible. This is accomplished by vomiting. If soda or dry mustard is available in the grub box, quantities of either diluted with warm water and drunk to excess will generally induce vomiting. Perhaps the simplest way is to drink an excess of warm water and poke a finger down your gullet.

Another good procedure to follow when you are thrown upon edible plants and fruits for survival is to eat small amounts of wild plants as they are found. This, too, helps the system to adjust. As an example, if you are moving through wild berry country, it's better to pick and eat the fruit as you travel rather than to sit in one place and eat until you are full. Of course, if you come upon a food supply in one area and suspect that other areas are sparse, you should take a quantity of food along. You can carry edible roots and wild greens in your pack and cook them at night over the campfire. Cooked tubers and roots are temporarily preserved and may be carried until a new supply is found. Just as you mark a spot in strange country until you find a new landmark, so you should mark areas of edible plants and fruits, preferably on a field-made map, until a new supply can be reached.

EMERGENCY FOODS

When traveling in wilderness country, the gradual change from an accustomed food supply to wild foods can be accomplished more easily if you always carry some form of emergency food. Dehydrated fruit, carried in a plastic refrigerator-bag to keep it clean, is a nourishing emergency food. Dehydrated soup, assuming there is anything to cook it in, is another. A half-pound package of raisins or chocolate candy bars are good emergency foods for short trips.

PINOLE

The ideal emergency food should be light, dry, and contain as much energy in proportion to its weight as possible. One of the very best is pinole. It is easily made, is indestructible, won't spoil, and has great food value for its weight. A pound bag of pinole will, under dire necessity, sustain a person for a week. If even small amounts of wild fruit, plants, and fish or small game can be added, it will keep one going for several weeks if necessary. The simplest form of pinole is parched corn. With a small bag of this food, Indians have crossed vast regions of wilderness country with nothing else save what they could glean from the land.

A more palatable form of pinole is made with a combination of kernel corn and brown sugar. Spread a pint of dry, sweet garden corn in a shallow cake pan and place in a hot oven (about 350 degrees), which will parch the corn without burning it. When the corn is a mild brown all over, sprinkle two table-spoonfuls of brown sugar evenly over the top, and heat again until the sugar just begins to melt. Cool the mixture and grind it in a home food-grinder.

The pinole should be put in a plastic refrigerator-bag, which in turn is sewed into a small canvas bag. The double bag will protect the contents and can be stored anywhere in the duffel without spilling.

When it is necessary to use this food in an emergency, small amounts totaling two tablespoonfuls are placed in the mouth and washed down with drinking water. This meager portion, supplemented by a few handfuls of wild fruit, will keep a person going all day. The corn, soaked to bulk by the water in the stomach, gives the sensation of at least a degree of fullness.

THRESHED WHEAT

Another simple concentrated food is threshed wheat. Dry wheat kernels, which can be carried in a pocket or small bag, will never spoil, have lots of food value for their bulk, and are pleasant to nibble on. A pound of wheat kernels will sustain life for a week, in an emergency. They are easily obtained from farmers or stock-feed stores in agricultural areas. A fair substitute for threshed wheat is cracked wheat, which is put up as a bulk cereal.

EDIBLE PLANTS

Arrowhead

Sometimes known as arrowleaf because of the pointed shape of the leaves, arrowhead is an aquatic plant whose leaves reach the surface of the water. It is found in the wetlands and swamp areas from central Canada to the Gulf of Mexico. The root, a starchy vegetable, is edible and may be prepared by boiling or roasting.

Barrel Cactus

This formidable-looking plant grows in desert regions. Shaped like a watermelon, it has a spiny surface and reaches a height of approximately 2 feet. The plant may be broken open with an ax or heavy knife for the moist pulp inside, which can be eaten or chewed for the moisture it contains.

Burdock

Widely distributed in the United States and Canada, this plant is regarded in agrarian areas as nothing but a weed and a nuisance. The leaves resemble rhubarb leaves and grow on long tough stems. The plant grows from 3 to 7 feet in height, and blooms with numerous hooked flower heads. It is simple to locate burdock in an area if any livestock are near, as the hooked flowers cling to the wool of domestic sheep and the manes and tails of horses. The roots of burdock are edible in their first year, as are the young shoots. The roots are either boiled or roasted, and the young shoots may be boiled and salted as greens.

CAMAS

A plant of the lily family occurring in the Northwest, camas, or quamash, grows with slender darkgreen stems and has blue blossoms. Adult camas have bulbs like small onions, and these bulbs are edible. Eaten raw, they have a flavor similar to a turnip. Before the Indians were driven from the prairies, they would dig whole fields for the camas bulbs and dry them. They were a staple of the Indian diet. The little railroad settlement of Camas, Idaho, was named after this plant. The western camas should not be confused with the death camass, which is poisonous and occurs in all the western states and most of the Southwest. The flowers of the death camass are yellow-white and grow in clusters.

CATTAILS

Often called tule, this plant is one of the family of bullrushes. It is found throughout temperate North America and reaches into southern Canada. It occurs both in freshwater and saltwater marshes, alongside ponds and quiet streams. Cattails grow from 3 to 8 feet high, and are common to waterfowl country. The name comes from the compacted seed-aggregations at the end of the long stem, which resemble a cat's tail. The edible portion is the tuberous root, which may be cooked as a starchy vegetable or in vegetable soup.

CENTURY PLANT

A member of the cactus family, this plant is widely scattered over the desert areas of the Southwest. The spiny plant grows to a height of 2 feet or more at the base, with a long pole-like stem carrying the bloom. The spike-like spines may be chopped away, leaving a pulpy base which looks like an overgrown pineapple. This may be roasted or boiled as one would prepare squash. The century plant played an important role in the southwestern Indians' long war with the whites. While the white soldiers had to extend their food lines wherever they chased the Indians, the red warriors lived to a large extent off these plants. Squaws would casually go on ahead, over the slow lines of retreat, roast great quantities of the plant in huge pits, and have food for the warriors when they arrived.

CHICORY

Also known as succory, chicory was introduced from Europe into the eastern part of the United States and Canada. Its root is often used as a coffee substitute or to adulterate coffee. The root may also be used as a herb.

CHOKECHERRY

Large alder-like shrubs often growing to well over the height of a man, chokecherry bushes bloom with long, tapering blossom-stems having numerous small, white blossoms. These blossoms are succeeded by tapering clusters of red berries which turn nearly black when completely ripe. The fruit is well named. The first cherries you eat pucker your mouth so that it is difficult to breathe without whistling a concerto. You will soon get used to this extreme tartness, however, and will find the fruit pleasant to nibble on. Each fruit has a large stone. There is no better jelly than chokecherry jelly, which is especially fine to garnish the meat of waterfowl. Chokecherry juice won't jell of itself, but must be added to apple juice. The pectin which apple juice contains will cause the combination to set. Chokecherry bushes have a wide distribution over southern Canada, northern United States, and in spotty scatterings considerably farther south.

CHUFA

One of the family of grasses, having a bearded-tuber root system, chufa ranges all across Canada and reaches southward into the tropics. The tubers may be roasted or boiled as a pot-vegetable, or roasted and beaten into a flour. Where cooking utensils are not available, the tubers may be rolled into wet leaves and roasted in the coals of a fire. The wet leaves help keep the tubers from burning.

CLOVER

Various parts of clover can be used as an emergency food. The dried heads can be pounded and used as bread food. The young leaves can be used as a salad or cooked herb. Tea purportedly having medicinal properties can be made from the dry flower-heads.

DANDELION

Widely distributed over the continent, dandelion, like burdock, is considered a nuisance. It is known also as lion's tooth because of the jagged leaves. Dandelions have a bright-yellow composite flower which grows on a long, bare stem. These stems, when broken, bleed with a milky fluid. The bloom has often been used in the making of dandelion wine. The young plants make good greens, somewhat bitter to the taste. As with other wild greens, dandelions should first be boiled or scalded in hot water. The water should then be drained off, and the blanched plants boiled again until thoroughly cooked. This takes away part of the bitter taste. Served with salt and pepper, and a bit of butter if available, dandelion greens taste something like spinach.

DOCK

There are approximately fifteen species of dock, some of which are scattered throughout temperate North America, reaching well into southern Canada. The young leaves are used as cooked herbs or in greens. Most species of dock are short, stout plants, with leaves from 6 inches to a foot in length growing out of stout leaf-stalks. The leaves are elongated. Dock lives near swamps and alongside roadways. It has a range from southern Canada southward over the temperate parts of the United States.

FIREWEED

As its name suggests, fireweed follows the great forest fires of Canada and Alaska, and occurs southward into the northern tier of the United States. It also grows in cleared areas in the same regions, and, because of road-clearing operations, now occurs along the borrow-pits of much of the length of the Alaska Highway. The plant grows to approximately 3 feet, and is characterized by the bright lavender-colored flowers. The new shoots are cooked as a pot vegetable, and Indians use the pith from the large stalks in making soup.

GROUNDNUT

Indian potato or wild bean are other names for this plant. The groundnut is a twining vine growing close to the ground and having elongated seed pods. Its range is from central Canada to the Gulf of Mexico. The roots of this plant are a series of tubers, or root enlargements, which sometimes reach a length of 3 inches. These tubers can be roasted, boiled, fried, or even sliced and eaten raw quite like Irish potatoes. Seeds from the pods are sometimes used as dry beans.

HOG PEANUT

Like the groundnut, the hog peanut grows with a long twining vine, and has underground fruits occurring in tough pods. These pods are boiled, which softens the skin so the seeds can be removed. The seeds, or fruits, are cooked similarly to dry beans. The range of the hog peanut is from southern Canada to the Gulf of Mexico.

INDIAN CUCUMBER

This plant grows with a long, slender stem, which has a circle of several leaves branching out from the stem near the top. At the stem's top is a smaller circle of fewer leaves near which are the black-purple berries. The root is a small tuber approximately an inch in diameter. This is the edible part and can be eaten uncooked. Indian cucumbers are common to eastern Canada, the Great Lakes, and southward to Florida.

JERUSALEM ARTICHOKE

A member of the sunflower family, this plant is native to the central portions of North America. It has a tuber root similar to the Irish potato's, which is the edible part. It may be boiled, baked, or roasted. If fire isn't available, the tuber may be sliced and eaten raw, with salt.

LICHENS

These are tiny plants that grow on rocks and sterile ground. They occur in the barren regions north of Hudson Bay, into the Arctic, and southward, and are often mistaken for moss. They have been known to prevent starvation among explorers. They can be picked off rocks and boiled into a jelly-like substance.

MALLOW

Usually occurring in the cultivated areas about farmyards and in fields, mallow is generally considered a weed. The young plants may be boiled and used as greens.

MARSH MARIGOLD

Sometimes called the American cowslip, this is not a true marigold but one of the buttercup family of plants. It ranges from Alaska southward to the southern states, and is found in rich meadowlands. It has a bright-yellow, waxy-looking bloom. The edible part is the plant's top, and only the tender tips should be used. These are prepared by double-boiling, draining off the first water, and as greens or pot herbs. Extreme caution should be used in eating marsh marigold not to eat any of the raw plant. *The raw plant is poisonous.*

MILKWEED

There are approximately forty varieties of milkweed common to North America. The most abundant is the common milkweed. The plant is light green in color and grows to a height of 2 to 4 feet. When the stems or leaves are broken off, the plant bleeds with a milky substance which gives it its name. In agricultural areas milkweeds are a nuisance. After the plants get a good start, they are hard to destroy. The seeds grow in pods reaching 3 inches in length, which have long, silky fibers attached, often giving the plant the additional name of silkweed. The edible part is the young shoots just after they emerge from the ground. These are prepared like asparagus or greens.

MUSHROOMS

Members of the Fungi family, mushrooms grow in damp shady places in the soil and in dead or decaying plants, mainly rotting tree trunks. There are several thousand known varieties of mushrooms, many of which are poisonous. Only botanists or people skilled in plant differentiation can tell the edible plants from the poisonous ones. There is no true distinction between mushrooms and toadstools, as many people believe, though amateurs generally consider that mushrooms are the edible forms, while the toadstools are poisonous. While incorrect, this may save many people from eating poisonous varieties. There is, unfortunately, no simple guide to help the beginner determine the edible from the poisonous mushrooms. His safest course is to reject all mushrooms unless he definitely knows them to be safe.

Here are some warning signs to look for when picking mushrooms:

Mushrooms having white or pale milky juice.

Mushrooms in the button stage.

Mushrooms having a scaly bulb or membranous cup at the base (the poison amanita or death cup is one of these).

Mushrooms having underside full of minute pores, and which grow from the earth.

Decaying mushrooms.

Woodland mushrooms having flat reddish tops and white radiating gill-spokes.

Mushrooms of yellow-orange color coming out of old stumps and having broad gills extending down the stems, and with surfaces which phosphoresce in the dark.

Such species as the *meadow mushroom,* the *shaggy mane,* and the *morel* are edible, but again one should be absolutely certain of the species before attempting to use it. Edible species are baked and slow-simmered in butter.

Mountain Sorrel

This plant grows in wide areas in the Arctic, Canada, and along the spine of the Rocky Mountains. It is a small plant with rounded leaves, resembling a small rhubarb plant. It has been used by Arctic explorers as a scurvy preventative, and for this reason named scurvy grass. It is prepared as a salad or cooked herb.

MUSTARD

Black and yellow mustard plants are of European origin but have become naturalized in North America and are common in farming country. It grows vigorously, to a height of 3 or 4 feet, and interferes with harvesting. The young mustard plants are edible, if made into greens.

PIGWEED

The lowly pigweed grows throughout the temperate parts of North America and is common in gardens, barnyards, and along ditchbanks. In some areas it is given the more aristocratic name of lamb's quarters, as it is also called in Europe. In some regions it is also called goose foot. Under favorable conditions of fertility, the plant will reach 10 feet in height. The leaves of the young plant are used for greens, and are prepared in the same way as dandelion greens.

PINE

The inner bark, or cambium layer, of pine trees was used by early Indians as emergency food. It can be eaten fresh as it is stripped off the tree, cooked as a herb, or dried and later mixed with other plants as the flour for famine bread. The white pine is considered the best species for the purpose.

POKEWEED

This is a smooth perennial herb with large petioled leaves, that is, leaf and stalk are in combination. The plant grows to a height of between 5 and 9 feet. It is often seen along the roadside in the United States and Canada. Pokeweed blooms with a white flower, which is succeeded by purple berries. The roots of pokeweed are large and branching, and are also poisonous. Only the young shoots of the plant should ever be eaten. These are prepared by cooking in two waters, as asparagus tips are prepared.

PRAIRIE TURNIP

The prairie turnip, or wild potato, is native to the Great Plains and the West. It derives its name from its shape, which is similar to the cultivated variety. The Indians used it extensively because of its starchy root, which was prepared as a vegetable. Some attempts were made to cultivate the plant as a potato, hence the name wild potato.

PURSLANE

The Purslane family comprises several species which are common throughout the United States and the warmer areas of Canada. Its location is often spotty. One of the best-known members of the Purslane family is the bitterroot plant common to Canada and the Northwest. This plant grows in mountain country and blooms with a single rose-colored blossom. The blossom will open only in sunlight. The roots of the plant are long and tapering. These are wholesome to eat, but have a bitter flavor which gives rise to the name. When the plant is cooked it gives off an odor like tobacco, and for this reason the plant is sometimes called tobacco root. So popular was the plant in the Northwest that the Bitterroot Range of mountains, separating Idaho and Montana, was named for it. The bitterroot is also Montana's state flower.

SEGO LILY

Also called mariposa, this small lily grows in mountain and semidesert areas, reaching a height of 15 inches or so. It grows on a long thin stem having the same light-green color as the plant. The plant itself has a small bulb which is edible when boiled.

SILVERBERRY

This is a small shrub bearing light silver-colored berries which are dry and pulpy to the taste. It is common to western United States, western Canada, and Alaska. In Alaska it is also known as wolfberry, while farther south in the Yukon it is called the donjekberry, after the Donjek River along which it is found in abundance. Like rolled oats, good for man or horse, the donjekberry was, in the early days of Yukon horse-packing, picked in quantities and packed into the back country to feed horses, in lieu of grain. The silverberry has a small kernel of nutrient inside each berry.

REED

This is a coarse kind of grass, growing from 6 to 10 feet high, and having jointed stems averaging about a half-inch in diameter. Its leaves are similar to thin corn-stalk leaves. The plant lives in shallow water, bogs, and marshes, and is found near both fresh and salt waters. The range is spotty inland, but generally covers from central Canada to the Gulf of Mexico.

The roots may be dug and prepared in the same manner as potatoes.

SLIPPERY ELM

The inner bark of this tree, like the bark of the pine, has been used as emergency food. It is either eaten raw or boiled with fat into a stew. The tree grows from the Great Lakes region southward and eastward to the Atlantic Coastal States.

SORREL

There are several species of sorrel, which in appearance is like small dock. Its range is principally in eastern Canada. The plant is used as a herb, to nibble on, and to quench thirst.

SOW THISTLE

This plant is a prickly-leafed thistle, common to cultivated agricultural lands, and is considered noxious because it is so difficult to eradicate once it has become started. The flowers are yellow, and the plant has a milky juice when it is cut or broken. The young plants can be boiled in two waters, as with dandelions, and used as emergency greens.

STINGING NETTLE

This plant is widely distributed throughout the temperate regions of the United States and Canada. It is both an annual and a perennial herb. The entire plant is thickly covered with fine, needle-shaped hairs.

When the plant is accidentally brushed or hit with the hand, these tiny hairs prick the skin, depositing a mildly poisonous fluid which causes the sting. This can be avoided when handling the plant by pressing the fine hairs downward against the stem. As with milkweed, the young shoots of stinging nettle are edible as greens.

SUNFLOWER

The seeds of the sunflower, common to the Great Plains region, were long useful to the early Indians for making flour. The seeds of the larger plants were first parched, then ground. Later they were used in the making of bread and in soups.

WATER CRESS

One of the few wild plants which may be picked and eaten on the spot, water cress is an aquatic whose leaves grow above the surface. It is perennial and of the mustard family. Water cress has a tart, tangy flavor which adds to the palatability of salads. It may be eaten as a salad, or used as a filling for bread-and-butter sandwiches. The plant grows in clear creeks and springs in the more temperate and mountainous areas of North America, and is best to eat before it flowers. The plant may be cut just below the surface of the water or simply pinched off with the fingers.

WATER HYACINTH

This plant is a transplant from South America and now appears in the sluggish streams of the South, where it has become a nuisance. In emergencies, the young leaves may be cooked and eaten as an herb, but the plant should not be eaten raw.

WILD GRAPE

Wild grapes grow in mountainous areas, and are tart, dark-blue little fruits usually growing in bunches. The leaves of the plant are light green in color and short.

WILD ONION

The wild onion grows with a straight stem and long, thin leaves. The bloom occurs at the tip of the stem. The plant may be recognized by its onion-garlic odor and flavor. The small bulb from which the plant grows is the edible portion, and cooking by boiling destroys some of its objectionable odor and taste. In their trek across the Great Plains to the Salt Lake Valley over a century ago, the Mormon pioneers ate large quantities of wild onions, usually adding them to stews.

WILD PARSNIP

Usually occurring where seeds from the cultivated variety have been scattered, wild parsnip can be prepared and eaten in the same way as tame parsnips. There is, however, a real danger connected with their use, which should never be ignored. That is their similarity to the water hemlock, which is probably the most poisonous plant in the United States. Both adult varieties send up their thick stalks having seeds in an umbrella-like cluster at the top. The stalks of the water hemlock, when cut longitudinally, show a number of transverse chambers which contain the poisonous substance. The poisonous water hemlock grows along streams, usually in wet meadowlands. In the United States it is widely distributed across the country.

WILD RICE

Most of the Atlantic coastal states from Maine to Louisiana, as well as southern Canada, the Great Lakes region, and the upper Mississippi Basin have areas of wild rice. It is found in tidal rivers and marshes, and is a favorite food of waterfowl. The plant grows from 2 feet to well over the height of a man. Seeds form in a tassel at the ends of the stalks, and ripen during late August and September. The seeds may be eaten raw or cooked.

WILD BERRIES

The bloom of many wild plants is edible. This includes the blossoms of wild berries and fruits such as strawberries, raspberries, huckleberries, etc. The blossoms of wild roses, buttercups (if cooked), wild geraniums, sweet william, and prickly pear are all edible. So is the bloom of wild white clover and red clover.

It is not safe to eat the bloom of plants which are known to be poisonous to livestock. Among the plants poisonous to livestock are the loco weed, larkspur, jimson weed, death camass, lupine, greasewood, and water hemlock. Also, several plants are poisonous to stock when certain parts are eaten, whereas man may eat other parts (usually after cooking) and find them not poisonous. Among these are the milkweed (mature plants and leaves) and chokecherry (leaves). These are both toxic to livestock.

The senses of taste and smell offer some guidance in the matter of detecting poisonous blossoms. For example, the jimson weed, a member of the Nightshade family, grows tall and rank; and the entire plant is highly poisonous. Its big, white, trumpet-shaped flowers, as well as the leaves of the plant itself, have a disagreeable odor. This should be a natural warning. If any bloom has either an objectionable odor, or upon being tasted has a sickening or unpleasant taste, it should be left alone.

The following wild plants produce berries that are edible:

BEARBERRY

Often called kinnikinik, this is a red berry which grows from the Arctic regions to the Southwest. It is useful only in emergencies. The berry is dry to the taste and about as appetizing as a piece of red cork, but it does contain some nourishment. It is said to be better cooked than raw.

BLACKBERRY

There are scores of species of wild blackberries, which are so called because of their coloration when ripe. The blackberry is an aggregate-type berry which grows from a brambly bush and is often called brambleberry. It thrives well in the temperate parts of North America, with a range extending into central Canada. The berry resembles a wild raspberry except for the darker color. Most varieties are sweet and luscious.

BLUEBERRY

Widely distributed over northern United States, Canada, and Alaska, the blueberry falls into two general classifications. On one type, generally spread over the eastern areas of North America, the berries grow in terminal clusters. On the other, found in the West, the berries grow singly on bushes, like western huckleberries. The berries of the western type are dusky blue in color and grow on bushes ranging up to 2 feet in height. After the first frosts, these bushes turn red, making the large patches look like scarlet splashes on the landscape. The plants like the high ridges and sidehills, and often grow in patches of several acres. The berries are very sweet and juicy.

DEWBERRY

A species of blackberry that grows close to the ground.

ELDERBERRY

Growing on large tree-like shrubs, this plant has a wide distribution in mountainous country. The blossoms and fruit form in large clusters at the ends of branches. The tiny blossoms are cream-white in color, and are succeeded by fruit which is dark blue, turning even darker when ripe. Hermits living in wild mountain country often make elderberry wine and jelly. Both are excellent. The stalks of the shrub are virtually hollow in the mature plant, and filled with pith. If the pith is poked out, the dry stalk can be made into an elk bugle. I have personally "bugled up" several bull elk on elderberry bugles.

GOOSEBERRY

This plant is found in the northern tier of states and across southern Canada. The fruit grows on prickly bushes ranging up to 3 feet in height, and turns dark blue when ripe. When completely ripened, it is palatable raw, and excellent when made into jam or jelly. The dried blossom ends should be rubbed off the fruit before eating.

GROUND JUNIPER

Grows on the open hilltops and slopes from Alaska to northern United States. The small juniper berries they produce are poor eating, but do have some value as an emergency food.

HAW

This is the fruit of the Hawthorn tree, which is native to Europe and Asia but has become naturalized in North America. The trees reach a height of 15 to 20 feet or more, having thorns protruding from their branches. The ripened fruit is blue-black in color, and reaches the size of a fingernail. The fruit resembles large serviceberries, with each growing on a stem of considerable length. Inside it is yellow, pulpy, and full of seeds. The ripened fruit often hangs on the tree after the leaves have fallen. Haws are not palatable but are edible. The thorn apple is a variety of hawthorn.

CRANBERRY

The high-bush cranberry is common to the northern States and Canada. Another, the mountain cranberry, is native to Newfoundland and Labrador. Still another species, the low-bush cranberry, grows in the muskeg areas of Canada and Alaska nearly to the Arctic. These berries grow close to the ground on vine-like bushes whose waxy, stiff leaves are evergreen. Each berry of the low-bush variety averages about the size of a small garden pea. The berries are yellow-green until they begin to ripen, when they turn bright red. They have a fine tart flavor and can be eaten raw. If sugar is available in camp, they can be made into jam by cooking equal parts of sugar and berries. The jam is wonderful as topping for hot cakes or as garnish for wild meat.

HUCKLEBERRY

Black huckleberries are native to the eastern part of the continent, and range from Georgia into Canada. They are characterized by their black color and the hard seeds of the fruit. Western or blue huckleberries grow throughout the mountainous areas of western North America, have tiny seeds, and are more allied to the blueberry. Depending on the species, the shrubs of this western variety reach a height of from 10 inches to 2 feet. They like the high ridges in conifer-timber areas, and the northern slopes of high mountainsides. Some species have tiny red fruit. Others bear dark blue-black fruit which is luscious and sweet. There is no better fruit eaten as is, fresh from the shrub, nor is there any better pie than a huckleberry pie. Bears love huckleberries. One way for the outdoorsman to locate the patches is to keep a sharp lookout for the bruins or their spoor. If the dung of a grizzly is blue, there are blueberry patches near.

Similarly, if the dung of a black bear is purple, huckleberries are within his circuit of travel.

MOSSBERRY

These small, nearly black berries grow on a low evergreen type of bush similar to that of low-bush cranberries. They are found in the muskeg regions of North America. The berries average about quarter-inch in diameter, and are very juicy and sweet to the taste. Many times they will be passed by because of their dark coloration, which, amid the dark-green leaves, blends well with the ground.

MULBERRY

The edible mulberries are of the black or red varieties. The red mulberry is native to North America, with a distribution from New England to Florida and Texas. The black mulberry is an import from Asia, and is currently cultivated in the South and in California for the delicate sweet fruit. Mulberry trees bear abundantly. The fruit, too tender and delicate to transport well, is fine when eaten raw or made into jams.

PAWPAW

This small, deciduous tree or shrub, also called papaw, is native to the United States in the area east of the Mississippi River. The tree blooms with purple blossoms, and bears a banana-like fruit of pulpy texture, which is good to eat after the first frosts. In Mexico and other tropical areas of the continent, the tree is known as the papaya. In appearance, this tree resembles a palm, with a tall trunk ending in a top of yellow leaves. The fruit, too, is yellow in color, and tastes something like a ripe melon or pear. It is one of the best-known fruits of Mexico and the American tropics, and is generally eaten fresh.

PERSIMMON

The persimmon tree is a transplant from Asia, and was brought into the South shortly after the Civil War. It is now cultivated in areas near the west coast for its use in making furniture. A native variety of the same tree grows in a region just south of the Great Lakes, all the way to the Gulf of Mexico. This native tree grows to a height of over 50 feet, and bears a fruit that resembles a plum. The fruit is bitter to the taste, and like the fruit of the pawpaw, must be ripened by frost before it is palatable.

RASPBERRY

Wild raspberries grow in the temperate parts of the United States, over wide areas of Canada, and in Alaska. They grow on small spiny canes, which give them their name. The wild variety is comparable to the domestic raspberry except that it is smaller and generally softer and more hairy. Like blueberries, wild raspberries grow in great profusion in many parts of Canada, and the natives there still gather them when they ripen in August, to can for winter. The fruit is sweet and juicy and is best when eaten directly from the bushes. Both grizzly bears and black bears love raspberries and gorge on the fruit. They can pick off each berry neatly with their mouths, without getting the spiny canes.

SERVICEBERRY

The serviceberry grows on bushes often reaching 10 feet in height, and has a distribution from the Gulf of Mexico to Alaska. The bushes have dark purple-red bark and dark-green leaves. Each fruit grows on a long stem, is purple outside and has a white meat, purple-stained, inside. The fruit has numerous large seeds, is somewhat mushy in texture, but has a fine flavor. In Canada the serviceberry is often called the saskatoonberry. During the early settlement of the West and Canada, this fruit was picked in large quantities and canned, either fresh or mixed with apples, and made into jam for winter consumption.

STRAWBERRY

Wild strawberries are similar to the domestic varieties in the general appearance of bloom, plant, and fruit. Both plant and fruit are smaller in the wild state, with the plants being more spindly and pale. They are found in the temperate areas of the continent, and generally grow in wooded mountain country, often in shaded areas.

EDIBLE NUTS

In addition to the fruits, many trees bear nuts that may be eaten raw or pounded into flour and made into nut-bread when needed as emergency food. Among the edible nuts are beechnut, butternut, chestnut, hickory, peanut, pecan, pine (pinion), sweet acorn, and walnut.

EMERGENCY DRINKS

Many of the edible plants or fruits have some portions which can be made into emergency drinks. Some of these are the following:

Chicory. The tubers are roasted, ground, or pounded, and brewed like coffee.

Chufa. Prepared in the same way as chicory.

Dandelion. Roots may be ground and brewed into a bitter drink.

Elderberry. Hot water poured over ripe elderberries and allowed to stand, then cooled, makes a refreshing drink, especially if sugar is available to sweeten it.

Goldenrod. Both the young leaves and the flowers of this plant are brewed into tea.

Labrador Tea The leaves of this small, lacey-leafed plant, also called mountain tea and Hudson Bay tea, may be brewed into a delicious tea.

Mint. The leaves of such mints as spearmint, peppermint, and Bergamot may be crushed, hot water poured over them, and made into flavorful drinks.

Mulberry. Crushed and immersed in water, and allowed to stand, mulberries make a tasty fruit beverage. Other wild fruits such as blueberries and huckleberries may be used similarly.

Sassafras. In early America, sassafras tea was given to all members of the family for the medicinal qualities it was thought to contain. The tea is made by brewing the roots of the sassafras tree.

Sweet Birch. The dried leaves of this tree can be used to make an emergency tea.

CHAPTER 12

Knots and Lashings

A knot is formed by intertwining parts of a rope or two ropes to hold them together. A hitch is the fastening used to join a rope to a solid object such as a tree, log, or pole. A lash is the binding used to hold one or more objects in place.

The common material used to do all this is rope or cord. Often other materials such as leather thongs, nylon filament, or string are used for the same purpose, either alone or in combination with rope.

HEMP AND NYLON ROPE

Before getting into the tying of knots and hitches, it is helpful to understand a few facts about rope. The two most common ropes used for outdoor purposes today are hemp rope and nylon rope in braided form. The size of either should be matched to the intended purpose; and size, in the use of rope, usually means strength. The strength of any rope also depends upon the material from which it is woven, and its age.

A basic formula for determining the breaking strain of new hemp rope is: diameter squared multiplied by

222

7200. The safety load is considered to be one-quarter of the breaking strain, in pounds.

As an example, a quarter-inch rope, or ¼ x ¼ x 7200 pounds, would break if subjected to 450 pounds of strain. The safe load would be 112 pounds. A half-inch rope of Manila or sisal hemp would break at about 1800 pounds, and could sustain a safe load of around 450 pounds.

Braided nylon rope will support approximately three times that amount. A safe load for quarter-inch nylon rope would therefore be 336 pounds, and for the half-inch size, 1350 pounds.

A factor to remember is that ropes generally do not break along their length, but at knots, assuming that the rope's strength is uniform. Any knot causing a sharp angle to the direction of strain weakens the rope at that point.

Generally, hemp rope is used for rough purposes, such as lashing duffel on pack stock, lashing bundles and other cargo, and for tent guys and pole lashings. Nylon rope is neater in appearance, and is used for lashing packboard loads, and for boat painters, outdoor clotheslines, etc. Nylon is slicker, and tends to give under some of the simple knots which would hold, by friction, with hemp rope. New hemp rope is hard to handle in lashing gear. Wet hemp can't be tied as solidly as when dry. And frozen hemp rope should be avoided like a plague.

STOPPER KNOT

Either type of rope, hemp or nylon, will fray or unravel at the cut end. For this reason, some type of knot, or stopper, must be used. The simplest stopper to use with hemp rope is a single overhand knot at

Fig. 1. Useful knots for the outdoorsman: (A) overhand knot; (B) square knot; (C) slip knot; (D) bowline; (E) sheet-bend; (F) water knot.

the running end of the rope. Hemp rope is formed of three twisted strands, which are then twisted together in the opposite direction. To tie a satisfactory end knot, untwist the strands for a few inches, but do not untwist each individual strand, otherwise the knot will be too soft for practical use. With the strands separated and laid lengthwise together, an overhand knot (Fig. 1A) should then be made so that after it is pulled as taut as possible the knot itself lies snugly against the untwisted part of the rope. The finished knot should be laid on a hard surface and rolled back and forth beneath the foot. This makes it snug and smooth.

WHIPPING AND BURNING

A good way to "stop" a braided nylon rope is to whip and burn the end. To whip the end of a rope, lay the ends of a length of strong cord oppositely along the rope end so they overlap for 3 or 4 inches (Fig. 2A). Then, while holding down the two cords along the rope, begin winding the loop around the rope, and back along its standing part (Fig. 2B).

When about 1 inch has been wound as taut as possible, each end of the cord is pulled tight from opposite ends of the winding. It will be seen that both ends pull under the winding. When pulled free of loops, the unused ends of the cord are cut off snug against the whipping (Fig. 2C). A lighted match, held for a second under the cut end of the rope, will fuse the nylon threads together, further keeping the rope from unfraying.

TURKEY-HEAD KNOT

If you want to be fancier, or to use a hemp rope for such purposes as threading through small-diame-

Fig. 2. Whipping the end of a rope.

Fig. 3. Turkey-head knot.

tered rings on horse hackamores, a turkey-head knot (Fig. 3) may be made in the rope's end.

To make a turkey-head knot, untwist the three strands from each other for about 6 inches, for a half-inch rope, but don't untwist each individual strand. Next, bend the strands downward so they look like spokes of a wheel running out evenly from the solid part of the rope. Mentally number the strands 1, 2, and 3, beginning at the right if you are right-handed.

Now take 1, loop it loosely under 2, and bring it up to vertical. Loop 2 around the adjacent 1 and also under 3, then bring it to vertical. Lastly, bring strand 3 under the adjacent 2, and also under the loose loop formed by strand 1, then up to vertical (Fig. 3A).

You now have a woven knot. Pull this as tight as possible and down against the untwisted portion of the rope. Make three more similar knots, pulling each succeeding knot taut against the under portion.

The result is four layers of woven strands, each lying tightly on top of the other (Fig. 3B). To finish, the knot is laid on the floor or hard earth and rolled firmly back and forth under the foot. The finished knot won't untie and is small enough in diameter to thread through tight places.

BRAIDING

Often similar sizes of rope or cord are not available for joining. Rope often has to be joined to string, leather thongs, or cord. Many times rope breaks and unravels, leaving only individual strands which could be used if they were strong enough.

For such reasons, anyone using rope should know how to braid. Many is the time I've seen the "straw strings" of threshed wheat bundles, and the twine used around hay bales, braided into emergency rope.

In the simplest braiding, three strands of material are knotted together with an overhand knot, and the knot hung onto a nail solidly set in a tree. Braiding is begun by taking the right strand over and across the center strand; then the left strand is passed over and across the center strand (originally the right strand), as in Fig. 4A. This motion is repeated until the desired length is reached.

When a strand runs out, it is spliced by laying another length alongside it, holding or whipping the two together, and braiding in the overlapping ends as a single strand. The ends, or fuzz, are later cut off the finished braiding. The finished product is a flat rope.

A far better rope is made by braiding four strands of material. To braid four, fasten all strands together with a knot, or whipping, and hang the knot onto a

Fig. 4. Two methods of braiding: (A) three-strand braid, (B) four-strand braid.

nail as before. Next spread the four strands and mentally number them 1, 2, 3, and 4, beginning at the right.

To begin, bring strand 1 down under 2 and 3, then up over 3, holding 1 solidly upon 3 with the thumb and index finger. Next, bring 4 down under from the opposite side, and under the two middle strands, bringing it up between them and the now-right strand taking the place of the original number 1; and firmly over and upon the middle strand next to it (Fig. 4B).

In other words, the strand numbers will change as each takes the place of another. But their positions won't. The procedure is to braid first with the right-hand strand, then the left-hand strand. Each in turn is brought under *two* strands, up between, over and across the strand adjacent to it. That's all there is to it, and the technique can be learned in sixty seconds, with four lengths of shoelace or fishing line.

If the tension is kept tight and uniform as the braiding continues, the result will be a neat round rope, which should be finished by rolling it between the palms. Rawhide or leather thongs braided this way can be made into fine emergency rope or stock halters of the hackamore type.

KNOTS

Most knots depend for their holding power on the friction created by two ropes, or the strands of a single rope, binding against each other. Simple knots will suffice for rough rope such as hemp, while slick rope material such as nylon requires more involved knots in order to hold. Often a combination of two knots is used for slick rope.

A half-dozen basic knots and their variations will suffice for every purpose. If the average outdoorsman will learn that many, and the specific purposes for which each is most suited, he will be better off than trying to memorize numerous specialized knots which he will soon forget because he has no use for them.

SQUARE KNOT

One of the simplest knots is the square knot (Fig. 1B). This is made by tying two overhand knots, one upon the other, but alternating the direction of the second half. To tie a square knot, take a rope end in each hand. Put the right rope under the left rope. Bring it full around, and point both ends upward. Next, take the now-right end (it was the left before) and bring it *over* the other end, down under and around, and tighten. If the knot is made by tying both parts identically, the result is a granny knot, which won't hold.

The square knot is useful for joining rope ends where mild tension must be kept on both ropes while the knot is tied. It is the knot used to tie your shoes, except that the loops are not pulled completely through.

In tying a square knot upon angular packages, it helps keep the tension to tie the knot, if possible, upon a corner. Often a variation called the "surgeon's knot" is made in order to hold all tension. This is done by making two turns around for the first part of the square knot instead of one.

Slip Knot

Another simple, usable knot is the slip knot (Fig. 1C). This is made by doubling the end of a rope back against itself, and tying a simple overhand knot with the rope end around the standing part of the rope. The noose will slip tight when the knot is tied around a tree or pole. The slip knot, plus a single half-hitch, is the best way to tie a saddle horse to a tree when it must be left for some time. The slip knot holds the rope against the tree so it won't slip down where Dobbin can step over it and entangle himself; and the half-hitch keeps the slip knot from untying, especially in new hemp rope or in the "hard twist" common to lariats.

Sheet Bend

For joining two ends of rope, no knot surpasses

the sheet bend (Fig. 1E). To tie a sheet bend, form the end of one rope into a small loop. Poke the end of another rope up through this loop, bring it around both parts of the other rope, and tuck the end under where it came up through the loop, but over both parts of the opposite rope.

If one rope is smaller in diameter than the other, use the smaller as the end to push up through the loop, and tie as before, except make one complete turn around the larger rope before threading the smaller under itself. Leather thongs can be joined to larger rope by this method, which is useful in tying rope to saddle strings, etc.

Even after wetting, or considerable strain, a sheet bend can usually be quickly untied by bending the loop end downward over the standing opposite rope.

BOWLINE

The very best knot for making a loop that won't slip is the bowline (Fig. 1D). To tie a bowline, make a loop around a tree and grasp the end in the left hand. Next, make a loop in the standing part of the rope between you and the tree, tipping the rope forward so that the part next to the standing end is on top. Lastly, poke the end downward through this loop, bring it under and around the standing part of the rope, and back through the loop from beneath.

The bowline is useful in any circumstance where a nonslipping loop, which may be easily untied, is desired. You can, for example, fit a loop formed by a bowline over a rock, ledge, or heavy branch; lower yourself down the rope to solid footing below; then flip the loop off the rock or branch and take your rope with you.

Fig. 5. Simple clove hitch for tying tent guy ropes (A).
Looped end (B) makes it easy to untie in wet weather.

CLOVE HITCH

The clove hitch (Fig. 5A) is one of the most useful knots for tying a rope to a pole or log. To tie one, toss the end of a rope over a horizontal branch or pole. Bring the end down, under, and up at the left side of the standing part. Cross the end over the standing part, make another turn down around the pole, bringing the end up again, and under its own loop to the right of the standing part of the rope.

WATER KNOT

A useful knot for joining rope together is called the water knot (Fig. 1F). It is made by laying two rope ends together so they overlap for a foot or more. Then an overhand knot is tied in each of the ends so that it encloses the standing part of the other rope. When pulled tight, the knot holds well, but it is hard to take apart.

Timber Hitch

The timber hitch is useful when working with logs (Fig. 6). It is made by looping the rope around a log, crossing the end over the standing part and back against itself, where it is then wound round and round that portion of the loop. When pulled tight, friction prevents it from unwinding.

Ring Hitches

Where medium-diametered hemp rope must be used to tie onto iron rings, such as halter rings and cinch rings, an overhand knot should be tied at the end of the rope, and the rope tied to the ring with another overhand knot. This simple knot will hold in

Fig. 6. Timber hitch for hauling logs.

any hemp rope, once the rope's initial stiffness has worn off.

For attaching small-diametered rope to small rings, which tend to cut the rope easily, it's best to make two or three turns around the ring, then finish off with two half-hitches, and again bring the knot at the rope's end snugly up against the finished knot. This type of knot distributes the strain evenly.

LOOPED KNOTS

Often knots must be tied so that they may be easily untied, even after they have been wetted by storm or water; and often when your fingers are half frozen. "Hard knots," such as a plain slip knot, should not be used where they must be quickly untied. Examples are tent ropes guyed to poles, or lead ropes tied to horses' tails in packstring work.

Usually any type of knot can be finished off, not by threading the end completely through at its final stage, but by looping it through. Half-hitches may be looped, either for the second part or for both parts by doubling the end. A bowline can be completed by looping. So can a sheet bend. So can a square knot, as in the loops left when tying your shoes. A clove hitch can be looped in its final stage, instead of threaded—and this, incidentally, makes a fine sour-weather hitch for tying tent ropes around a side pole.

When rain or snow wets such looped knots, they are handily untied simply by jerking the final loop, which loosens the tightest part of the knot and makes untying easy. Looped knots will hold as firmly as otherwise, if used where constant tension is applied.

Fig. 7. Two wraps and double half-hitch, end looped.

TYING ROPE UNDER TENSION

Often the ideal knot for a purpose cannot be tied because it is necessary to apply tension to the rope during the tying. The best hitch for tying a rope under tension to a solid object is to make two wraps around and two half-hitches (Fig. 7). For example, in hoisting a weight with the rope over a branch, tension is held while two turns of the rope are made around the pole; then two half-hitches hold that tension and finish the hitch. Again, when steadying the heavy ridgepole of a large tent with a guy rope, you can quickly take two turns around the stake, finish off with half-hitches, and not lose an inch of slack. If, in such cases, both parts of the double half-hitch are made with looped rope, the entire hitch can be quickly jerked free.

LASHINGS

Knots and lashings used to join poles and small

logs together are somewhat different than knots used to join two lengths of rope or tie a rope to an object.

SHEAR-POLE LASH

One of the most common lashings is the one used for joining two shear poles for erecting tents. Lay the two poles side by side, attach the rope end with a clove hitch to one of the poles, and make three overhand turns around both poles. Make two turns with the rope around these loops at right angles and between the poles (called frapping); and finish off with a clove hitch around the opposite pole. When the poles are spread, forming the shears, the twisting tension will bind them firmly together.

A similar binding for shear poles can be made without the use of the two clove hitches. Simply make three turns around both poles, two more turns of frapping between the poles and around the loops, and join the rope ends with a square knot (Fig. 8).

Fig. 8. Shear-pole lash.

Fig. 9. Diagonal lash.

If enough rope is available, this same type of hitch can be used for joining any number of poles together, as in making a raft or a pole tripod. The rope is looped around all poles at the desired position. A couple of frapping turns are made between each pair of poles and finished with a half-hitch, and the two ends are tied with a square knot.

DIAGONAL LASH

The other basic lash is for tying one pole at right angles to another pole. This may be done in two ways. The simplest is to make three turns with the rope around both poles, diagonally, at the junction; then finish with frapping. Pulled tight, this takes up any slack and pulls the binding tight to prevent slipping (Fig. 9). If you are lashing a pole frame, each corner should be lashed in the opposite direction; otherwise, because the tension is the same at both ends, the frame will sag into a parallelogram. In other words, make one diagonal binding pointing to the right, the opposite one pointing left.

Fig. 10. Square lash.

SQUARE LASH

A second way of binding a crossbar to another pole requires more rope but is more solid (Fig. 10). Attach rope with a clove hitch to the crossbar. Next wind the rope down under the lengthwise pole, up the opposite side, over the end of the crossbar, down under the lengthwise pole again on the opposite side of the crossbar, up over the crossbar to its other side . . . and repeat for three or four turns. Finish off with two turns around the rope itself between the poles, and another clove hitch around the opposite pole.

LASHING POLES SIDE BY SIDE

Often you will want to join several small poles side by side, as in making a pole bed frame or table top. The poles need not be secured as firmly as when making a raft (Fig. 11).

First, lay all the poles side by side. Loop the rope at the middle and, beginning at one side near the ends, place the loop around the first pole. Then, push one end down between the first and second poles, the other end up between them. Secure the second pole by pushing the end of the upper rope down again through the space between the second and third poles, the opposite end up between them. It's just like stitching a double overhand-stitch in cloth with two needles. Finish at the opposite side by pulling the rope tight, and tying off with a square knot. A similar lash at the opposite end of the poles will secure them.

WEAVING STITCH

Where several crossbars are to be laid upon side-rails, but with space between them, they may be secured by a weaving "stitch" made in this way: Tie the rope with a clove hitch to one end of a rail. Place

Fig. 11. Lashing poles side by side.

Fig. 12. Weaving stitch.

the rope under the first crossbar, up and around it in a half-hitch, and bring the rope under the siderail to the next crossbar. A similar half-hitch is made around the second bar, but on the opposite side of the side-rail. The turn around the third bar is made as for the first. When all crossbars have been lashed, the rope is drawn tight and finished off with another clove hitch. Tension on the rope binds all cross members downward against the rail, and longitudinally against each other (Fig. 12).

EXPRESS HITCH

The lashing of duffel and gear into compact bundles which won't spill their contents and which may be handled easily is vital for most outdoors travel and camping. Containers that fit the larger items represent the best packaging; but for the inevitable and numerous small items, the best single way of packaging is to wrap them securely into a canvas manta (a 6-foot square of canvas) and tie them up with an express hitch (Fig. 13). Smaller bundles may be wrapped in smaller pieces of canvas and hitched similarly.

First, the items are fitted together as compactly as their shapes will allow, and placed in the middle of the manta. Next, the sides of the canvas are folded over. If the side is longer than the bundle, it should be folded under itself rather than extended over and onto the opposite side. With both sides folded in, the bottom is folded over. The top should always be folded last, so that the flap covers the other folds— this to prevent rain or snow from wetting the contents.

To begin the express hitch used in securing the package, make a slip-knot loop, or a lasso-type loop with the smaller loop tied with a bowline knot. Loop this around the top part of the package, with the knot resting over the folded top-flap. Pull tight, and while holding the tension, make a half-hitch around the

Fig. 13. Express hitch.

package at its center. Pull and hold this tight, while making a third half-hitch around the package near its bottom end.

You now have three loops around the package. Next bring the rope down under the package, and up to the first loop at the back. Make a half-hitch around this cross-loop; continue to the second cross-loop and make another half-hitch; do the same at the third loop, then bring the rope over the package's top, down to the first cross-loop, and tie off with half-hitches around that part of the rope leading downward from the first loop.

Rectangular packages are easy to tie with an express hitch. Odd-shaped bundles may be tied up in the same way, however. A good way to increase the rigidity of the hitch, with odd-shaped bundles, is to make two turns around each cross-loop instead of a single half-hitch, when bringing the standing part of the rope around the package after the three loops are made. When drawn tight, the rope twists these turns diagonally, so no part of the rope slips in any direction.

Such an improved express hitch is often used for tying a rock solidly enough to be used for an emergency boat anchor. Another hitch for tying a rock for the same purpose, if a long rock can be found with a straight or thin middle, is a slip knot and a half-hitch. When pulled tight, and the rope wetted, such a combination will hold well.

PACKBOARD LASH

Packboards have a series of screw eyes anchored solidly into the standards. To bind a packboard load, first attach a 6-foot length of heavy cord or light rope to each of the opposite top screw eyes. Next, lay the

Fig. 14. Packboard lash.

wrapped load on the packboard so that the top flap is outside and pointing down. Place the load an inch higher than it is intended to ride, to accommodate for sagging during travel. Then lace the load alternately across with the cords, just as you lace your shoes (Fig. 14).

To finish the tie, place your knee upon the rope binding on the load, so it won't slip, and tie a bowline knot in one rope, shortly after it has passed through the final screw eye. Thread the opposite rope through the loop formed by this, and pull the two ropes tightly together. Finish with two looped half-hitches. Tension may be kept by doing this, while some would be lost in finishing off with a square knot.

The same lashing is used for a toboggan load, except that the ropes at the toboggan's sides become the screw eyes of the packboard.

CARE OF ROPE

Rope is valuable outdoor equipment; in some cases, lifesaving equipment. Care in its use and storage will insure its being usable when needed, and certain precautions and rules should be observed.

First, never cut a length of rope unless it is absolutely necessary. Cut rope will unravel unless knotted, and unraveled rope is ruined rope. Short lengths are never as useful as longer lengths, and knotted or spliced rope is never as satisfactory as unknotted rope. It is far better to coil up unneeded rope, after lashing, and leave it long enough for another purpose.

Another good way to preserve the length of a rope, is to "knit" the surplus. This is done by beginning at the final knot of any job, making a slip knot, reaching through the loop formed and bringing in another loop, making still another loop through this one, just as in crocheting. When the surplus rope is all knitted, pull the end through the final loop so it won't unravel, and tie it in a coil to the final knot of the lash.

After using a length of rope, it should be coiled neatly and hung off the damp earth away from gnawing animals. One way of coiling rope is to grasp the end in the left hand, raise that hand to vertical, then wrap the rope around the uplifted elbow and between the thumb and fingers until it is all coiled. With the coil finished, the loops are knotted snugly together with two or three half-hitches around all strands.

Where larger rope is used, it may be coiled into longer loops by holding one end in the left hand and making successive loops of the desired size with the right hand, which are hung over the left forearm until all rope has been coiled. With these coils completed, three turns are made around the entire coil, drawing all strands together tightly against each other. The end is then drawn through the coil just above these lateral turns. This will hold the coil in place until the rope is needed again.

Where possible it is best to hang coiled rope inside to protect it against weather and rodents. When this is impossible, rope should be placed on something high, and canvas draped over it. Like canoe paddles and the handles of camp tools, rope accumulates salt from the perspiration of humans or pack animals. Animals like porcupines will gnaw and ruin rope for the salt contained in this perspiration.

Occasionally you can be *too* careful in your consideration of good rope. A young fellow in Wyoming found it necessary to "tail" his packstring—that is, he tied one loaded animal to the tail of the beast ahead of it. One of these horses was a beautiful buckskin, with a long, nearly white, magnificent tail.

Because of the arroyos through which the string passed, tension was hard and often abrupt on the tails of the animals. Back on level ground again, the young fellow tried to untail the beasts, but found the buckskin's tail so tightly twisted in the rope that he had to cut the hairs. He really did a good job, with the result that the animal's long flowing tail was cut off square and short.

At camp, the owner and outfitter was understandably angry. "I suppose it didn't occur to you to cut the rope, instead of Buck's tail?" he asked.

The youngster was unapologetic. "A horse's tail will grow out again," he assured his employer. "A rope won't."

CHAPTER 13

The Ingenious Outdoorsman
What He Can Make

The farther one goes into the wilderness, and the longer he remains there, the greater becomes his need for improvising certain items of equipment. Basic items of gear become damaged or wear out. Equipment for every purpose cannot usually be taken along owing to weight and difficulties of transportation. And often specialized pieces of equipment cannot be purchased but must be made, often on the spot, to fill special needs. Tap an experienced outdoorsman and you find an ingenious and inventive person. Following are some of the ways outdoor living can be made easier by improvising camp equipment.

CAMP LIGHTS

The best camp lights yet developed are the gasoline lantern and the battery-operated flashlight. Emergency lamps help to prolong the life of these types of lighting and serve as independent means of illumination when the need arises. The most inexpensive and portable are wax candles. A half-dozen candles of half-inch diameter should go along on any lengthy outdoor trip.

Candles may be used in many ways. The simplest is to light the candle, then tip it so that several drops of melted wax will land on a table at the desired spot. Set the candle base into the soft wax and hold till it cools and sets. The lighted candle then won't tip over. Another way is to push the candle into the top of a bottle and use the bottle as a lamp base. Again, one blade of a pocketknife may be shoved into a tree, the blade at its other end pulled to an upright position, and the candle impaled on the uplifted blade.

It is possible to focus the light from a candle by

Three simple candle holders that can be made in the outdoors with only a pocket knife and a tin can.

making a simple lantern. Cut two inch-long slits, one across the other, on one side of a #10 tin can midway along its length, and fit a wire or cord bail to the can's opposite side. The right-angle corners of tin formed by the cuts are pushed inward so that the candle can be shoved through. To hold the candle snugly, bend the points of the tin in or out.

In use, the can is held longitudinally, the open end focusing the light into a beam. As the candle burns down, it is shoved farther up into the can. This type of tin-can lantern is called a "palooser," because so many were once used in the Palouse country of the Pacific Northwest.

Surplus wax from candles and butt ends should not be thrown away. They can be melted and used for a tin-cup light. This is made by cutting down a small tin can to one-half its height, but leaving an inch-wide strip along the seam. Bend over the raw edges of this strip as well as the circular cut-edge of the can. Then bend the rimmed strip into a handle, as on a tin cup. The wax pieces are melted in this cup around a wick made either of cotton cord or three strands of string braided together.

POTATO-SACK PACK

Packs for lugging duffel about are not difficult to improvise. One of the simplest for small items is made by sewing a seam across the open end of a 100-pound potato or seed-grain bag, then cutting an 8-inch hole through the exact center of both parts of the flattened sack. To finish, tie a short cord or light rope to each of the four corners. The items of duffel are placed through the center hole, into each side of the sack, and the sack lifted over the head and set down over

Potato sack with hole cut in middle becomes an emergency pack.

the shoulders. Part of the load rides at the rear, part of it in front. The corners are tied at each side by the four cords.

This emergency pack will carry reasonable loads. The seam across the bag's end can be sewn with any available string. A usable needle can be made by straightening one of the metal keys used for opening canned meat; or the cord can simply be threaded through the mesh of the bag with the fingers. Wearing such a pack makes one appear somewhat bosomy, but for temporary use, for loads up to 15 or 20 pounds, it is quite comfortable.

CAMP TABLE

A camp table for comfortable outdoor dining can be built on a framework of four posts set solidly into the ground 30 to 34 inches high. These posts should be set on the smokeless side of the fire. Dry pine posts 4 inches in diameter are ideal. They should be placed at each corner of a rectangle forming the desired size of the table, say, 3 feet by 5 feet.

Next, attach a pair of crossbars to each pair of end posts so their upper surfaces are just even with the post tops. They may be attached with spikes, if available, or lashed with rope, buckskin thongs, or wire. Onto these crossbars, small poles or saplings 2 to 4 inches in diameter are laid closely together and hitched solidly with the weaving hitch. It helps to get the straightest saplings possible, and to smooth their upper surfaces to prevent utensils from slipping through the finished table top.

A fine addition to such a table is to make seats integral with it. This can be done by spiking or lashing another pair of crossbars to the legs, long enough to extend about 18 inches past each side of the table and approximately 14 inches off the ground. Next, flatten the upper surfaces of six poles having diameters of about 4 inches. Lay these lengthwise along the table's sides, three on each side, on the protruding ends of the lower crossbars and lash or spike them close together. In a large, permanent camp, such a table-bench is often built first, then a large wall tent pitched over it.

CAMP BED

Some sort of framework should always be made at camp on which to place your bed. Today's bed is apt to be a good sleeping bag laid on an air mattress. This combination, as well as beds of blankets and boughs, should be raised off the ground. Moisture will soak up into the bed, and even though a rubber air mattress keeps it off the sleeper, moisture clings to mattress when it is rolled up, subsequently getting into the bed itself.

One simple arrangement for a bed frame is to lay two 3-foot logs at either end of the bed, allowing an extra foot of bed length. That is, lay them 7 feet apart for a 6-foot bag. Onto these, lash 4-inch poles alongside each other until a 3-foot width is covered. The outside poles, one on either side, should be of larger diameter than the others to prevent the sleeper from rolling off. If sufficient cord or rope isn't available for lashing the poles, they may be laid into shallow notches cut into each end log. When the weight of the bag is on them, they will not slip out of place.

RAISED FIREPLACES

For cooking at a semipermanent campsite where no stove is available, it is practical to raise the fireplace off the ground to a comfortable cooking height. This may be done in two ways: One is to stake off a 2-foot square of ground with 30-inch stakes of green wood—like a picket fence enclosing a square. Six inches below the top of the stakes, lash four crossbars, one on each side, to keep the stakes from spreading. Into this space, dirt is shoveled to the full height. Gravel or rocks are then laid over the dirt top to make a foundation for the cooking fire, which is built on top.

A second method is to build a miniature log cabin enclosing an area 2-by-2 feet square. The logs are notched on their undersides and laid on a pair of cross logs. This is continued until the desired height is reached; then the enclosure is shoveled full of earth. If enough green logs are not available, dry logs may be used except for the top layer.

Burlap bag slipped over orange crate makes an efficient camp cooler. Shallow pan of water feeds moisture through cloth wick onto burlap.

CAMP COOLERS

The easiest way to improvise a cooler is to dig a pocket in a spring and place the food containers into the small pool. In a creek, it's best to form a cairn of rocks at the edge of the water, leaving just enough opening for the water to come in. Cans set directly into the creek are apt to float away.

A lid for such a cooler can be made from a large, flat rock. If none is available, the split half of a thick log, with the flat side down, makes a good cover. A heavy cover keeps direct sunlight out, and keeps any predator from getting into the cooler.

You can make a simple cooler by tying all canned goods into a burlap sack, putting it into a creek, and anchoring it with a strong rope to a stump on the bank.

Many foods, such as bacon, butter, fruit, and meats, cannot be kept cool in this fashion, however. But if a burlap sack and an orange crate are available, a fine cooler for all foods can be made. Stand the crate on end and attach a rope to the upper end. Cut a hole in the sack's bottom and thread the rope through. Food packages are placed on the two shelves of the

Cooler can be made of wooden slabs cut from a log and inserted in burlap bag which has an opening flap cut as shown. Cleat nailed to slabs keeps them from tilting.

box (middle partition and bottom end), the sack is lowered over the crate, and the cooler is suspended by the rope from a high limb. Sprinkle water over the burlap sack and set a tin can full of water on top of the box. If a small strip of burlap or cloth is then placed in the filled can with one end draped over the edge and onto the burlap sack, it will siphon enough water to keep the sack moist. Evaporation of this moisture will cause the container to remain cool, even during the heat of midday. Additional water may be sprinkled on, if needed.

If no crate is available, a cooler can be made by slabbing out four boards from a section of log. Make each board a foot square, if a log that size is available. Then cut a strip about 10 inches wide out of the sack, leaving it "hinged" at the bottom. The boards are placed inside the sack and nailed into position like the shelves of an upright cupboard—one at the sack's bottom, the others spaced below. The bag becomes the sides and back of the cupboard. The rope is tied to the upper board. A willow cleat nailed to all shelves at the face, or open side, keeps the shelves from tipping and joins them solidly together. In use, the food is placed in this upright cupboard, the flap is closed, and water is sprinkled over the bag. A can of water with a cloth wick on top, as with the orange-crate cooler, will keep the burlap moist.

WASHSTANDS

A simple stand for the wash basin can be made by driving three saplings firmly into the ground just far enough apart so they will catch the under rim of the basin when the tops are "sprung" a trifle.

A fancier washstand can be made by lashing three

Three ways to support a wash basin at camp: (1) on stick platform lashed to flattened sides of a tree; (2) on three saplings driven into the ground; and (3) on tripod of three saplings lashed halfway down.

saplings together a foot or so from their tops. The bottom parts of the saplings become the legs, which are spread apart to form a tripod. This also spreads their tops into a triangle of three pole ends on which the wash basin is set.

Another good washstand is made by slightly flattening two opposite sides of a large tree at a height of 34 inches, and nailing or lashing two saplings, one at each side, which will stick out horizontally for 15 inches in front of the tree. Onto these saplings poles

NOR
STA

Clock-compass that tells time and indicates north can be made in camp of a pole and twelve stakes.

are lashed, making a small table having its back edge against the tree. The wash basin is set upon this. This arrangement is also fine for shaving, since the mirror can be handily hung on the tree above the stand.

CLOCK-COMPASS

You can build a combination clock-and-compass with only a small pole and some stakes. Choose a small spot of ground exposed to the sun at all times during the daylight hours. Smooth the surface until it is level. Next, wait for a starry night and take an 8- to 10-foot straight pole, and drive into the ground at an angle so that its tip points directly at the North Star. At noon some day as you loaf around camp, drive a stake into the ground near the far end of the shadow cast by the slanting pole. That's 12 o'clock on your woods clock. Drive stakes similarly for each hour of the day and you have a permanent sun dial.

EMERGENCY SNOWSHOES AND BINDING

During winter travel, a broken snowshoe presents a problem. If the break isn't too bad, a repair often can be made by splicing a light slat to the broken sidebar. However, an emergency shoe in the shape of a board can be slabbed out of a 3-foot length of dry log. Roughly shape the board to size, cut out a semicircular hole for the toe, and with a knife bore two holes, one at either side of the toe hole. Thread a length of rope through these holes, around both snowshoe and pac, for an emergency binding. The lightest possible wood should be chosen, and the snowshoe shaped according to the width and strength of the wood, and only large enough to support one's weight. Cedar is the best wood for this, as it slabs easily.

A different type of emergency snowshoe can be made of green alders or willows. Two sidebars of suitable length are placed side by side and bound at both ends with fishing line or cord. The saplings should be flattened with a knife at the ends to prevent them from slipping. Next, lash an alder crossbar tightly at the position where the ball of the foot nor-

Emergency snowshoe improvised from two saplings and a number of short sticks.

mally rides over the standard snowshoe lacing, spreading the sidebars sufficiently to get the desired width. Lash smaller crossbars behind this one, an inch apart, across the space where the foot will ride, and a final crossbar just forward of the toe opening. Finally, a burlap bag or a piece of clothing, such as a leg of a pair of Levis, should be sewn around the frame to cover the bottom of the shoe.

An emergency snowshoe binding, either for the above shoe or for a commercial model, can be made of a length of cotton clothesline, cord, leather thong, or rope. Cotton clothesline and sash cord are best, as they won't stretch when wet. Double the length of line at the middle and place this loop around the heel of the pac. Bring each end forward, and under the crossbars at either side of the toe; then up and across the toe, and back through the cords on either side of the arch. Crisscross them over the front of the foot, and tie them at the back of the pac. This emergency binding is easily twisted out of, if necessary.

BIRCHBARK KETTLES

Birchbark kettles are made of birchbark that has been soaked in water until it becomes soft. One of the best is the basket-kettle shown in the illustration. For sewing cord you can use spruce or tamarack roots, leather thong, or nylon cord. Holes are punched with an awl, if available, or a knife blade. A rim of bent willow or birch is sewn all around at the kettle's top in a continuous overhand stitch, to give rigidity and a carrying rim to the finished vessel.

All seams are waterproofed with emergency glue which can be made in the outdoors by boiling together 15 percent bacon fat or animal suet and 8

Pattern for cutting birch-bark kettle and completed kettle laced with thong or strips of root fiber.

percent resin found in such conifers as spruce, balsam fir, and pine. The addition of the animal fat makes the product less brittle. Fish glue can be made by boiling in water the heads, fins, and tails of fish, until nothing except a sticky gelatin-like substance remains.

CAMPER'S SOAP

Soap is a necessity for trips into the woods, especially for prolonged stays. If you exhaust your supply, you can make your own by pouring scalding water several times over wood ashes, and using the resultant liquid in the wash water for washing clothes. Pioneer women in the West often had no other form of soap for the purpose. They would keep all ashes from the kitchen stove in a wooden barrel. Hot water was repeatedly poured through these ashes and drained off through a hole at the bottom of the barrel. The lye of the ashes, largely potash, was the cleaning agent.

Another recipe calls for boiling this same liquid, strong as it can be made, with small amounts of bacon grease and other animal fat. The mixture is boiled until most of the water is evaporated, and then allowed to set overnight. The soap will rise to the surface and can be skimmed off.

The tallow of a freshly killed deer can also be used to make soap. Pour 2½ gallons of scalding water over 2 gallons of wood ashes. Stir occasionally, and let the mixture set overnight. Skim off the froth, and drain or pour off the clear liquid as needed. Meantime, render a half-pound of deer tallow, and boil down the melted fat in the wood-ashes liquid, in a small cast-iron, enameled, or galvanized container. When the approximate 3 quarts of liquid has been slow-boiled away with the tallow to the final pint, allow the remainder to set overnight. The soap will rise to the top as a crust.

Bacon rinds, surplus grease, and other animal fat can be made into a better soap with the addition of ordinary household lye. Add four pounds of such cracklings, rinds, or grease to 4 quarts of cold water and 13 ounces of lye and let soak for three days in an enameled kettle or pot. Next, add 5 quarts of cold water and cook the mixture over a fire for thirty minutes, or until all cracklings dissolve. Allow the mixture to stand overnight, after which the soap will rise to the top and can be cut away in bar-sized cubes. These are set upon a log to dry.

Deer tallow can be combined with lye to make a fine-grade soap which will rival the commercial product. Dissolve 1 can of lye in 7 cups cold water. While the mixture is still hot, add 4 pounds of clean deer tallow, broken or cut into small bits; ½ cup borax;

½ cup household ammonia; and 1 cup Chlorox (this particular product must be used, not a substitute).

Let the mixture stand for a couple of days, or until it granulates, stirring once in a while with a wooden paddle (not metal). During the stirring, the large lumps may be broken up. The resulting soap is like cheese curd and may be further granulated, after it has completely dried, by running it through a food grinder.

PRESERVING ANIMAL SKINS

The skins of game animals may be used in a variety of ways, either as rawhide or as buckskin leather, for fashioning articles of use to the outdoorsman.

Deer skins and similar hides should be worked on when they are fresh. Otherwise, they must be salted well and dried out to preserve them until they can be tanned. Before tanning a dry hide, it must be loosened by soaking. This is done by immersing the complete hide in a solution of salt and water (1 pound of salt to 2 gallons of water), for from six hours to two or three days, depending upon the stiffness of the hide.

MAKING RAWHIDE

For making rawhide, the hide must be fleshed of all remaining meat and fat. Pare off the larger pieces, then scrape the flesh side of the hide with a blunt knife, horse rasp, or similar implement, holding the skin firmly over a smooth log set at a workable height. This should be done in the shade, as full sunlight tends to "burn" the hide.

The next step is to remove the hair. This can be

First step in making rawhide or buckskin from an animal hide is to scrape off remaining meat and fat with blunt-edged tool.

done in several ways. One is to stir a gallon of wood ashes into a tubful of hot water, allow the water to cool to room temperature, and soak the hide in the mixture for several days. Periodic testing will show when the hair is loose enough to slip easily.

Another way of loosening the hair is to use slaked lime. Place two pounds of caustic lime into a wooden tub or barrel and slake by *slowly* adding small amounts of cold water. As the lime slakes, add up to a gallon of water, then cover the container and let it stand for a day. Next add 10 gallons more water, stir thoroughly, and immerse the hide in the mixture. Often it is necessary to weight the hide down with a rock to keep it completely covered.

Several times each day, churn the hide around in the mixture with a wooden bat, so that the lime keeps well off the bottom of the barrel. Do this without getting the hands into the solution. Normally, within four to five days the hair will slip easily from the hide.

The Indians used to loosen the hair by simply burying the hide in the earth while it was still fresh. Depending upon the "greenness" of the hide and the
temperature, this takes from two to six days. The hide
should be buried 6 to 8 inches deep, and spread out
completely flat. A good way to determine how long
to leave the hide buried is to dig up a corner each
day and test the hair by pulling on it with the fingers.
For this reason, it is best to bury the hide with the
hair side up. When the hair slips easily the hide
should be dug up and the hair removed immediately.

After loosening the hair, the damp hide should be

After hide has been treated with lime solution or buried in
the earth from two to six days, most of the hair can be
easily removed.

Remaining bits of hair are then scraped from hide with edge of a sharp rock.

placed over the log and all hair pulled out, or rubbed and scraped away. Use the edge of a sharp rock to do this, as well as to remove the dark, filmy layer of "scruff" which covers the skin itself.

If lime has been used to loosen the hair, the hide must next be de-limed in a solution of 1 quart vinegar to 6 gallons of water, and in sufficient quantity to cover the skin. Soaking the hide in this solution for two days will get rid of the lime. During this time it should be churned about periodically. Afterward, the hide should be washed repeatedly in clean water to remove all traces of the acetic acid in the vinegar.

To finish such a cleansed hide into rawhide, it is then stretched tightly and allowed to dry slowly in the shade where air will circulate around every part of it. This can be done by stretching the hide inside a frame made by lashing four poles together. The hide is sewn to all four poles through small holes made in the outside edges. If a board platform is available, the hide can be stretched as tight as possible and tacked along its edges to the board The board is then stood up on edge. When it dries, rawhide will be extremely hard, but it can be softened by soaking it overnight. This will leave it soft enough to be worked into articles.

Rawhide is useful for making chair seats and backs, ornamental drumheads, knife and ax sheaths. Some cowboys still use a rawhide lariat for catching horses and mules inside a corral, where a quick, stiff loop must be snaked out to catch a skittery animal on the first try, and there is no time for a soft lariat to build a loop. All professional steer ropers use a rawhide "burner" instead of a metal honda for the tiny end loop in a rope lasso. These burners are shaped of wet steer rawhide, formed inside the loop and allowed to dry out. Rawhide has long been used as the covering for the horns of stock saddles. I have a riding saddle which was custom-built for me thirty-nine years ago, and the rawhide around its horn is still in good shape. This, too, is steer rawhide.

When rawhide lacing dries out it is almost transparent, and makes a substantial and good-looking lace for leather sheaths to enclose sharp-edged tools. Laced in while still wet, it can be shaped with the leather to take the form of the tool. When dry, it provides a hard protective cover for the cutting edge of the tool.

MAKING BUCKSKIN

For most uses, however, it is better to finish the hide by tanning it into buckskin. This involves two more steps: tanning and softening the raw hide.

A simple tanning solution is made of household

When hide has dried after soaking in tanning solution, it is softened by working it over a blunt-edged post set in the ground at a convenient height.

white soap-chips. After the hide has been cleaned, oil the flesh side lightly with deer tallow and hang it over a pole in the shade for a day. Next, dissolve 3 pounds of soap-chips in 10 gallons of warm water, and soak the hide in this solution (kept at room temperature if possible) for from three days to a week, until the hide will permit the soapsuds to be squeezed through it. At this stage, rinse all the soap from the hide by repeated washings in clean water. When the hide has dried to the stage where it is still mildly damp, it is ready for softening.

To soften a hide into buckskin, it must be worked over a thin, blunt surface to break down every fiber. A good implement at camp for doing this is a 5-inch post set into the ground at a workable height—18 inches is just right. The top of the post should be thinned down to leave a blunt edge like a shovel blade or the end of a boat oar. With a movement much like polishing shoes with a cloth, the hide is pulled back and forth across the wooden edge, flesh side down, until it is soft all over. This takes considerable effort.

To finish, the hide is smoked slowly over a hard-

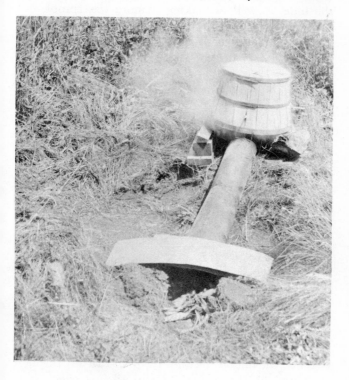

Hide is finished by smoking it over a smudge fire. Here smoke was piped upward into basket which contains hide suspended upon two saplings shoved through slits. Basket is raised off hot pipe; shield over fire regulates draft.

wood smudge fire. One way of doing this is to use the softened hide as the "wrap" for a small smokehouse. Another is to pipe the smoke upward from the fire into a box or basket in which the hide is loosely suspended. The hide should be shifted occasionally so it will be evenly smoked, and care should be used that it never gets hot. Smoking darkens and softens the hide, as well as making it more waterproof.

Lastly, a very light film of Neatsfoot oil may be rubbed onto the flesh side of the hide, but it isn't really necessary for good buckskin.

TANNING SKINS WITH HAIR

Often the outdoorsman will wish to tan small skins with the hair on. The procedure for tanning small hides with the hair on is similar to the steps followed in making buckskin. The hides are softened and fleshed in the same way, but not de-haired. The hides are then put into the tanning mixture. A good one for small skins consists of 1 pound alum dissolved in 5 gallons of boiling water, to which is added 2½ pounds of table salt.

When this is dissolved and cooled, the skins are immersed and left from five to ten days, depending upon the size and thickness of the skins. Coyote skins, as an example, require about five days. During the tanning period, the skins are moved about periodically in the solution.

When the hide is the same color all the way through (as tested by slicing a thin strip off one edge), it is tanned. The skin is then hung to drain, and all of the solution washed out by repeated rinsing.

The skins are then hung in the shade to dry completely. They are next softened again by sponging

Finished buckskin, having been smoked and softened, is darker than original hide and waterproof. Light film of Neatsfoot oil may be rubbed onto flesh side.

warm water over the flesh side, then rolled up over-night to sweat. After sweating, the skins are softened by breaking the fibers over a blunt edge.

A final step is to rub a dressing of some kind of warm animal fat into the flesh side, to keep the skins soft. All excess oil or fat is then removed by rubbing sawdust over the skins. They are then ready for use.

CUTTING LACES

Both rawhide and buckskin are used for lacings to braid rope and cord, or for leather thongs. The neatness and uniform strength of the lace depends upon an even width.

Two methods of cutting a lace from a circular piece of leather. In camp two knives stuck in a flattened log serve as a gauge for cutting lace in continuous spiral. At home two boards may be used as shown below.

The best guide I've found for cutting continuous uniform lengths of lacing from leather or damp rawhide is simply two knives stuck solidly into a flattened log or table top. One knife does the cutting, the other guides the width.

The cutting knife, which should have a razor-sharp edge, is stuck firmly into the log at about an angle of 80 degrees. The knife used as a gauge should be set the desired width of the lacing from the cutting blade, say, a quarter-inch, and at the same angle, but with its edge in the opposite direction. It is best if the guiding blade is of greater width than the cutting blade. A butcher knife and thin pocketknife make a good combination.

The lacing is cut in a spiral around the edge of a piece of leather which has been trimmed so it is fairly round in contour. To begin, cut a 2-inch length of lacing with another knife, starting it from the left side of the leather, for a right-handed person. This length of lacing is placed between the two knife blades. Holding the end in the left hand, and the leather in the right, both are pulled against the sharp edge, which cuts it as the other blade gauges the width. By working fairly close to the blades, and keeping the uncut leather flat as it goes between, a continuous spiral length of lacing of uniform width can be quickly cut.

Where nails and flat boards are available, a similar gauge may be made by nailing a 1-inch board on a half-inch board so that the edge of the top board is over the center of the bottom board. A sharp knife is then shoved up through the bottom board at the desired width from the edge of the upper board. The edge serves as a guide as the lacing is cut by the blade.

PRESERVING SNAKE SKINS

Snake skins are difficult to tan, but may be preserved by a salt-alum solution similar to that used for small skins. The snake skin is softened, then soaked in the lime solution used for de-hairing deer hides until the scales come loose. These are scraped or brushed off with a stiff-bristled brush, then the skin de-limed as above. It is then soaked for three or four days in the alum-salt solution used for small skins which has been diluted to 50 percent strength with water.

Next, to the alum-salt solution, 5 grams of sodium carbonate (dissolved in warm water) are added slowly, a drop at a time. The skin is kept in this solution five to six days, and periodically stirred.

The tanned skin is then drained, and soaked twelve hours in a solution of 1 part sulphonated oil to 3 parts water.

Lastly, the snake skin is removed, squeezed dry, stretched gently, and tacked in shape on a flat surface. When completely dry, it is removed and gently worked over a blunt board until it is pliable. It may then be ironed into shape with a warm flat-iron, and painted with liquid celluloid to give it a gloss.

PRESERVING FISH SKINS

The best way of preserving fish specimens is, of course, to have them mounted. This entails at least a fundamental knowledge of taxidermy.

The skins of fish, however, may be preserved by a rather simple process. First, the fish is wiped off with a solution of alum (1 teaspoonful to a gallon of water) to remove the mucous, or slime. Next, the fish is skinned completely by making only one incision in the hide along midships of the unwanted side, running from the tail to gill coverts. Fins and tail are left integral with the skin, and are cut off at their base. The head is also left with the skin, with the eyes, cheek muscles, and all meat around the gills removed.

Next, the skin is fleshed with a dull knife, scraping toward the head, and the cleaned skin is dipped into a strong solution of grain alcohol (2 parts alcohol to 1 part water). This solution is drained off, then a weak formaldehyde solution is painted onto the fins, tail, and head, but *not* onto the skin. For preserving the skin itself, a deadly poisonous solution of 1 ounce of sodium arsenite to a gallon of water is swabbed onto the flesh side of the skin and allowed to soak in.

Lastly, the skin is shaped as desired, and allowed to dry. During the drying process, the fins and tail are spread to position between flat pieces of cardboard, and held there with paper clips. This preserves their natural shape, without letting them split.

ESKIMO TANNING METHODS

Often other parts of game animals, besides the hide, can be used in making outdoor equipment. One such part is the leg tendons of large game animals such as caribou, elk, moose, etc.

Leg tendons are prepared and used in the sewing of hides and skins, and make good emergency and permanent "thread." As an example, I have a pair of Eskimo-made mukluks whose inner boots were hand-sewn with a curved needle and split caribou tendon. The sewing, done by my Eskimo guide's wife, rivals machine sewing in evenness and delicacy of stitch, and the tendon thread is as strong as when the mukluks were made four years ago.

To give you an idea of how these tendons were

prepared, as well as how the Eskimos, who have few outside materials to work with, go about tanning hides, I'm going to quote from a recent letter from this same Eskimo guide. With this man's limited opportunities to learn and use English, he writes remarkably well. I'm simply setting it down verbatim, to preserve the full flavor.

Dear Clyde.

I'll do my best to answer your questions. First we do have three ways of tanning and making leather of seal skins.

1. For bleaching a seal skin. You prabably see some white seal skins hanging on the outside racks while you was up here. In order to make a bleached seal skin here is what they do. After skinning a seal they don't bother to wash the blood or oil off the skin, but they do rub more oil on the hair and roll the skin in small roll and place it in a can or any container and cover the skin with blubber and place the container where the heat will reach the container (with skin in it) and leave the skin in the container for about a week. In a week's time the hair will slip off the skin as long as the container is in a warm place. After the hair slip off the next move is to get wooden pegs and peg and stretch it and freeze dry, and keep it outdoors all the time. This is done in winter only. And in about three weeks the skin is completely dried and white, and this leather is used for mukluk lace's and mukluk bottoms and tops.

2. This is done for making waterproof mukluks. In order to do this, after the skin

is dried, first they get a piece of lime stone (which is plentiful near by) and place it in a burning stove in order to get it softer to grind it in powdered form (today some women use Dutch Cleanser for this purpose) and spread this powdered stone all over the skin just so it get between hair and to the skin and they get a sharp edged rock and use it as a scraper and work it back and forth till the hair is scraped off. And the next thing is to get a metal skin scraper and scrape the access fat off as well as softening the skin. Then the skin is ready.

3. Tanning the skin for jackets, pants and mukluks not getting the hair off. After the skin is dried scrape the access fat off as well as getting it soft after scraping is done, get a handful of flour and place it in a bowl add water and mix it till it is thin and spread this flour on the skin and fold the skin and let it lay for over night and as the skin is drying it is worked with hands in order to get it soft and thats that.

And for the sinew and tendons. First clean the meat off the sinews, after cleaning them get a can or bowl of water and soak the sinews for about overnight or till the sinew turned white and blood off then it is time to get a piece of board and stretch them and place them to dry. After dry place them in cool place, when overdried will break off when they are bended. same to tendons. And for splitting, start on from the thinest part and peel off the desired size you want. And for using this sinew for sewing, place the

thinest part in the eye of the needle that way
the sinew will not split while sewing . . .

Obviously, these types of "native tan" are most
useful in cold weather and climates when there is less
danger of putrefaction. However, hair seals are nearly
one-half blubber, or fat, and this fat is the tanning
agent. I happen to know, also, that many Eskimos,
for a more permanent tan for all seasons, use human
urine as the tanning solution.

CATGUT

Commercial catgut is made, not from the intestines
of a cat, but from those of sheep, horses, and burros.
Processing is an involved and tedious series of steps
including the removal of all fat, soaking in alkaline
baths, scraping, smoking in the fumes of sulfur, and
drawing the ribbons of gut through a metal aperture
to get a uniform size in the finished strings. These
are used for stringing musical instruments, and for
tying off incisions in surgery.

A simulated catgut can be made of the intestines
of deer, elk, moose, and other game animals by somewhat the same process. The gut is scraped with a blunt
knife until all fat is removed. Next, the intestine is
soaked overnight in a solution made by pouring 3
gallons of boiling water over a gallon of wood ashes,
and cooling. The gut is next drained and cleaned by
washing in several changes of clean water, then placed
for three days into the alum-salt tanning solution
used for small hides. When the tanning is complete,
the gut is washed again and cut into thin ribbons.
These may be used as is, or twisted and dried into
string suitable for sewing buckskin, leather articles,

Samples of designs that may be cut with tools made at home from heads of spikes.

and canvas. Smoking catgut, as with buckskin, improves the product.

LEATHERCRAFT

Very often an outdoorsman will want to make his own knife and ax sheaths. These should be made of stiff, heavy steer hide for the protection it offers cutting edges during rough handling. Heavy, factory-tanned leather may be laced with rawhide or buckskin and decorated to suit one's taste.

Begin by laying out a full-sized pattern on paper. Brown wrapping paper makes a good design paper. Some experimentation may be necessary to get exactly the right size. This is done by fitting the paper around the tool and cutting to shape, allowing for a lacing edge or seam.

TOOLING A DESIGN

Next comes the matter of the design itself, and here the artistry of the individual has full play. In general, any design should be in keeping with the shape of the article. For a long sheath or case, the design should be long, such as a trailing vine and leaves, not a series of polka-dots.

The design need not be a realistic depiction of anything in nature. The best designs are abstract, and often in the form of flowing leaves, flowers, and stems. The best way to get a good design is to practice a few times on a piece of paper the same size as the finished work. When a good design is made, keep it for transferring to the leather. Don't leave too much "background."

Generally speaking, the leather item is tooled on only one side—the side exposed when the item is worn or used. The design must fit this space.

Having created a suitable design, your next step is to transfer this design to the full-sized pattern. This is done by blacking the underside of the paper on which the design is drawn by rubbing the edge of a soft lead pencil all over the paper. Next, the paper is laid in place on the pattern, and the lines retraced with a pencil. This will transfer the design onto the paper pattern.

The next step is to transfer the pattern onto the leather. First, lay the flat leather on a smooth surface. Professionals use a marble slab, but this isn't necessary for the beginner. Next, sponge off both sides of the leather with water until they are damp but not wet. Make sure there are no pencil marks on the back of the paper pattern, then lay it in place on the face side of the wet leather. Once in place, it can be held by taping the edges with cellulose tape. Now go over all lines of the pattern with the pencil, bearing down quite heavily so as to leave the imprint in the leather. Make sure that every line of the design is traced. A dry ball-point pen makes a good tool.

Next, while the leather is still damp, cut around

Pattern for a holster has been cut from a piece of leather and design traced from original sketch on paper. Swivel knife was used while leather was still wet to cut around all outside lines to separate the design from the background area.

every outside line of the design with a swivel knife. This is a knife which can be made to revolve in the fingers while being held solidly with another finger. It has a blunt taper to its edge, so it will cut only a shallow groove in the leather. It is the only tool the beginner actually needs to buy—if he's good at improvising others. Cutting around all marks of the design outlines the pattern, forms a border, and separates the design from the background areas.

The next job is to stamp in the background. This

is done with some pattern of background tool. It may be a crosshatch pattern, basketweave, simple dots or a stipple. Any number of tools that can cut background designs are available from most hobby stores or leather-working companies which advertise in the outdoor journals.

The most fun, however, is to make your own. This is a simple job. Take a 40-penny spike, or 60-penny spike, and file or grind the head perfectly flat. The spike head may then be ground along the edges into a square, triangle, or thin rectangle, depending on the desired design. For working into corners of the leather background, at least one tool should be triangular in shape.

Next, take a triangular file and cut a crosshatch pattern on the flat head of the spike, making all cuts about $\frac{1}{16}$ inch apart. Then cut off the spike's sharpened end so as to leave a tool of about 3 inches long. If you set this tool on a dampened scrap of leather, and hit the end with a hammer, you will be surprised to see what a pleasing design it leaves embedded in the leather.

Other designs may be filed or punched into spike heads. Another good one for backgrounds leaves a series of closely-set dots of raised leather. This one is made by driving the sharpened end of a center-punch into the spike head, making the punch marks in a crosshatch arrangement and as close together as possible. This head, when punched into wet leather, leaves raised dots which make a pleasing background design.

With a suitable tool, the background area all over the design is then stamped into the leather. Professionals use a mallet and machine-built tools for the job. The beginner needs only his own spike tools, a

Design has been completed by stamping in background with homemade tool and modeling the edges to give embossed, three-dimensional effect. Holster will then be laced with leather thong.

hammer for pounding, or even a wooden "mallet" made by cutting off a section of a tree branch having a smaller branch growing out of its side for a handle.

As you stamp in the background, the leather will dry. Before it gets too dry, sponge off the surface again and continue the work. Sponging occasionally, until the surface is just damp, prevents watermarks on the finished item.

When the background has all been stamped in, the shape of the design is modeled in. A modeling tool may be purchased, but the handle end of a small spoon can be made to serve. Briefly, in modeling, all edges of the design are smoothed down so they appear to raise gradually, from the level of the stamped background, giving an embossed, three-dimensional effect.

When all design has been modeled into the best possible shape, so that it appears to stand out from the background, a final border all around the entire design may be made if desired. One good design for this is simply a continuous row of tiny dots. These are made with a spike tool which has been ground or

filed to a very thin strip of metal, into which are
punched tiny holes, with the center-punch, at uniform
distances from each other. The border mark is laid
off by running the tip of a stylus, or blunt point,
along a straightedged ruler around the border of the
design, keeping the leather damp. The border of holes
is then stamped in with the thin tool. Fancier bordering tools can be made as desired.

LACING THE WORK

When the entire design is finished, the leather is
allowed to dry out. The edges of the leather are cut
to fit the outline of the intended sheath or case. The
item is then folded into shape, and laced. If it is a
knife sheath, two vertical slits should be cut in the
leather at a point where the belt will go, each slit
finished at both ends with a punched hole to prevent
tearing. Otherwise, a separate belt loop can be riveted
onto the sheath.

Lacing stitches vary from simple to involved. A
good one for the beginner is a simple overhand lacing, with the lace going around and around the
doubled edges of the sheath, through holes punched
at uniform distance inside the edge. Where the leather
edges come together, as in a knife sheath, the holes
should not be punched opposite each other in the
opposite edges. If this is done, the finished article will
twist. Instead, the holes should be punched so each
hole in one edge comes between two holes in the opposite edge.

Rawhide thongs processed as described, and soaked
until they are soft enough to be workable, make good
laces. Buckskin also makes fine lacing for many
leather articles used in the outdoors. If you want to

These two knife sheaths were fashioned of homemade leather and designed with spike-head tools. Ends of lacing were properly concealed.

be real fancy, get a lacing leather known commercially as tooling calf.

In lacing, beginners don't know what to do with ends. A good way to handle the beginning end is to lay 2 inches of it, before it enters the first hole, between the edges to be laced; then lace around both edges and the lace itself. This way the lace end will be concealed in the finished item. The remaining end lace may be similarly concealed. To do this, lace the final 2 inches of the article loosely with, say, a half-inch of slack in each overhand stitch. Next, bend the end of the lacing down through this length of loose lacing and between the edges to be laced together; and lastly, pull the lace's end through between two lacing stitches. Then, by starting where the lacing is tight, and pulling tight each stitch, the end will be concealed except for a loop at the end and the tip of the lace itself. By pulling on the lace end, it can be drawn through, pulling the loop inside the laced work. The lace can then be snipped off close and its edge tucked under. This, in addition to making a neat job, prevents the lacing from coming loose.

With any single overhand lacing stitch, it is best to punch holes of considerably smaller diameter than the width of the lacing, and to space such holes exactly the lace's width apart. In use, the small holes contract the lacing tightly, but the lace outside the holes spreads flat and covers the entire edge, making a neat, smooth seam.

The final step is to dye and finish the leather. Steer hide may be dyed any desired color with leather dye, then waxed to finish. One of the finest and most appropriate finishes for outdoor items such as knife sheaths is a product named "Antique." This brown stain is smoothed onto the finished article, allowed to stand for a half-minute, or until the desired depth of the brown color is reached, then quickly wiped off with a clean cloth. The longer Antique remains on the leather, the darker it will stain. To preserve the finish, buff the leather occasionally with any good shoe polish or wax.

Outdoor Identification Section:

I. Trees
II. Animal Signs

Tree Identification

Trees furnish the outdoorsman with fuel for his campfire, boughs for his bed and shelter, logs for his raft and his cabin, timber from which to slab out camp furniture, shade for his rest and travel, and even some edible food for his stomach. In addition, the woods furnish cover for the game he may seek, and slow down the moisture in watershed country so that he may have clear, stable, and fish-populated streams.

But in a deeper way, the magnificent forests of America give inspiration, meaning, and courage to the outdoorsman. There is nothing more straightforward or honest than the unvarying reach of a great fir tree toward the heavens. There is no greater lesson in courage than that given by a mighty oak, buffeted by all adversity, carrying its scars with dignity, and silently living on. And what could better depict eventual achievement and accomplishment than a 6000-ton redwood tree fourteen centuries old?

A tree is defined as a plant having a central trunk, which at maturity reaches a height of 10 feet or over. In the light of this definition, there are over 800 different kinds of trees in the United States alone. It is next to impossible for the average person to know them all. It does, however, add to our enjoyment of trees to be able to call some of the better-known species by their first names.

CLASSIFICATION OF TREES

Trees may be broadly grouped in several ways. One way is to classify them as either broadleaf trees or conifers.

The broadleaf trees are generally hardwood trees, and, as the name suggests, have large leaves. They include such species as oak, maple, and basswood. The conifers have small leaves, or needles, suited to enduring cold climates, and are so named partly because of the shape of the tree. Conifers have a large central bole, and branches that reach out horizontally. As these branches rise toward the tree's top, they shorten in length, giving the entire tree a cone-shaped appearance. This, plus the fact that most conifers are cone-bearing trees, gives them their name. The seeds grow in these cones, which are produced by the branches. When the cones have ripened, the heavy scales open and the seeds are distributed by wind. The conifers include such species as pine, fir, spruce, and yew.

Most conifers are evergreens; that is, the tiny green leaves stay with the tree throughout all seasons of the year and shed gradually. At least one species of conifer is not an evergreen—the larch, or tamarack, which sheds its leaves annually like deciduous trees.

AMERICA'S FOREST AREAS

To get an idea of the general forest areas of North America, imagine an ellipse of area roughly one-fifth the width of the United States, lying in a north-south direction, and covering the Great Plains region of the United States from the Mexican border well into the Prairie Provinces of Canada.

Such a broadly defined area is the relatively un-forested region of the continent. So far as the United States is concerned, this belt of plains separates the forested parts of the nation into two major areas—the eastern forests and the western forests. Generally speaking, the eastern forests have been depleted to a greater extent than have the western forests, and the greater part of the cut timber today comes from the western area.

Going back to the above ellipse of plains area, it will be apparent that the western forests and the eastern forest belt tend to join northward beyond the plains region. Also, the lower end of the Pacific and Rocky Mountain forests tend to meet the end of the eastern-southern forests toward the Texas area of the Gulf of Mexico.

In effect this divides the continent into several broadly separated regions of forests. In a broad way, the trees of one region will differ from those in an-other. There is, of course, considerable overlapping of species; and within each general belt of forest there is, further, an admixture of species. However, by separating the continent into different regions, and considering the trees of each region separately, the identification of individual species becomes easier.

Northern Forest Belt

One of these divisions is the northern belt of forests, and the trees there are largely coniferous. This vast division of the continent covers parts of the

New England States, and in a westward direction covers the upper Great Lakes area to Minnesota. From there the region is principally northward, covering a great share of Canada, and joins above the Canadian prairie country with the western forests. From there the northern belt of conifers continues into Alaska and covers a major portion of this new state.

The major species in this extended belt include the pines, firs, hemlock, larch or tamarack, spruce, and the arborvitaes, commonly called cedars.

There are several species of pines, including the famed white pine, red or Norway pine, jack pine, and pitch pine. The most important fir is the balsam fir. The three main species of spruce are the white spruce, the red spruce, and the black spruce.

Mixed in with these major species are, of course, numerous hardwoods and aspens.

ROCKY MOUNTAIN BELT

Generally south and westward from this belt is a belt of forests coincident with the Rocky Mountains. This forested area broadly includes all the country along the chain of mountains from Mexico well into Canada where the overall region joins with the northern coniferous forests.

In the Rocky Mountain region there are four major kinds of trees—the firs, pines, spruces, and larch, which is the western brother of the eastern tamarack.

The principal fir here is the Douglas fir. Two other firs are the Colorado fir and the white fir. Pines may be divided into white pine, yellow or ponderosa pine, and lodgepole pine. There are two main species of spruce, the Englemann spruce and the Colorado, or blue spruce. As with the northern belt of forests, there are numerous other species of trees mixed in with the major trees of the Rocky Mountain region.

PACIFIC FOREST BELT

Farther west than the Rocky Mountain belt is the Pacific region of forests. As the name suggests, this is a coastal region extending generally from the Mexican border along the Pacific and well into Alaska. The timber here is largely coniferous. Trees include such species as Douglas fir, redwood, pine, hemlock, fir, spruce, and arborvitae. Douglas fir is the main fir in this region, but noble fir, grand fir, and red fir are also found in the Pacific forests. Pines include ponderosa, white pine, and sugar pine. The principal spruce is the Sitka spruce.

CENTRAL HARDWOOD BELT

East of the Great Plains area in the United States is a broad belt of forests reaching southwesterly from the New England States all the way to Georgia and Texas. This general belt joins the northern belt of conifers to the south of the Great Lakes, and includes parts of Canada east of the Great Lakes. It covers also the lower Mississippi Basin, extending into the eastern parts of the Great Plains States themselves. This vast area is principally an area of hardwood trees.

The hardwood forests include numerous species including oak, chestnut, beech, hickory, birch, walnut, elm, gum, tulip, maple, locust, sycamore, basswood, wild cherry, ash, willow, and poplar. Oak is the most important tree of this hardwood group, economically speaking. Oaks are of many species, but are classified into two major groups, the red oaks and the white oaks. White oaks have rounded leaf-tips, while those of the red oaks are pointed. Elms include the American and the slippery elm. Maples include several species such as the silver maple, boxelder maple, and the hard or sugar maple, which is the most important maple for lumber. Ash includes several species, generally according to color. The white ash is most important.

SOUTHERN FOREST BELTS

To the southeast of this wide hardwood area is another belt of conifers. This area reaches from Virginia to Florida, and westward along the Gulf of Mexico inland, as far as Texas to the west. It includes major portions of the states of Mississippi, Louisiana, Georgia, and Alabama. The trees of this region are principally pine, cypress, and red cedar. Pines include the longleaf pine, shortleaf pine, slash pine, and loblolly pine.

A final forest belt is that of the evergreen hardwoods found in the subtropics. This area includes parts of Florida and the Gulf Coast States. Trees include mahogany, cedar, rosewood, citrus, and pine.

Mexico has only a small fraction of its land area forested. Trees include mesquite in the desert regions, the hardwoods in higher low-country, and pine along the higher crest of its spine.

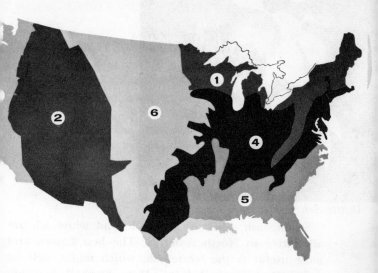

America's forest areas: 1. Northern forest belt, 2. Rocky Mountain belt, 3. Pacific forest belt, 4. Central hardwood belt, 5. Southern forest belt, 6. Plains belt.

The following section contains many of North America's most important trees, alphabetically arranged. All photographs courtesy of the U. S. Forest Service, unless otherwise credited.

White Ash

ASH

Swamp ash, blue ash, red ash, and white ash are all native to North America. The best known and most useful is the white ash, which might well be called the "baseball tree." More baseball bats are made from this species than from any other tree. The white ash grows to a height of 70 or 80 feet, with graceful, drooping foliage. The trunk is often free of major branches up to a considerable height. The majority of the leaves occur at the ends of the branches. These leaves are compound, with each set of leaves growing out of the central stem opposite to each other, with each individual leaflet averaging up to 6 inches long. The winged seeds average from 1 to 2 inches in length. The white ash is found from southeast Canada to the Gulf States, and as far west as Minnesota.

Gray bark of the white ash has deep, diamond-shaped fissures and narrow, forking ridges. The leaves (above), which grow opposite one another, average 6 inches long with usually seven on a stem.

White ash is a heavy-limbed tree, the largest of which grow to a height of 100 feet or more and a butt diameter of 5 feet. It is broad and rounded in open country, straighter and taller in forest areas.

ASPEN

The quaking aspen, as it is often called, is a member of the poplar family, and is well named. The round leaves of this tree will move and flutter even with no detectable breeze. The tree grows over much of the continent, and though normally short in height, will, where it must compete for sunlight among the conifers, often reach a height of 60 feet or more. In Canada, where it is abundant, it is often called silver poplar. The aspen is short-lived and multiplies by sending up root stalks at considerable distance away from the main stem. With the first frosts, aspens turn a beautiful golden color, and are most striking when seen among evergreens. The aspen is important to the outdoorsman. The smoke from dry aspen splits has a pleasant odor which is one of the joys of the outdoors. Living aspen trunks are pale green with nearly black markings.

Nearly round leaves of quaking aspen are 1¼ to 3 inches long, shiny green above and dull green beneath. The fruit, maturing in May and June, is light green in color and nearly ¼ inch long.

Quaking aspen's smooth, thin bark is greenish-white. With age it darkens and becomes furrowed.

BASSWOOD

The American basswood is also called a linden, or lime tree. Basswood grows over a wide area including southeastern Canada and the eastern half of the United States. Mature trees will reach 100 feet in height and reach maturity in about that same number of years. The tree has upward-spreading branches which flower with yellow-white blossoms containing honey. The dark-gray bark has deep furrows; the inner bark was once used by Indians for making rope. The wood is light in color, and is used where a light, soft wood is necessary for making furniture and toys.

Mature basswood has gray, furrowed bark with scaly ridges. Heart-shaped leaves, 4 to 8 inches long, are coarsely toothed; fruits are nutlike in appearance, ½ inch round.

BEECH

This is a deciduous tree native to Eurasia and North America, and is found in the southeastern part of Canada and the eastern part of the United States. The trunk of the beech is statuesque in appearance and covered with a smooth silvery bark. Its leaves run from 3 to 6 inches in length and are shaped like a pointed ellipse. They are sharp-toothed at the end of their veins. Beechnuts form in small husks and, when ripe, drop to the ground, serving as food for several species of wildlife. Beech buds in the spring are long and pointed. Mature trees reach a height of 100 feet. The wood is useful for making boxes, novelties, and furniture. The beech is often used as an ornamental tree.

Beech leaves have parallel veins ending in sharp points, are dark blue-green above, light green beneath. The blue-gray bark is thin and smooth.

Paper Birch

BIRCH

There are several species of birch. Two of the most important are the yellow birch, found in the northeastern part of the United States and adjacent Canada, and as far west as Minnesota; and the white birch. The yellow birch has played an important part in the making of furniture, boxes, and veneer wood for interior finishes in buildings, but the supply is diminishing. The white, or paper birch, so called because its bark peels off in light-colored, paper-like strips, has a range from Maine to Minnesota as far south as the tip of Lake Michigan and north to Canada. The paper birch is sometimes mistaken for an allied species, the gray birch. The paper birch has had a long romantic past in that it has been the principal material for covering birchbark canoes. In temperate climates birch trees will reach a height of 60 feet. But as the tree is found north-

Leaves of the paper birch are oval, 2 to 4 inches long, coarsely and usually doubly toothed. They are dull dark green above, light green and sometimes hairy beneath.

ward into the severe climates of northern Canada and Alaska, this height greatly decreases. The birch there is called the arctic birch, and in North America is the tree farthest north before all trees give way to tundra. I have hunted in arctic birch regions of both Canada and Alaska where the trees were not over 3 feet tall, and the small, waxy leaves were about the size of a thumbnail.

ark of the paper birch (left) and yellow birch (right) curls n thin, papery strips. Paper-birch bark is white and mooth; yellow-birch bark yellowish or silvery-grey, turn-ng reddish-brown on old trees.

Red cedar (left), a towering western tree, has reddish-brown bark that is thin and fibrous (below). Bark of white cedar (bottom) is also reddish-brown but has narrow connecting ridges.

CEDAR

There are several cedars, some which are called cedars but which are really arborvitae or juniper. One is the northern white cedar, or arborvitae. This tree grows in much of Canada and the United States, in the same general region as the white pine. The white cedar grows to a height of over 50 feet. The heavy foliage is in the form of flat sprays of leaves, with tiny leaves "braided" along the small branches. Another similar species is the southern white cedar, which grows in wet ground from the Northeast States to the Gulf of Mexico. This is sometimes called the swamp cedar. Still another cedar is the red cedar, spread widely over most of the United States. This species is not a true cedar but a juniper, and is identified by the clusters of small bluish berries which grow along the branch-tips. Another is the common juniper, which grows in semiarid soil and rolling hill country over much of North America. This species has very sharp, short needles, and bears the typical blue juniperberries.

Cedar wood is light, but in some species splits badly, making it difficult to use as length-lumber. Cedar wood is, however, highly resistant to damage from soil and weather, and for this reason makes good fence posts and shingles for buildings. For a comparable reason, Port Orford cedar of the West Coast has long been used for making boats. The red cedar of western North America is highly prized as a wood for making fancy furniture, ornaments, and especially for making cedar chests.

Leaves of red cedar (left) are shiny dark green, scale-like, ⅛ to ½ inch long. Atlantic white-cedar leaves (right) are shorter, dull blue-green in color.

CHESTNUT

The chestnut is a species closely allied to the beech. The American species was once common to the hardwood belt of forests, principally coincident with the Appalachian Mountains. The tree grew to a height of 70 to 100 feet, with long leaves having very sharp edges. The chestnuts were formed inside big burrs that had sharp stickers on the outside, which would open after frosts. An Asiatic blight has decimated the American chestnut, and recent attempts to rehabilitate it, or to produce disease-resistant strains, have not been successful.

Fruit of the chestnut is a spiny bur about 2 inches in diameter (left), containing two or three edible nuts. Leaves are narrowly oblong, 5 to 9 inches long, parallel veined, with slightly curving teeth.

Dark-brown bark is irregularly fissured into broad, flat ridges.

Eastern Cottonwood

COTTONWOOD

There are three main species of cottonwood: The eastern cottonwood found in the eastern half of the United States; the swamp cottonwood, which was once found over the central part of the Mississippi Basin, along the Gulf to the north end of Florida, and up the Atlantic seacoast; and the black cottonwood, found principally in California and in the Northwest, and northward into Canada.

The species is fast-growing and will mature in less than two decades, reaching a height of 100 feet. The cottonwood tends to follow river courses. The leaves are triangle-shaped, glossy, pale-green in color, and have toothed edges. In the fall after frost, when the leaves turn golden in color, a row of cottonwoods along a river course makes a sight which is nothing less than spectacular. The name comes from the way the seed is formed and matures. The cottonwood tree produces strings of seed capsules whose small seeds have white, cotton-like attachments. These are

Bark of the eastern cottonwood is yellowish and smooth in young trees, becoming gray and deeply furrowed with age. Leaves are triangular, 3 to 6 inches long, coarsely toothed, smooth, light green, and shiny.

blown from the tree during wind, and scatter the species. Wood from the cottonwood is light but warps badly as lumber. It does, however, make good excelsior, and light containers. It is also useful as firewood. Standing cottonwoods are highly useful as shelters in open country against wind.

Smaller than the eastern species, black cottonwood has heart-shaped leaves and grayish-brown bark.

CYPRESS

The cypress is a swamp species having needles for leaves, and bears round cones having woody scales. The bald cypress, like the western larch, sheds its leaves annually. The cypress ranges southward from the lower New England States to Florida, across the lower portions of the Gulf States to Mexico, and over much of the swampy areas of the Mississippi Basin. The cypress grows in water or mud along the shores of swamps. Its massive trunk flares like a fluted cone. Cypress trees will grow to over 100 feet in height, and reach 10 to 12 feet thick at the base. Some species have a large spreading top, others are shaped like a conifer. The wood is yellow or orange in color, and is highly impervious to water and decay. Doors and arches in Europe which were made of cypress have endured for a thousand years. In America the wood is used for outdoor purposes where resistance to weather is required.

Bald cypress has reddish-brown or gray bark with long fibrous or scaly ridges. The yellow-green leaves, which are shed in the fall, are crowded feather-like on slender, horizontal twigs. Cones are ¾ to 1 inch in diameter and have hard scales.

American Elm

ELM

Of the half-dozen species of elm which grow in North America, the American elm and the slippery elm are the best known. The American elm is classic in shape. Trees sometimes reach 100 feet in height and 6 feet in diameter. The trunk remains undivided for the first 20 to 30 feet, then the branches sweep upward and outward, drooping downward similar to the shape of an umbrella. The leaves are roughly elliptical in shape, having pointed ends and toothed edges. The leaves are not symmetrical at their bases; the larger half is on the convex side of the curving stem.

The slippery elm is named because of its slippery inner bark. Its range is not as broad as that of the American elm, but is limited to the eastern half of temperate North America. Its leaves resemble those of the American elm, but are considerably larger.

Leaves of the American elm are not symmetrical in shape. Dark-green and smooth above, leaves are pale and usually hairy beneath. The flat, single-seeded fruits (right) are ⅜ to 1 inch long.

Gray bark of American elm is deeply furrowed, with long, forking, scaly ridges.

FIR

The firs were once considered in the same family of trees as the pines, though they differ in two respects. The cones of firs have scales with flat, rounded apexes; and their leaves do not grow in bundles, or clusters, as do the true pines. Firs range in distribution from eastern Canada nearly to Alaska, and from the Northwest almost to the Arctic Circle. Two of the most important species are the balsam fir of the northern belt of forests, and the larger Douglas fir (not a true fir) which reaches its greatest importance in the Pacific coastal forests. The balsam fir is a typical "Christmas tree," with thick spreading branches beginning shortly above the ground. It reaches a height of 30 to 50 feet, and has shiny blue-green needles which, when crushed, give off a pleasant "piney" odor.

The Douglas fir ranks at the very top for lumber in North America, and in the West represents more than one-half of the standing timber. Douglas firs are among the tallest trees, with exceptional specimens reaching over 350 feet. Some trees are 15 feet through at their bases. The tree grows tall and stately, having relatively few branches for a considerable distance up the trunk.

Bark of balsam fir is gray or brown with many resin blisters. Needles are flat, rounded at tip; cones are upright

Balsam fir (above) has thick, spreading branches starting near the ground. Douglas fir (right) is taller with few branches near the ground.

Bark of Douglas fir (left) is reddish-brown, thick, deeply furrowed into broad ridges. Needles (right) are short-stalked, flat, dark yellow-green or blue-green. Cones are light brown with thin, rounded scales.

Blue gum, or eucalyptus, trees shed their brown bark in long strips, exposing the grayish bark underneath.

GUM

Two species of gum are among our more important trees. One is the sweetgum, or red gum, which is distributed over the eastern part of the United States, from the lower New England States to central Florida, across the lower Mississippi Basin, and as far west as Texas. Other areas also occur in Mexico and Central America. Sweetgum trees reach a height of 90 to over 100 feet. The blue gum, or eucalyptus, is an imported variety now found in California, the Southwest, and along the Gulf States to Florida. The tree is an evergreen, with brown bark and willow-like leaves averaging up to a foot in length. The brown bark strips off in shaggy lengths, exposing the grayish underbark beneath, and makes the tree appear to be constantly molting. The leaves and fruit of the eucalyptus give off a sweet-smelling odor.

HEMLOCK

The eastern hemlock is a pyramid-shaped evergreen, which may reach 100 feet in height and over 3 feet in diameter at the base. The short, flat, linear leaves occur on opposite sides on the branchlet, averaging about a half-inch in length, and give a lacey, soft appearance to the foliage. The foliage is dark-green on top, with the underside of the leaves being a silvery-gray. The eastern hemlock grows on rocky hillsides, and ranges in distribution from Nova Scotia southward to Alabama and Georgia, and from Nova Scotia westward as far as Minnesota. The western hemlock occurs in a coastal belt from Washington, along the coastline of British Columbia, and into the southeastern part of Alaska. This species is larger than its eastern cousin, with trees often reaching well over 200 feet in height. Western hemlock likes cool, moist areas. A fast-growing tree, it often grows in large stands exclusive of other timber. It is becoming important as a pulp wood.

Western hemlock's bark is reddish-brown, deeply furrowed into broad, flat ridges. The dark-green needles are short-stalked and flat.

Bark of eastern hemlock, smaller of the two species, is brown or purplish and deeply furrowed. Needles are similar to those of western hemlock.

HICKORY

Shagbark Hickory

There are several species of hickory, most of which are distributed along the Mississippi Basin and eastward. All species can be identified by their compound leaves and the nuts the trees bear. Differences among the species are found in the bark, nuts, and number of leaflets. The shagbark, a common hickory, is so named because of its coarse, shaggy bark, whose individual bark-plates curl away from the trunk like long scabs ready to peel off. The shagbark grows to a height of over 100 feet. Beneath its rather disheveled exterior is a heavy wood of tough quality. Your ax and shovel probably have hickory handles. The leaves of the shagbark usually have five or seven leaflets, while those of other species of hickory may have seven or nine.

Shagbark hickory gets its name from gray, shaggy bark which curls away from trunk. Leaves, usually five, are long, elliptical, finely toothed. The thin-shelled nuts are edible.

LARCH

The American larch, or tamarack, grows from Maine westward beyond the Great Lakes, and over a northward range which covers most of Canada. It is common to wet, boggy ground, but also grows on adjacent hillsides. The average-sized tree is apt to be 50 to 70 feet tall, though like the birch, the tree dwindles to almost shrub-like stature at the northern limit of its range in Canada. The leaves of the larch are shed annually; otherwise it resembles the evergreens. These inch-long leaves appear in tiny knots or spurs along the branches, and number from 6 to 16 from each spur. The small half-inch cones look like miniature rose blossoms. The trees at a distance often look meager of foliage because of the intermittent arrangement of the leaves.

The western larch, the tallest and most important North American larch, grows in the Rocky Mountain Northwest as well as in the eastern part of the Pacific belt of forests. It is an important lumber species yielding a heavy softwood which is very durable.

Bark of the larch is reddish-brown, scaly, deeply furrowed into flat ridges with many overlapping plates. The needles, which are shed in the fall, grow in clusters at the end of stunted branches.

The tall, stately larch is an important lumber tree, the wood being used for poles and construction. Stand above is 185 years old.

MAGNOLIA

The magnolia goes by several names such as swamp magnolia, sweet bay, swamp laurel, and laurel bay. The species is evergreen, having tough slick leaves 3 to 6 inches in length which are glossy-green on top and gray underneath. The trees grow to a maximum of around 60 feet, but are shorter in the northern extremities of their range. This range covers a strip of the east Atlantic Coast from the southern part of North Carolina down to central Florida and around the coastal area of the Gulf of Mexico well into Texas. Spot areas appear much farther north. The coastal strip extends inland only approximately 100 miles, though farther up the Mississippi Basin. The bloom of the magnolia, which has been immortalized in song and story, is a creamy-white, cup-shaped flower averaging 2½ inches across, and has from 6 to 9 petals which are shaped like spoon blades. The tree is striking in appearance. For 30 feet or more the trunk may be free of branches. From there on up the branches are bunched to give a bulky compact appearance.

MAPLE

Sugar Maple

There are numerous species of maple in North America, with at least six species reaching commercial importance as lumber. These are the sugar or hard maple, black maple, silver maple, red maple, boxelder maple, and bigleaf maple. The maple has three distinguishing features. First, the leaves tend to grow opposite each other on the branchlets. Secondly, many species of maple such as the sugar maple, Norway maple, and silver maple have leaves which are deeply indented, and have five distinctive and sharp-pointed lobes. The lobe separations on some species such as the boxelder are barely separated. The third identifying characteristic of the maples is the pair of two winged seeds which grow together, and which resemble the winding keys of wind-up toys. These seeds are often called "keys" for this reason.

The sugar, or hard maple, is the most important of

Leaves of the big-leaf maple are very large, 6 to 12 inches in diameter, dark green and shiny. The bark is gray-brown, thin, smooth.

the group. It is found in every state east of the Great Plains, and in the southern parts of adjacent Canada. The sugar maple, in addition to its value for lumber, also yields a sap which is boiled down into maple syrup and sugar. Adult trees will occasionally reach 100 feet in height, and many will yield 20 gallons of sap per year. Of all the lumber produced by maples, bird's-eye maple is perhaps most valuable and is used in fancy woodwork and gun stocks.

Other species of maple have identifying characteristics. The red maple gets its name from its red buds and twigs of winter, and its scarlet leaves in the fall. The bigleaf maple of the Pacific slope has leaves which often reach a foot in width—hence the name. And the silver maple is so called because its leaves, though dark green on the upper surfaces, have a silvery-green under-surface.

Leaves of the sugar maple are 3 to 5 inches in diameter, dark green above, light green beneath. Bark is gray, furrowed.

OAK

White Oak

Just as maples are identified by their winged seeds, so are the oaks characterized by their acorns. Of all the hardwoods in North America, the oak is most important, partly because of its quantity, and largely because of the wide variety of uses to which its tough, long-lasting wood may be put. The variety of uses for oak wood ranges from timber for ships, mine tunnels, and boats, to furniture, boxes, and crates. There are over sixty species of oak in North America, with at least one-third of the species important in a commercial way. The commercially important oaks are found eastward of a line extending from Texas to the northern end of the Great Lakes.

For lumber purposes, oak is divided into two groups, the "white oak" and the "red oak." White oak, chestnut oak, and swamp oak furnish white-oak lumber; and the marketed red oak consists of such species as northern red oak, swamp red oak, and southern red oak.

For purposes of identification, the white oaks have lighter bark, rounded leaf-tips, and the acorns are borne on first-year wood. The red oaks have darker bark, pointed lobes on their leaves, and the acorns are borne on second-year wood.

Some of the more important oaks are the white oak, live oak, black oak, and northern red oak. The white oak is the most important oak for lumbering. The tree reaches a height of 60 to 100 feet, is slow in growing, with full maturity coming after several hundred years. White oaks may reach 8 feet diameter at their bases.

The live oak of the Southern and Gulf States is a wide-spreading tree having the tradition of being the ship-builder's tree. The angular, knee-like timbers necessary to ship construction were made from the limb-tree junctions of this massive tree.

The black oak, actually one of the commercial red oaks, is named because of the dark color of its bark. Perhaps the black oak's best-remembered asset has been the use of its bark in the tanning of hides. The northern red oak began to receive serious attention from lumbermen when the supply of white oak began diminishing. Its strong, close-grained lumber makes railroad ties, posts, and furniture.

Scrub oak, which often reaches no more than 10 to 15 feet in height, is found in many places in the West and Southwest, where it grows in thick patches, often covering an entire mountainside.

Acorns of the northern red oak (left) are ⅝ to 1⅛ inches long and nest in shallow cups. Black-oak acorns (right) are smaller, ⅝ to ¾ inches long, and are half enclosed by deep cups.

Acorns of the white oak (left) are ¾ to 1 inch long and have a shallow cup. The bark is light gray and fissured into

PINE

Sugar Pine

The pines are one of the most important trees of the conifer group. In North America there are nearly three-dozen species of pine. Pines grow largely in the mountainous regions of temperate North America, but in the colder areas are found at lower elevations. In the tropical parts of the continent, they are found only at the higher spines of elevation. Pines are identified by their hard, woody cones and by their leaves. The leaves, which are needle-shaped, are often referred to as "pine needles." Unlike the spruce and the fir, which bear single needles, pine leaves come from the branches in bundles or clusters of from two to five, with the lone exception of the singleleaf pine. Pine leaves vary in length with the species from an inch to 1½ feet. Among the important pines of North America are the lodgepole, longneedle, pinion, ponderosa, red, southern, and white pine.

Lodgepole Pine

Tall, straight, free of branches for most of its height, lodgepole pines grow to a diameter of from 8 to 12 inches. The bark is gray-green, with numerous small chip-like scales on its outer covering. The species ranges over the Northwest, along the Pacific Coast, and into adjacent Canada.

Bark of the lodgepole pine is brown and thin, with many loose scales. The stout needles, which grow in clusters of two, are 1 to 3 inches long, yellow-green in color.

Longneedle Pine

The most important of the southern pines, the longneedle is distinguished by its long leaves, as the name suggests. Needles will reach up to 18 inches in length. The wood of the longneedle pine is strong and is used in abundance for heavy construction purposes. This pine is also known as the turpentine-and-rosin tree, for its production of these items.

Needles of the longneedle pine grow in clusters of three. They are very long, 10 to 15 inches; the cones are 5 to 10 inches long, dull brown and prickly. The bark is orange-brown, extremely coarse and scaly.

Pinion Pine

Scattered throughout the more arid hills of the Southwest, this is a small, bushy-type tree averaging 15 to 20 feet in height. It is known mainly for the "pine nuts" it produces, which have long been a staple part of the diet for Indians in that area. Even today, in spot areas, the local Indians still gather the small, sweet nuts in autumn, and sell them to stores within the region.

Ponderosa Pine

As the name indicates, this is the big, or ponderous pine. Adult trees will reach a height of 200 feet and a diameter of 6 feet at the base. The ponderosa has deeply furrowed bark of orange-russet color, with a bole generally free of branches for a considerable distance above the trunk. Needles are in clusters of two or three, and will grow from six to ten inches long. The cones of the ponderosa are brown-colored and grow to five inches in length. The range of this species is comparable to that of the western lodgepole pine, though more extensive.

Needles of the ponderosa pine grow in clumps of two or three and are 6 to 10 inches long, dark green in color.

Western Wood Products Ass'n

Ponderosa pines are tall and straight, reaching 200 feet in height. Bark is brown or blackish, furrowed in deep ridges, becoming yellow-brown on older trees and fissured into large, scaly plates.

Red Pine

This is a medium-sized pine which grows in the northeastern part of the United States and Canada. Its name was taken from the reddish-colored bark. The wood of the red pine contains more resin than that of the white pine, and is classed as a "hard pine," as against the soft wood of the white pine.

Bark of the red pine is reddish-brown, with broad, flat, scaly plates. Needles grow in clusters of two and are stout, twisted, ¾ to 1½ inches long. Cones are small, light yellow in color.

Southern Pine

Loblolly Pin

Southern pine, or yellow pine, is a name given collectively to the four major species of pines found in the southeastern part of the United States—the shortleaf, slash, longleaf, and loblolly pines.

Bark of the loblolly pine is reddish-brown, deeply fissured into broad scaly plates. Needles grow in clusters of three, are 6 to 9 inches long, pale green. Cones are reddish-brown, 3 to 5 inches long, with stiff, sharp prickles.

White Pine

The white pines may be divided into two widely-separated species, the eastern white pine and the western white pine. The range of the eastern species includes the northeastern part of the United States, around the Great Lakes, and into adjacent Canada. The once-large forests of the eastern species have been largely decimated. The eastern white pine has long slender cones and sweet-smelling needles which grow in bundles of five. The western white pine grows mainly in the Northwest and adjacent Canada, with Idaho having the largest remaining stands. Mature trees reach several hundred years of age, and up to 175 feet in height. Leaves of this species also come in clusters of five. Because of its soft texture and easy-working qualities, western white pine lumber is in much demand for paneling and woodwork. Rustic knotty-pine is a choice lumber for cabinets.

Western white pine (right) and eastern white pine (below) are both important lumber trees. Bark of western tree is gray, smooth, becoming fissured into large, flat scaly plates. Bark of eastern pine is gray or purplish and more deeply fissured. Needles of both grow in clusters of five.

Western Wood Products Ass'n

REDWOOD

The giant redwoods, or sequoias, of California are not only our largest trees but are considered to be the oldest and largest living things on earth. Some specimens are estimated to be over 4000 years old, with individual trees reaching up to 6000 tons in weight. The trees are named for the russet color of their wood. A smaller species of redwood, growing within the same area, is used for shingles, chests, doors, and furniture. The wood is brittle but very resistant to weathering and age.

Redwood trees grow to enormous heights, 200 to 300 feet, with record tree measuring 364 feet. Bark is reddish-brown, thick, and deeply furrowed. Needles, ¼ to ¾ inch long, grow in two rows.

SAGUARO

The saguaro is a cactus, but grows to such prodigious size and height that it may be listed here. It is often called the "Joshua tree" because of its "arms," which extend from the main trunk, seeming to implore the heavens as did the Biblical character. The plant takes up water after a desert rain and hoards it for dry weather beneath its spiny covering. As drought increases, the saguaro wrinkles. The species is found in Mexico, scattered in California, and principally around Tuscon, in Arizona. Mature plants may stand up to a height of 30 feet or more.

The ribbed trunk of the saguaro is spined with sharp needles. Reaching 2 feet in diameter, the trunk hoards water in its internal cavity for dry weather.

SPRUCE

Several species of spruce are common to North America and are found over wide areas of Canada, northward into the Yukon and Alaska, and southward into the northern tier of states. Spruces are generally dark in color and have short stiff needles which grow all around the branchlets. These needles are four-sided and in cross-section are nearly square, as against the long, rectangular shape of a cross-section of fir needles. The needles are slightly curved. Eastern varieties of spruce include the red, white, and black spruce. A spruce imported from Europe, the Norway spruce, is now widely spread in Canada. Two western species are the Engelmann spruce and the Colorado spruce. The Engelmann grows in high mountainous country from the Southwest to the Yukon, and is a most important lumber variety. Its wood is light but strong, and is much used in airplane construction. The Colorado, or blue spruce, is native to Colorado, but has been transplanted into other areas, largely as an ornamental tree. It has a silvery sheen to the dark color of its leaves.

Western Wood Products Ass'n

Bark of the Englemann spruce is grayish or purplish-brown, thin, with loosely attached scales. The needles (above) are ⅝ to 1⅛ inches long, dark or pale blue-green. Cones are 1½ to 2½ inches long and pointed.

Blue spruce of the Rocky Mountain region has gray or brown bark furrowed into scaly ridges. Its dark leaves have a silvery sheen and branches curve upward at tips.

Norway spruce is a straight, cone-shaped tree reaching 150 feet in height. Branches rise at the tips, have many offshoots.

White spruce rarely exceeds to 70 feet in height. Branc are long, densely cloth sweeping out in graceful, ward curves.

SYCAMORE

Unlike the pines, the sycamore likes low, open country, and is found from the Northeastern States westward to the Plains States and southward to the Gulf of Mexico. The leaves resemble those of some maples in that they have five lobes and are sharp-edged. The leaves grow alternately along the branches, not oppositely as do the maples. Perhaps the most distinguishing feature of the sycamore is its bark. Due to flaking off of old bark, with patches of new bark appearing beneath, a combination of brown and cream-colored areas make the lower trunk appear speckled like the rump of an Appaloosa horse. The sycamore is one of the largest of broadleaved trees.

Sycamore leaves are heart-shaped, 4 to 8 inches long, and coarsely toothed. The bark is smooth, peeling off in large flakes, showing patches of brown, gray, and green on the trunk.

Black Walnut

WALNUT

Two species of North American walnut are the butternut and the black walnut. Both occupy the larger share of eastern United States, though the limit of range on the south is somewhat inside the Gulf coastal area. The butternut tree has a short trunk and low sweeping branches, with trees running to 40 or 50 feet in height and 2 feet or over at the base. The leaves are compound, with eleven to seventeen leaflets. The black walnut is one of the more important woods used in furniture, cabinets, and principally in gun stocks. It is a fine-grained wood, doesn't split easily, and takes a high finish. Black-walnut trees are larger than butternut trees, often reaching a height of 100 feet. They have umbrella-like crowns, compound leaves, and bark of dark-brown color. Mature nuts of this species are round in shape, reach up to 2 inches in diameter, and are enclosed in an outside husk.

Bark of black walnut (left) is dark brown to black, thick, with deep furrows and narrow, forking ridges. Leaves are compound, 12 to 24 inches long. Bark of the butternut (right) is light gray, furrowed into flat ridges.

The butternut, smaller than the black walnut, has a short trunk and low sweeping branches.

Leaves of the butternut are compound, 15 to 30 inches long, with 11 to 19 leaflets, which have no stalks.

Butternuts grow in clusters of three to five fruits. Egg shaped, with thick husks, they are edible, having a sweet and oily taste.

Weeping Willow

WILLOW

There are over 100 species of willow in North America. In addition, willows form hybrids easily, which adds to their total numbers. In general, willows are fast-growing trees which grow into large spreading shapes from short trunks, or from trunks which tend to separate. They are identified usually by long slender leaves which grow alternately along the branchlets, and the flowers which grow in catkins. Three of the best known willows are the black willow, the pussy willow, and the weeping willow. The black willow grows across southern Canada, and the eastern half of the United States with the exception of the extreme southeastern part. Pussy willows are found in the same overall region, and are identified by their soft, grayish buds resembling tiny rabbit tails, which grow on small trees reaching 15 feet or so in height. The weeping willow is found in most

Bark of the weeping willow is grayish-brown and fissured. The leaves are lance shaped, 3 to 6 inches long, and grow on long stems.

Black willow has irregular, spreading branches and a dark trunk. It grows in eastern half of the U.S.A.

of southern Canada, and southward to the Gulf States, and likes moist ground. This species is noted for its exceptionally long branchlets, which droop often nearly to the ground, giving the tree its "weeping" appearance. As an example of how fast this and other willows grow, we planted a weeping willow on our acreage twenty-eight years ago by simply planting a cutting into moist ground. This tree now reaches 35 feet in height, and its diameter 6 feet up the trunk is 30 inches.

Bark of the black willow is dark brown or blackish, deeply furrowed, with scaly, forking ridges. Leaves are long, slim, pointed, finely toothed, shiny green above, pale beneath.

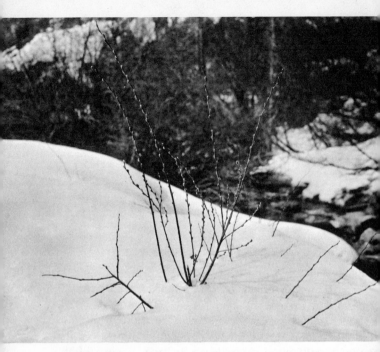

Pussy willow grows as a shrub or small tree. Branches
are gathered in March and April for furry, gray buds
which are valued for their decorative qualities.

Signs of the Animals

In his travels through the woods, and along streams and seacoasts, the outdoors lover sees only a small percentage of all the animals that inhabit the wilderness. There are many reasons for this. Many of the smaller wild animals are prey for larger animals; and consequently, in order for a species to survive, it must be furtive in all movement and activity. This semiconcealment keeps it from the eyes of man. Again, many of the smaller animals are nocturnal and do much of their moving about after man has gone to sleep. A bigger reason why man sees only a portion of the animals about him is the fact that man's activity and noise are interpreted by animals as evidence of an enemy. To protect themselves, they remain concealed.

To the more observing person, the signs that animals leave record their habits and their numbers. The fresh burrow, earth, and tracks in the sandy desert is a printed record of the jackrabbit, ground squirrel, or badger, depending upon the characteristics of the spoor. The felled aspen tree, teeth marks, drag trail, and wet "slide" into the mountain creek all tell the alert that fall is coming, and the beaver is storing green, succulent branches near the underwater entrance to his pond home, against the coming freeze-up. And the scarcely audible *tick-tick* in the trees above, on a still morning, means that somewhere in the leafy branches a squirrel is sorting seeds and nuts from the cones.

These and the many other signs of the animals tell the alert observer of forest activities, a cycle of living and true industry, and give him a sense of belonging. And since man himself is but an animal of a higher order, an awareness and an understanding of his woodland brethren add not only to his enjoyment but to his own significance.

THE ELK

A handsome, majestic animal with tremendous antlers and awesome bulk, the elk, or wapiti, is now native only to the West. He spends his summers high in the mountains and his winters at lower altitudes where the weather is not so harsh. Most of his signs are visual, but there are audible ones as well.

Elk tracks can be identified by their size and roundish shape. Dewclaws register when animal is walking in soft ground or snow.

Aspens with black patches on their trunks are a sure sign that elk have stripped bark during winter feeding.

Tracks of a mature elk are large, up to 4½ inches long, and roundish. Dewclaws usually only register in mud or snow or when the animal is running. When walking, the elk leaves tracks that seem to be more in a line than when he's galloping.

Elk feed on grass, twigs, leaves, and bark, the bark of aspens being favored winter fare. You will often find these trees well scored where the animals have stripped off chunks of bark with their lower incisors. If you happen to come to an area where aspens have grown blackened trunks as far up as an elk can reach,

Patches of flattened grass in high country are often evidence that elk have bedded down there during summer.

you can be assured you've stumbled on a spot where elk have spent the winter year after year; their repeated gnawings have caused the trees to develop these rough, darkened boles. Also in winter, elk browse on shoots and twigs of trees, cleaning the branches as far up as they can reach.

Broken branches and torn bark are other tree signs to look for. These are left by the bull elk when he rubs his antlers against tree trunks and bushes to scrape off the velvet that has been covering them since they started growing in March or April, and to polish and sharpen them in preparation for battles with other bulls in defense of his harem. Sometimes saplings used for this purpose are killed. Why aren't winter-dropped antlers a good sign of elk wanderings? Rodents, and sometimes elk themselves, usually chew them up in short order.

In winter, elk paw sizeable holes in the snow to get to food, and you may even find their beds in the snow as well. In summer, look for areas where the grass has been depressed if you want to see places where these animals have been sleeping.

During the summer, when elk are in the high country, it will pay you to keep an eye on the banks of shallow ponds and lakes. Often you will find tracks there where the animals have come to drink, swim, and enjoy themselves. During the rut, before these tremendous deer have started for the lower country, the bulls frequently cool off their fiery enthusiasm by pawing away the wet ground and thrashing around in the mud. Sometimes these old wallows collect water and are visible for several years. Like deer and moose, elk often dig up the ground for minerals, and only your knowledge of tracks will tell you for sure what animal has done the excavating.

Elk droppings vary according to time of year. In summer they're flat, tending to be circular and about 5 or 6 inches across. In winter, they take on the pellet-like form common to those of the rest of the deer family.

The elk makes a variety of noises, most well known of which is the bugling of the bull in the fall. It is like a musical arpeggio of four distinct tones rising to a virtual whistle, then sliding downward to end in a

Winter droppings of the elk are pellet shaped, similar to those left by other members of the deer family.

series of grunts. It can be heard at dusk and at daybreak for nearly a mile in hushed wilderness country. It is the challenge cry of the bull during the rutting season.

Another sound associated with the rut is a horrendous one. It is the noise made when two of these many-tined monarchs join in battle, something that happens when one bull is trying to protect his harem of up to thirty cows from another bull with acquisitive ideas. The noise is a clashing and crashing of antlers that drowns out all other sounds of the forest community. It is accompanied by grunts, groans, and bellows of outrage. After a time, one of the animals calls it quits and looks elsewhere for female companionship.

Other sounds made by elk are a soft bark as the mother calls to her calf and sometimes a squeal or two as mother and youngster converse. A sharp, loud bark usually is a sign of alarm, and a lot of squealing and rumbling indicates that a startled band of mothers and young is trying to get back together, each parent with the proper offspring.

This is classic whitetail country—the fringes of thick forests where deer can feed on bushes and saplings.

THE WHITETAIL DEER

This handsome animal ranges from southern Canada down through Mexico and Central America, and west to the Rockies. He is also found in parts of Idaho, Colorado, Wyoming, Arizona, and New Mexico. He varies considerably in size, from a maximum of up to 400 pounds for a large northern whitetail to a minimum of about 100 for the little Coues deer. The tiny Key deer of Florida are less than half of that and are extremely rare.

The Coues deer, who lives in southwestern Arizona, Mexico, and parts of Texas, is also referred to as the fantail, the Sonora whitetail, and the Arizona white-tail. Unlike his northern cousins whose coats change from reddish brown in summer to grayish in winter, the Coues keeps his brownish gray all year.

The study of a whitetail's tracks will tell you a lot about what he is doing. When the animal is walking, it places the hind foot practically on top of the heart-shaped print of the front one, and the groups of two are slightly staggered. Dewclaws do not show. When galloping, the whitetail makes a separate and distinct print with each hoof, the toes are spread out so that the familiar heart shape is gone, hind feet print in front of front ones, and the dewclaws show, those of the hind feet being farther behind the hoofs than those of the front ones. In this gait, the prints also show as a staggered line. When bounding, this deer brings his four feet down closer together, and they form a rather triangular grouping. As in the gallop-ing gait, hoofs are spread and dewclaws show.

Drag marks behind tracks in snow may mean a large whitetail buck has passed by.

Generally speaking, but this is by no means infalli-ble, a buck, particularly a big one, shows more of a drag mark than a doe. This can be noticed in snow or in the disturbance of dead leaves on the forest floor. Furthermore, it is quite natural that a larger animal will leave a trail that shows prints farther apart from the center line than will a small one. An-other indication that a set of prints might have been made by a big buck is in the tracks themselves; those of a large male tend to toe out, but, like the other ways of telling the sex of a deer by its track, this is not always 100 percent accurate. In all of nature, each animal within a species has its own individuality, and just as there are women with big feet and men with small ones, so some does leave big prints and some bucks do not. Generally speaking, if you're following the trail of a herd of deer and you see the tracks overprinted by a conspicuously larger set of tracks, you can be reasonably sure a large buck has been bringing up the rear of a group of does and fawns.

Look for tracks at deer crossings, which are usually relatively narrow areas through which deer regularly pass in their travels from place to place. A saddle, or notch, in a ridge is a favorite deer crossing, for deer, like humans, tend to choose the easiest route across rough terrain.

There are many other signs of the whitetail, some of them varying by season. For instance, if you're hunting and see that the soft bark has been scraped and gouged from a small cedar or willow sapling, you may assume that there are bucks around. These marks are made in late August—usually well before hunting season—when the buck tries to scrape the velvet off his antlers. A more valuable sign to the hunter, because it is made in the fall, is evidence of brush and small growth that's been broken, stripped, and generally beaten up. Bucks violate bushes in this manner by hooking them and sparring with them with their antlers in the general pugnacity of the rutting season. It is a sure sign you're in buck territory.

Another seasonal sign is the wallow. Like elk, whitetail bucks will occasionally wallow in mud during the rut, but they're by no means as addicted to the habit as are their larger relatives. If in doubt about which

Whitetails often browse in winter on the bark of cedars, stripping the trunk to the limits of their reach.

animal made the wallow you're looking at, check for hair, and don't forget to look over the surrounding tracks.

Antlers are usually shed sometime in January or February, and, as is usually the case with cast antlers and horn, they're chewed up by rodents for their calcium and lime. However, the deer themselves also gnaw cast antlers. If you find the remains of an antler, check the tooth marks; those left by the rodents are smaller than the mouthings left by deer.

Food of the whitetail is enormously varied. In spring and summer it is made up of grasses, buds,

SIGNS OF THE ANIMALS 355

berries, mushrooms, fruit, many green leaves and shoots, water lilies, and, occasionally, a fish stolen from an angler's camp or actually caught. A deer catches a fish by stabbing at it with a hoof until it is so battered and bruised it can be picked up in the animal's mouth.

In fall, twigs, acorns, apples, leaves, and low-growing plants are consumed. In winter, where the snows are deep and the weather severe, deer yard up, perhaps several bucks as well as five or six does and their young. They stay together in a small area browsing on sprouts and twigs of cedar and spruce, suckers, and what shrubbery they can find. Edge areas along meadows and woodlots, where trees meet open spaces, are favorite feeding spots owing to the low bushes and second-growth saplings that usually grow there. Deer usually feed in these areas during the night, climbing into the high ridges at dawn and bedding down for the day. If the winter is hard, many deer will perish of starvation. In southern climes and areas of mild winters, whitetails generally do not yard up.

When the low-growing feed has been eaten, the animals reach up to nibble away the twigs of the

In the fall, broken saplings and trampled ground tell the passerby that two bucks have fought a battle.

overhanging branches. Since a big buck can reach up higher than a small deer, the young and the does are the first to feel the pinch of hunger, many of them eventually dying. Also, in rearing up on their hind legs to reach a succulent branch, a deer can get his neck caught in the fork of a limb and hang or strangle himself.

Scats of deer are the familiar pellet variety, tending, however, to be softer, larger, and more shapeless when the animal is eating his soft summer fare.

Watch for deer beds in winter as well as summer. In summer they appear as depressed spots in grass or leaves. In winter, they are depressions in the snow. Usually you'll find them on hillsides where their makers can keep an eye out for danger.

Most common sound made by the whitetail is a sort of whistling snort, emitted when the animal is alarmed. Contrary to the belief in some circles, both bucks and does snort and can be heard for considerable distances when they do. Another sound, rarely heard at any distance, is the low conversation between a doe and her offspring.

A deer noise that occasionally can be heard in the fall woods is the clashing of antlers when bucks fight over does. During the rut, bucks fight furiously among themselves, and the clashing of antlers, low grunts of indignation, and the thrashing around in an area of perhaps a half an acre is as readily recognizable as is the sight of the terrain after the fight is over.

Don't forget that deer like water lilies, and they wade out in ponds and lakes to get them. While you're sitting around camp on a still evening, keep an ear cocked toward the shore; you may hear a deer pulling up the succulent stems.

Baby deer, usually twins, are born in May or early June, but by that time their father has long gone. He will stay by himself throughout the summer while his antlers are growing. By late August they're formed, and, in the north at least, the buck goes into the rut sometime in October. By this time, the young are weaned, but they generally stay with their mother until the following spring.

In November, the rut is in full swing and lasts about a month for each individual buck. He seeks a female but only stays with her a few days before dashing off to find another.

Winter droppings of whitetail (above) and mule deer (below) are pellet shaped, generally under an inch in size.

Tracks of bounding mule deer show hind feet placed close behind forefeet. Prints are larger than whitetail's.

THE MULE DEER

The muley lives in the Rocky Mountain area from Canada to Mexico, and in parts of his eastern range he is found at the western limits of the whitetail's range. He is also very similar in habits and life history to his eastern cousin.

The mule deer is a somewhat bigger animal than the whitetail, about 475 pounds being tops for this brownish-gray creature. Also, he is more of a mountain animal, spending his summers at around 8,000 feet and migrating seasonally into the valleys where the winter weather is less harsh. These two ranges may be as much as 150 miles apart but are usually closer to 50. Certain mule deer, however, live in the southwestern deserts.

The trail of a galloping mule deer shows one prominent difference from that of the galloping whitetail. The muley bounds in high leaps, but when he comes down his hind feet are behind the front ones. The galloping whitetail puts his hind feet down in front of the front ones when going all out. This leaping, bouncing-ball gait of the muley permits him to look over the countryside and spot danger when in high midstride. He might cover 4 feet vertically and 20 feet or more horizontally in a single leap. Walking, his track is similar to that of the whitetail, but his hoofs are a bit bigger. Also, a muley that spends much time on rocky ground is apt to have the points of his hoofs more rounded than will an animal who has spent more time on less abrasive soil or sand.

The muley doesn't fight as much as the whitetail, and you're not going to hear the clashing of antlers as much among this species during the rut. During courtship, a buck may get together a harem of three

A frequent sight in the southwestern desert—a jojoba tree with its branches stripped of foliage by browsing mule deer.

or four females, but if a larger male drives him off, he'll shrug and wander away in search of other does.

Watch for salt licks. Like all deer, the muley loves salt, and the clay in which it's deposited will be worn and eroded by many tongues.

Diet of the mule deer is varied, but he commonly eats more grass and herbs than does the whitetail. Twigs and leaves of all sorts of brush and berry bushes are eaten greedily as well as the leaves of aspens, oaks, mountain ash, bitter-brush, and willow. These deer are also fond of mushrooms, fungi, and mistletoe where available in their range. In winter, the branch tips of juniper, mountain mahogany, and fir are nipped off and chewed up.

By the end of January in the north, and a month or so later in the south, the bucks lose their antlers and settle down for the winter. Small groups—a buck, a doe, yearlings, and fawns of the season—now get together to form large herds. With the coming of spring, the animals start for their summer quarters, munching the new grasses as they wander along. Fawns, usually twins, are born in late June or early July, after the does have reached the summer range. Bucks wander off by themselves until the two-month rut begins in October.

The muley, along with its many similarities to the whitetail, also makes a snorting whistle when alarmed. It emits a coughing grunt when fighting and now and then lets out a low, growling noise.

An observant autumn hiker might note the velvet clinging to a rock and know that a mule deer scraped and sharpened his antlers there in late August.

THE BLACKTAIL DEER

There's little to distinguish the signs of this animal from those of other deer. Tracks, droppings, tree and bush signs, all are just about identical. Range and some personal habits, however, differ.

The blacktail lives in a narrow coastal belt that goes from about central California north to the southern tip of Alaska and east to the western slopes of the Sierras and the Cascade Range. This is the area of heavy spruce and redwood forests, and its undergrowth is dense. Because it is so dense and so high, the blacktail makes his escape from enemies by stealing through it on well-known trails rather than by bounding off as do frightened muleys and whitetails.

Northern and inland animals tend to migrate to a certain extent from the high alpine meadows in the summer to the more hospitable valleys in the winter. Those living in the dense forests of the lowlands feed on the same sort of shrubbery enjoyed by the mule deer and on moss, mistletoe, fungus, and acorns. There's no grass in these dense forests. Leaves and twigs of alder, cedar, hemlock, and other trees are eaten in winter. Sometimes, when winter food becomes unbearably scarce, blacktails will forage along the shore for kelp and various seaweeds.

These deer are splendid swimmers, and those living along the coast of their range often swim from island to island in water that also has icebergs floating in it.

The blacktail mates in November in the north, a month earlier in the south.

A walking blacktail leaves well-spaced tracks.

In the North Woods country, water is apt to mean moose.
Here he finds his favorite food—aquatic plants.

THE MOOSE

This tremendous animal, weighing from 900 to
1,800 pounds for a huge Kenai specimen, is known,
of course, for his huge, palmated antlers, the 4- to
10-inch "bell" that hangs under the base of his jaw,
and his rubbery-looking snout.

His tracks are similar to those of an elk, but they
are larger (up to 7 inches or so) and are more pointed,

with a tendency to splay. Sometimes dewclaws show, particularly when the animal is trotting. Usually a bull's tracks are toed out, while those of a cow are straight. A moose trail shows staggered prints.

Moose love aquatic plants, so if you're in an area of ponds and marshes anywhere in his range (Maine, some of the western and northwestern states as well as wooded Canada and most of Alaska) keep your eyes open for tracks and signs of torn-up water lilies and ploughed-up pond bottoms.

Another visual sign of the moose that's concerned with his feeding is the mess he leaves of fir trees, aspens, and willows in winter. He strips branches as far up as he can, often standing on his hind legs and reaching up as high as 18 feet or so. Sometimes, when he is particularly interested in the branches of a sapling, he will jump on it, force it down by sheer weight, and nibble away at its top. Watch for small trees broken this way and also by the moose's having pulled the branches of such small trees until the trunks have snapped. This winter activity is accom-

Moose tracks are large, up to 7 inches long, and form a staggered trail. They are more pointed than the elk's.

During fall rutting season, bulls often leave torn-up ground and broken trees as evidence of furious battles.

panied by numerous tracks, usually within an area of several acres, showing that a bull, a cow, and a couple of young have yarded up there. Practically all the trees in the locality will be found stripped to a surprising height.

Moose chew on aspen bark, as do elk, and the only way you can tell for sure which animal has done the gnawing is to have a knowledge of wintering habitat and other signs. Their browsings on twigs do not show the neat, clipped-off ends left by rodents with their sharp teeth.

In winter, scats of moose are in the familiar pellet shape of the deer's, though more pear-shaped, and they are much larger and more numerous than are those of deer. In winter, these droppings are very dry and somewhat smooth. In summer, scats may be without recognizable form and resemble those left by a milk cow. As winter comes on again, however, and food becomes dryer, scats become more pelletlike.

Beds in snow or grass can be confused with those of elk because of the size of the animal that made them. Look for tracks and droppings to verify any beds you come across. Another sign, one that can be smelled as well as seen, is the moose wallow. At a time when he is interested in attracting a lady friend, the bull paws a shallow pit perhaps 4 feet across in the soft ground. Then he urinates in it and wallows in the soggy mess. These wallows aren't hard to identify because of the tracks around them and the stench they exude.

Bulls drop their antlers around midwinter, to start new ones in early spring. Shed antlers are, of course, another sign, but so many members of the woods fraternity chew on them that they are rarely seen.

Another visual sign would be a quarter of an acre or so of woods torn up and scarred from the battle of two rutting bulls. The rut begins along in Septem-

er signs to look for in se country — droppings an inch long, tooth s on aspen trunks where al has chewed bark.

With his enormous reach, the moose strips willow saplings 10 feet tall of their foliage. He'll bend even taller trees to the ground and clean them bare.

ber, lasts about six weeks, and results in many battles that leave the trees, brush, and ground looking as if they'd been attacked by a maniac on a bulldozer.

When two bulls fight for the favors of the cows, they clash their antlers, shatter the foliage, and grunt with the efforts they're making to drive one another away with their heavy headgear. If you hear such a racket thundering through the fall woods in moose habitat, tread warily.

Listen too for the splashing of water and the showering of spray when you're in wet moose country. The animals wade out into lakes and ponds to get the floating vegetation, but for underwater plants moose go beneath the surface and come up snorting and blowing with mouthfuls of the stuff.

During the rut, the bull grunts as he wanders around in search of female companionship. The cow bellows, bawls, or whines as she tries to attract a bull. When cow and calf converse, the noises are quite low.

THE CARIBOU

A sign of caribou in the north country—
antler velvet clinging to broken bushes in
the fall.

With his towering, regal sack, snow-white neck,
and beautiful dark-brown body, the caribou is perhaps one of the world's handsomest animals. On
this continent, he ranges throughout most of Alaska,
the tundra and forests of Canada, and a very small
part of northern Minnesota. These creatures are
divided into the woodland caribou of eastern Canada,
the mountain caribou, inhabiting the Rockies, and the
Barren Ground variety, which lives in the far North.

There are many visual signs of the caribou, not
the least of which is his very distinctive track. Hoofs
are rounded, and the crescent-shaped halves spread
when the animal puts his weight on them. Front hoofs

tend to spread a bit more than hind ones and, at about 4 inches across for a good bull, are a little bigger. When the animal is walking, dewclaws, or pasterns, of the front feet show quite far behind the hoofs. Hind hoofs are put down just a little bit short of the front ones, and the dewclaw marks look as if they belonged to the hind feet rather than the front ones.

Males and females both grow antlers, though those of the females are not the least bit impressive when compared with those of a handsome buck. Mature bucks shed theirs sometime in November, and the does and immature bucks lose their racks in spring. By September, the bucks are getting rid of the velvet on their new antlers by cutting and slashing at bushes and young trees. The stuff hangs in the scarred and broken brush as another visual sign of the caribou.

It's long been a popular belief that these animals use their palmated brow tines, called shovels, for scraping snow away from the lichens of which they are so fond. This is not true. In the first place, antlers have usually been shed when the snow is on the ground, and in the second place, their position in relation to the noses of their owners would make scraping with them extremely difficult. They paw the winter covering away with their front feet, and you'll often see areas in caribou habitat where they have dug large holes in the snow to get to moss and various grasses as well as lichens.

Caribou love lichens and eat them year round, but

Full-grown caribou leave crescent-shaped tracks about 3 inches long. Under animal's weight, hoof halves spread wide apart.

Exposed lichens in snow-covered terrain show where caribou dug holes with their front feet to get at favored food.

grasses, willow limbs, aspens, blueberry bushes, and other shrubs are also consumed. Look for stripped limbs and evidence of chewed-off twigs on bushes. Look also for signs that fungus has been nibbled at. Caribou are very partial to it.

Scats of these 300-pound animals are often in the pellet shape of other deer, but they can be soft and in a mass when the creatures have been eating juicy greens.

If you're wandering around in the north country in winter, keep an eye out for a cloud of vapor in

Winter droppings of caribou, similar to those of other deer, are pellet shaped and usually under an inch.

the distance. This will indicate that a herd of caribou is on the move. The cloud is caused by the body heat of the animals and by the vapor of their breaths.

Watch too for beds in the snow and for caribou hair. The animal sloughs off his winter coat in huge tatters and shreds, usually in spring.

Caribou migrate seasonally from summer to winter feeding grounds, and the sight of a tremendous herd of the moving animals is not one to forget easily. Neither is the sound. When a caribou walks or trots, there is a definite *click* in his ankles, and when a large herd is under way the sound, mingled with occasional grunts and groans, is audible for some distance.

During winter, bulls begin to leave the cows, and by late spring the latter are in separate groups. Young,

Strange winter sight in caribou country is cloud of vapor caused by body heat and breath of a traveling herd.

Depressions in the snow indicate that caribou have bedded-down during winter feeding.

usually one but sometimes two, arrive in June or late May. In the fall, however, the bulls have their fighting equipment back, and an audible sign of this is the crashing made when they polish their antlers and occasionally engage in battles among themselves in defense of the harems they're beginning to acquire.

Caribou are not particularly vocal, but now and then you might hear a low grunting. This is generally used as communication between a doe and her offspring.

Some say the caribou is not very bright, and certainly his occasional, helter-skelter dashes from one direction to another defy reason. But be that as it may, his high, springy lope, his magnificent antlers, and his distinctive, clicking walk are part of the wilderness that is shrinking too fast.

THE ANTELOPE

Often called the pronghorn, this animal of the arid plains regions of the western United States is among the fastest-moving creatures on earth and one of the most graceful. He likes the company of his fellows and is usually seen in bands of up to 100 animals, though in early fall the bucks begin to get together small groups of does as a harem. Twin fawns are the rule, and they're usually born eight months after the mating. Mature bucks rarely weigh over 125 pounds, and does are somewhat smaller.

Antelope uses white rump patch of erectile hairs to flash warning signals to herd when danger is near. These signals are tip-off to distant observer that antelope are in the area.

Antelope tracks are rather heart shaped and deer-like, front hoofs being slightly longer than the hind ones. There are no dewclaws. When going full speed —and it has been estimated an antelope can hit 70 miles an hour—leaps can be as much as 20 feet or more.

The pronghorn is mainly a weed eater rather than a grass eater, the bulk of his diet being dandelions, chicory, and other range weeds along with nibblings of desert shrubs such as sagebrush and juniper. Scats vary from pellets to longer masses.

The white rump patches on these basically dark-tan animals consists of erectile hairs, and when prong-horns are alarmed the patches stand out like huge fluffs of white cotton. At the same time, the startled creatures release a scent that a hunter can smell hundreds of feet away. By the time he smells it, however, the antelope are well on their way to safety.

Heart shaped and similar to those of the mule deer, ante-lope tracks never show marks of dewclaws; the antelope has none.

Antelope droppings are either pellet shaped and less than an inch in length, or soft and elongated, depending on the season.

These swift animals are not particularly vocal, though when alarmed or ill at ease they sometimes make a loud, snorting whistle like that of a whitetail deer. When a doe is calling to her offspring, she may give a low bleat.

One of the great peculiarities of the antelope is his branched, hollow horns, which he sheds annually, usually in late winter. He is the only hoofed mammal with such horns known to shed them. Once dropped, they're munched on by rodents and even by the antelope themselves for the calcium they contain. If not chewed up, they disintegrate quite quickly. Both sexes have horns, but those of the female are seldom over 5 inches long while those of mature bucks average 10 or 12.

The resounding crash of two rams in a head-on charge may be heard in sheep country during the autumn rutting-season battles.

THE ROCKY MOUNTAIN BIGHORN

Great, brown, blocky animals with long coarse hair nothing like the wool found on domestic sheep, these nimble-footed creatures live in the high, windswept mountains of North America from southern British Columbia and Alberta south through the Rockies. Because of their magnificent, close-curled horns, they are at, or near, the top of every trophy hunter's list.

The Rocky Mountain ram weighs about 200 pounds, but large ones can reach 300. Ewes are smaller.

Tracks of the bighorn are rather like those of a whitetail deer, but the edges are straighter and the tips tend to be squared off rather than sharp. Hoof print of an adult male may be 3½ inches long, and when the animal is walking he puts his hind foot on the print left by the front one. Bounding, he comes down with all four feet together. Not quite so sure-footed as the mountain goat, the bighorn is, however, faster as he leaps around the rocky cliffs and shale slides of his habitat.

There are other visual signs of the bighorn. Between feedings during the day, these beautiful creatures lie down to contemplate their domains and to chew their cuds. Their beds at this time are informal affairs, often prepared simply by scratching a few times in the ground with their forefeet. Their night beds, however, are another story. Usually on the lee side of a ridge, they are shallow, platterlike depressions about 3 feet long, and the rams often use them for a long time. If you come across something like this and don't recognize it by sight, just sniff and look a bit more closely. Bighorns often urinate in the beds when leaving them in the morning, and they leave their accumulated droppings around it. These latter, incidentally, tend to be pelletlike when the animals are feeding on dry food, massed together and softer when the diet is soft and succulent.

Bighorn's tracks are similar to those of whitetail but the edges are straighter; tips are square rather than sharp.

Shallow depressions on lee side of ridge are sheeps' night beds. These are usually deeper than animals' daytime resting places.

Sheep also use caves, particularly when the weather is very bad. Aside from the obvious visual signs, use your nose when exploring a cave suspected of having harbored sheep. And anywhere in sheep country, look for coarse, long hairs that have been caught in the rocks.

Sheep love salt, and they will gravitate to salt licks, particularly in spring and early summer. They can be recognized by the maze of tracks and trails leading to them and by the holes and smooth spots worn in them by the tongues of the countless animals using them. Sheep also get salt by eating decomposed rock with a high salt content.

Bulk of the bighorn's diet is grass and herbs, but the creatures occasionally browse on the buds of willow, spruce, fir, and aspen. Where the snow is not too deep in winter, look for evidence of pawing. The animals in the central Rockies have to get grass in winter, and they'll paw through almost a foot of snow to reach it.

The bighorn is not a very vocal animal, but in summer there is much conversational bleating between ewes and lambs. Mature sheep snort to warn one another of danger, and when rams get angry they gnash their teeth.

Rams stay by themselves during the summer, usually in small bands of animals of the same age. About the middle to the end of October, however, they start looking for the ewes. By the middle of the following month, the rut is going full blast. Some rams assemble harems of up to seven ewes, and some of these harem masters are belligerent in the defense of their womenfolk if a strange ram appears on the scene. It is then that the spectacular battles between the rams take place.

A battle starts with the two combatants snorting at one another fairly close together. Then they walk away from each other 30 or 40 feet, turn as if on a prearranged signal, and charge each other head first. The crash when their massive horns meet can be heard for a mile or more. If you are in sheep country in the late fall, you might be lucky enough to hear this sound and even to see a battle in progress. The repeated chargings may last for a few minutes or a couple of hours. Both rams are usually on their feet when it is over, and sometimes the two wander off together as if nothing more serious had taken place than a mild difference of opinion. Occasionally, however, a few rams that have nothing better to do join in the fight, and the result is a pitched battle during which horn tips get broken, nose bleeds occur, deep gashes are given and received, and a contestant or so may be killed by being pushed over a cliff or getting his skull fractured.

A traveler on the arid southwestern desert is apt to see the decaying skulls and horns of desert bighorns baking under the torrid sun.

THE DESERT BIGHORN

This animal is a southern extension of the Rocky Mountain bighorn, and he inhabits the hottest, most arid, most rugged country the southwestern United States, Lower California, and Mexico have to offer. He is also hard to spot because his gray-brown coat blends perfectly with the brown, rocky hills in which he lives.

The desert bighorn is a bit smaller than the northern variety, and he probably weighs, on the average, about 50 pounds less. Because he lives in an area of burning heat, his hairs are shorter than those of the cold-weather bighorn. He also has a more slender neck, and his rump patch isn't quite as white as that of his somewhat bigger cousin.

Since the desert sheep lives in a climate so vastly different from that enjoyed by other sheep, it is natural that some of his habits would be different too.

In the main, however, signs of him are similar. He makes a similar bed, he leaves his droppings around it, he battles in conventional sheep manner, his tracks are the same, and he also wanders into caves.

One difference, however, is that the rut gets under way earlier in the desert, usually around the first of September, and the lambs are usually born around the first of February. Another difference is in watering habits. Northern sheep have plenty of water, but the desert variety lives where it is not only scarce but somewhat nonexistent. Where there are no holes of accumulated rainwater, the southern sheep depends on dew, fruit of cactus plants, and the water stored

Signs of bighorn sheep, both desert and mountain, are few, but one may occasionally see wisps of their hair clinging to a rock.

in such cacti as the barrel cactus and the saguaro. It is a mystery how they do it without getting skewered, but they will nibble as much as 6 inches into the huge saguaros for the moisture. Since grasses aren't as plentiful in the desert ranges, the sheep there are mainly browsers, living chiefly on such shrubs as mountain mahogany, buckbrush, and Mormon tea. They travel great distances, however, for the succulent greenery that springs up briefly early in the year.

Because rain is so scarce in this rough country, tracks can be very confusing. You can see one that looks as if it had been made only a couple of days before you came across it, but in reality it may have been made months before.

Also due to lack of moisture, the desert bighorn's horns—which are also of the close-curl type—tend to be drier. As a result of this, they crack and flake, and it is not uncommon to find pieces of them in ram beds and where the animals have been fighting or have bumped against rocks. Watch for this sign of the desert bighorn.

Like those of deer, the shape of wild-sheep droppings depends on available forage. This is type left by animal on thin forage.

anging high among the northern peaks, the pure white
*all sheep often surveys the world from a bed outside
is cave.

E DALL SHEEP AND THE STONE SHEEP

The Dall sheep is one of the handsomest of North
merican game animals. He is pure white with yel-
)wish-brown horns that flare out more than do
10se of the bighorn. Also, he is a smaller creature by
r. Horns tend to be slenderer and rather triangular
 cross section.

Range of these truly majestic animals is from the
)rthern reaches of Alaska south and southeast
rough parts of the Yukon into northern British
olumbia. Like all sheep, they tend to travel exten-
vely, to seek less snowy altitudes for their winter
nges, and to have a sweetish odor about them that
 well recognized by outdoorsmen of the north.

Food of the Dall is principally grass and sedge though many other lichens and plants are nibbled at now and then.

Bighorns broom their horns—rub the tips until they wear them off—so the ends will not obstruct their vision, but this is not done as frequently among the Dalls because their horns flare out more and do not tend to block the animals' vision as much as do the close curls of the massive bighorns.

Tracks of the Dall sheep are slightly sharper than those of the bighorn and are more tapered toward the front

As soon as the wilderness traveler gets south of Alaska and east of the Dalls' Yukon range, he begins to see the Stone sheep. This animal ranges much farther down into British Columbia than does the Dall, of whom he is such a close relative that he is a subspecies. In spite of that, however, he looks quite different. This beautiful creature is the darkest of the sheep, though his colors vary tremendously. He can be anything from a practically black animal to one that is light with a dark-brown saddle. Where the ranges of the Dalls and the Stones overlap, the sheep tend to be lighter with some darker markings, but in the southern part of his range the Stone is quite dark.

Stones average smaller than the bighorns, as a gen

eral rule, but a bit larger than their white cousins. Horns are similar in shape to those of the Dall, being outward flaring and more slender than those of the bighorn. Instead of being yellowish like those of the Dall, however, they are dark brown.

Both of these varieties of sheep have habits and leave signs like those of the Rocky Mountain animal. They fight like them, leave similar tracks and droppings, make similar noises, and generally do not leave any evidence that marks them strongly apart. As a wilderness wanderer, you should pay careful attention to the ranges of the four types of sheep if you wish to interpret sheep signs toward identification of the kind of sheep trail you may be following.

THE ROCKY MOUNTAIN GOAT

One of the few animals on this continent that remains white all year, the Rocky Mountain goat is known in the United States as a dweller of the highest crags in the western mountains. This creature with the needlelike, back-curving horns, which are found

A sure sign that a goat has passed by: as they descend from the rocky heights during their summer shedding, they often leave bunches of white wool draped on bushes.

in both sexes, is also at home in parts of western Canada.

Goats—occasionally come down off their windswept, rocky pinnacles in early summer when they're shedding, and the sign of a shedding goat's passing is unmistakable. He leaves huge gobs of white wool draped all over the brush. When he's got rid of it all, he looks much thinner than he will in winter when he has his hairy pantaloons, beard, and great shaggy coat back again.

Tracks of the mountain goat in snow show foot drags behind the hoof prints, which are spread and somewhat squarish in appearance.

Because the goat lives in an environment that's largely perpendicular, his concave hoofs have a hard outside and a softer inside. He can hook the horny edge over the smallest of rocky protuberances, thus getting a foothold as he picks his way slowly and sedately along the face of a cliff that would make a bighorn sheep shudder with apprehension. Besides this, his toes open at the front, giving him double purchase. Because the cloven hoofs tend to spread when the animal is moving along, tracks appear squarish and are usually over 3 inches long in a mature billy. On the trail, prints usually show in groups of two when the animal is walking. In snow, foot drags are often apparent. When he bounds, the goat's tracks show all four prints closer together.

Goats sometimes seek refuge in caves, making snow beds outside. Look for traces of hair, tracks, and droppings.

In summer, goats feed on grasses, herbs, and flowers, and at this time their droppings are in 4- or 5-inch masses. In winter, when goats eat twigs and what dry grasses they can find, scats are in hard, separated pellets.

To see more signs of goats, look for mineral licks in the animals' range, dusty beds, and also for hollows in the dust where these 150- to 300-pound creatures have rolled and wallowed. Sometimes they make beds in snow, and occasionally they take refuge in caves. Tracks, droppings, and perhaps a few long, white hairs within should be the tip-off.

Mature male goats are usually solitary animals, but in November they get the mating urge. In late April, May, or June, young are born. Twins aren't rare, but one is the usual number of offspring. Mother and kid then join a group composed of other nannies and kids, young males, and young females to browse on the mountain slopes.

One last sign. If you're way up in the high country and see what you think is a patch of snow high above the timber line, get out your spotting scope. That patch of snow may be the goat you're looking for.

Droppings of the mountain goat are generally smaller than those of deer and sheep. Soft pellets like these indicate later summer feed.

THE BLACK BEAR

This animal is the smallest of our bears—200 pounds on the average though 500-pounders have been taken—and the one with the widest distribution, from Alaska throughout Canada and most of the United States.

Tracks of this bruin are strangely human in shape, and frequently the little toe doesn't show up, making the animal seem to be a four-toed creature, which it is not. Sometimes the claw marks don't show either.

Feet are put down in such a way that the longer (up to 7 inches) hind foot leaves its print several inches in front of the front foot, which may be 5 inches long and is usually rounder than the hind one. Tracks show up as a double row of prints, one side being those left by the right feet and the other being those put down by the left ones. When the animal is loping, all tracks are more close together.

Blacks leave many visual signs besides their tracks. One of the most common is the markings left on what most persons refer to as a bear tree. Bears rub themselves on trees, usually pines or firs, and as they rub this way and that, some of their hairs remain clinging to the bark. Frequently, while rubbing, a bear will reach up to claw and bite the tree. Often evidence of this will be at such a height that you'll realize the bear was standing on his hind feet when he did it. Watch for hairs, claw and bite marks, and oozing pitch for indications of a bear tree.

If you should see an aspen with scabs on its bark quite a way up the tree, suspect the black bear. This

Black bears often strip the bark near the bottom of pines, spruces, and firs to get at the syrupy juice beneath.

A torn-up berry patch signifies a recent bear visit. Bruins strip the branches, eating twigs, leaves, fruit and all.

facile climber often goes up aspens, and in so doing his claws gouge the soft bark. The tree grows scabs over these cuts that remain as long as the tree is standing.

Still another tree sign left by the black bruins is one that can result in the death of the tree. These bears strip bark off pines, spruces, and firs near the bottom, sometimes girdling them, to get at the syrupy juice just beneath it. Look for vertical tooth marks when you see this sort of tree damage.

Watch too for turned-over rocks and old logs torn apart. Bears like ants and many varieties of beetles, and they look for such tidbits beneath stones and in rotten or decaying wood. Ant hills are frequently torn apart and their makers eaten with relish. These animals also like roots, bulbous plants, seeds, pocket gophers, ground squirrels, and other small, ground-dwelling creatures; so keep an eye out for prominent diggings where such tasty morsels have been sought. Big holes, flung dirt, and claw marks should be an easy indication of the lumbering beast that did the excavating.

Black bears also climb trees for birds' eggs and nestlings. They are fond of honey too and never miss an opportunity to raid a bee's nest. In fact, blackie likes pretty much of everything that he doesn't have to work too hard to get.

Scats of this creature tend to be rather uniform in diameter and often appear as disjointed segments consisting most frequently of grasses, roots, wood shavings, pine nuts, and berry seeds when berries are ripe. If the animal has been dining on another animal (carrion, usually) scats will be mostly hair. Some berries, notably strawberries, will produce a semiliquid mass.

If you are in bear country and find your garbage can tipped over and the contents scattered over the countryside, look for a black bear somewhere in the vicinity.

A black bear leaves a trail of paired sets of tracks, the longer hind-foot print appearing in front of the forefoot.

Black bears like to ru
against trees, leaving trace
of their hair as well as cla
and bite marks. Pitch oozin
from a tree is a good sign t
look for.

A bear bed is a rather hastily constructed affair. When tired, the animal simply scoops out a depression and flops down in it. The long winter sleep, however, is another matter, at least for bears with a modicum of interest in their own comfort.

When cold weather comes along, they den up in caves, under ledges, in hollow stumps, beneath the root structures of blown-down trees, or in holes they have dug themselves. Often the den faces south. Lazy bears, and there are lazy bears as well as lazy people, simply wander into some thick brush and pass a dreary winter shivering with the cold.

The bear usually sleeps till April or May. While sleeping fitfully, the female gives birth to any number of cubs up to four. She awakens long enough to bite the umbilical cord and lick her children clean, but as they struggle up to the milk that awaits them on her underside, she goes back to sleep and slumbers for another couple of months.

Black bears don't make much noise, but now and then a mother bear will grunt or growl at her offspring, and they, in turn, will whimper if separated from her. An angry bear will roar and snarl with such volume that he can be heard half a mile away. A wounded or hurt bear will moan, wail, sob, and howl with all the anguish of a man in deep agony.

One sound you might listen for is the noise made by nuts as they rain through tree branches. Bears love acorns, chestnuts, and beechnuts, and they climb trees to shake the nuts to the ground where they later eat them.

Scats of the black bear are often in disjointed segments, about 2 inches long, usually containing traces of vegetable matter on which the animal largely feeds.

Grizzlies like to dig for marmots, tearing up large areas of earth and displacing rocks in search of burrowing prey.

THE GRIZZLY BEAR

This huge bear with the dished-in face has been practically run out of the United States, being now only found in small numbers in the high, wild areas of Wyoming, Idaho, Montana, Colorado, and in Yellowstone Park as well as Glacier National Park. Farther north, in Alaska, British Columbia, and the Yukon Territory, he is far more abundant.

If you should be wandering around anywhere in the grizzly's range, and stumble over the half-eaten carcass of a deer, moose, or elk that has been loosely covered with leaves, twigs, or other forest litter, get away as fast as your legs can carry you. You are already a shoo-in favorite to get chewed up, because you've probably stumbled on the jealously guarded food cache of a grizzly bear. It is possible you've come across a mountain lion's larder, but don't bet on it. Get out. Likewise, if you smell decaying flesh, move away fast unless you've put the stuff there in the first place as bait for a trophy bear.

The grizzly is a very large animal, averaging from 500 to 750 pounds, though they have been recorded at 1,000 or more. This bear has a big hump on his shoulder, and his color varies tremendously from yellowish brown to dark brown with light hairs along the back. This latter coloration gives the grizzly another name by which he is frequently known—silvertip.

His habits are very similar to those of the black bear, with, however, several important differences. For one thing, he eats more meat, though he is basically a vegetarian feeding on berries, grasses, buds, tubers, and roots. Like the black bear too, he is very fond of burrowing animals, and an area worked over by a grizzly digging for marmots is an area full of excavations big enough to bury a sofa. He is passionately fond of carrion, and when he is after fresh meat he can kill an elk, deer, or moose with one blow of his massive paw.

After he has killed it—usually an old or sick one—he'll feed on it and then cart the remains off somewhere and cover them, as mentioned earlier, returning to dine on them until the carcass is completely consumed.

All bears leave similar tracks, but the grizzly's is larger than the black's, the hind foot often measuring 10 inches.

A large hole in the ground near timberline may be a grizzly's den, which he digs in August in preparation for the winter.

Unlike the black, the grizzly does not climb trees, but he leaves claw marks and telltale hairs on their trunks.

Grizzly tracks are similar to those of black bears. Prints of the grizzly bear, however, are generally larger. Hind prints may be 10 inches long by almost 6 inches wide. Front ones are apt to go 5½ by 5½. Old, established trails are sometimes made up of zigzag pits on either side of the center line where the bears have been stepping into each other's prints for years. This trait is not as marked in the black and grizzly, however, as it is in the brown. Often an old grizzly trail is merely a deep set of parallel ruts.

When near salmon rivers of the West Coast, keep an eye out for the remains of eaten fish. The big bears come down to the rivers during the spawning runs and scoop the big fish out onto the beach where they devour them. Sometimes they grab them from the water with their powerful jaws. Nearby tracks should positively identify the anglers.

A grizzly usually dens near timberline, in a rocky cave, beneath the roots of a big tree, or in a self-excavated hole. He starts looking for a likely spot in August, and when the weather turns nippy he enters it, curls up, and sleeps until April. The sow gives birth in her den just as does the female black.

Occasionally the bear comes out of his den before the snow has gone, and this gives rise to something that has been reliably reported that might be considered a definite sign. Look for snow slides. Most bears have their playful moments, and on at least one occasion a grizzly was seen repeatedly sliding down a snow-covered hill on his broad rump. He appeared to be enjoying himself vastly.

Scats of the grizzly are similar to those of the black, but they are generally larger. During berry time, they might be semiliquid.

The grizzly makes noises that vary from grunts, snorts, growls, and coughs to full-fledged roars. Like the black, he carries on horribly when hurt.

Brownies often tread in tracks left by predecessors, and their trail may appear as a well-worn path in the wilds.

THE BROWN BEAR

This truly tremendous animal is the largest terrestrial carnivorous mammal in the world. A full-grown bear may weigh 1,500 to 1,600 pounds and have a reach when standing of 12 feet. Basically his habits and diet are very similar to those of the grizzly, to whom he is closely related. In fact, where their ranges overlap, it is sometimes difficult to tell whether a given specimen is a brown or a grizzly.

The true brown, however, has a small range—the

outhwest coast of Alaska, including many of the slands and the heights of the coastal mountains. Some f these giant bears inhabit northwest British Colum- ia, but the largest animals are generally found in the Aleutians or on Kodiak Island.

The brownie's track is just like that of the grizzly, but it is much larger. The hind foot may measure 6 inches long. One interesting thing about an estab- ished trail of this animal is that it frequently appears as a series of zigzag pits sometimes as much as 10 nches deep. These are formed on a well-used trail because each bear steps into the same prints made by his predecessors. Another interesting thing about rails such as this is that they often follow a perfectly traight line and, where they go up a mountainside, are visible from a great distance. If a trail like this, particularly one in mossy tundra, has been abandoned or some years, it will grow up in clumps of grass, because seeds collect in the pits. This won't tell you where bears are, but it certainly will tell you where they've been.

You will find well-worn bear trails along salmon streams, because this variety of bear greatly enjoys fish and comes to the rivers during the June spawning

Brown bear leaves largest track. Hind foot, which he places in front of forefoot like other bears, may measure 16 inches.

Fisherman of the bear family, brownie visits salmon streams during spawning time, litters the bank with unfinished meals.

runs. Look for uneaten fish as well as the streamside tracks. The animals customarily litter the banks with far more salmon than they can eat. Also along the streams, look for resting places scooped out among the alder thickets and willows. Sometimes you'll even find a mattress—a pile of moss 10 or 12 feet across that the bear has assembled to make his nap more comfortable.

The brown's diet is similar to that of the grizzly but he frequently eats a lot of shoreside sedge. In spring he feeds almost completely on grasses, later digging up roots and feeding on berries. Regarding the latter, watch for berry patches that have been heavily torn up. Bears eat berries by stripping the bushes and eating leaves and twigs along with the fruit. Ground-burrowing animals are also game for the brownie, and any dead animal is much relished. He even eats dead whales that have washed up on shore.

Scats of the brownie are similar to, but larger than

loose of the black. It is well to remember too that a
fresh diet, as well as one of berries, will make
them loose.

Young brown bears can climb trees, but when they
grow older they give up such nonsense. They do,
however, rub themselves on trees, tear out bark with
their teeth, and reach up to claw them as do
other bears.

A brown usually goes to bed in late September in
a den chosen much as the grizzly chooses his, and he
doesn't reappear until about mid-April.

Females mate only once every two or three years,
and it is only during the breeding season of a month
or six weeks in May and June that the sexes show
any affection for one another. Young are born in
the den and stay with the mother no more than
two years.

Padding across the snow-covered ice of his Arctic habitat, the polar bear leaves a massive trail—his only sign.

THE POLAR BEAR

This animal is the bear of the Arctic wastes and pack ice. He may run as large as the brown, but generally he doesn't. He ranges throughout the Arctic from northern Alaska, over the Arctic Ocean pack ice, and into Hudson Bay and the coastal areas of northern Labrador.

The polar bear has a long, slender neck and is generally a more graceful animal than is the brown bear. The only part of him that's not creamy white is the tip of his nose. Five-toed paw prints are not easily distinguishable because the pads are covered with fur.

The ice bear is a terrific swimmer and a fantastic traveler. Sometimes he comes ashore where there's vegetation, but this is rare. Usually he gets his groceries from the ice and sea, feeding on seals, walruses, fish, porpoises, ducks, and marine vegetation. When these animals come ashore to catch spawning fish in the cold, northern streams, they will eat a lot of grass and land vegetation. The bears gather from great distances to feed on dead whales, and that's about the only time they tolerate one another's company except during the brief courting season in June or early July.

Chances are, unless you frequent zoos, that you'll not see a polar bear or even see a sign of one unless you are hunting him. If you are, watch for the massive trail in the snow-covered ice that could only have been made by a tremendous animal. He is the only tremendous animal in his range, and he travels alone.

Unlike other bears, the polar does not hibernate—with one notable exception. The female—who has young at two-year intervals—hibernates in piled-up masses of ice or in hard-packed snow, but only when she's expecting cubs.

Polar bear's tracks are difficult to distinguish because foot-pads are covered with fur, but a well-formed impression would look like this.

THE GRAY WOLF

In most of this country (Alaska excepted), you will look in vain for signs of this handsome animal. He's been harassed to the point where his numbers are limited to parts of Wisconsin, Michigan, and Minnesota. In sections of Texas, Oklahoma, the Mississippi Valley, and Florida, a smaller species of the wolf is known as the red wolf. In Canada and Alaska, the gray wolf—also called the timber wolf—comes into his own and may reach a length of 7 feet and a weight of 175 pounds.

Tracks of the four paws usually show fairly close together but are spread out in a staggered line when the animal is loping, are more closely bunched in a bounding gallop. They're very similar to dog tracks, though much bigger. The front tracks are larger than those of the hind feet, measuring 4 to 5 inches in length. Toes of the hind feet do not spread as much

Wolf tracks resemble dog tracks but are much larger, sometimes measuring 5 inches in length. These were made in dry mud.

Trail of wolf tracks approaching a caribou carcass reveals the animal's wary nature. He advances from one point of cover to the next until he reaches his quarry.

as those of the front ones. If you're doing your observing in the north country, you might easily confuse the tracks of a wolf with those of a husky. It's also good to remember that usually dogs do not have the same suspicious nature that a wolf has. When approaching an object, a dog will usually come up to it directly, but a wolf will advance in a devious path that takes advantage of every bit of cover. Watch for his pattern when trying to determine whether the tracks you are following are those of a dog or of a wolf.

In northern wolf country, watch for caribou. Where there are caribou, there will almost certainly be wolves

A wolf den in the bank of soft soil often extends 25 feet, ending in a roomy chamber.

not far behind. These predators, whose color vary drastically from light to dark, follow the herds on their migrations. Don't look for much in the remains of prey, however, which is a sort of negative sign in itself. These powerful creatures have jaws of almost unbelievable strength. If they pull down an animal of any size, they'll crunch up and swallow the biggest bones, leaving only blood, a few hairs, and horns or antlers. Big animals, however, aren't the staple of wolves. Their main diet is gophers, rabbits, and squirrels. Of the bigger animals, usually the young and aged are pulled down.

Keep an eye out for dens. They are usually dug in a bank of soft soil, and they may extend 25 or more feet to end in a roomy chamber. The male does not use the den but keeps watch on its entrance when he is not out collecting food for his burgeoning family, additions to which are forthcoming any time from April through June. Six is the average litter, but there may be twice that number. Wolves also den in caverns, hollow trees, or enlarge an abandoned den of a coyote, badger, or other burrowing animal.

You may be in wolf country and never see one of the creatures. They're secretive and smart, but they're not above broadcasting signs of their presence vocally as well as visually. They have a sound that once heard can never be forgotten. It has all the loneliness of the wilderness in it and all the longing of a hopeless dream. This howl has none of the short, yapping bark. It is long and deep, and you'll usually hear it when you're back in camp snugged down for the night. Mating call of the male is throaty, and when he is chasing game he will utter a guttural note, the direction of which is often hard to determine. A high, plaintive cry is often used near the den.

Wolves also den in rock caves on hillsides which provide a wide view of the landscape—and approaching foes.

THE FOX

The most widely distributed fox in North America is the red fox, a graceful animal that has learned to adapt himself readily to the trappings of civilization and the conversion of the wild countryside to farm-land. Areas of the deep Southeast, the Gulf Coast, and parts of the Southwest are the only ones in this country that he avoids.

Signs of the red fox aren't hard to discern. His tracks, almost in a straight line, are rather delicate, showing four claws and the imprint of pads. In winter, however, there's so much fur on the animal's feet that the individual pads may not show up in the snow. Prints of the rear feet are often superimposed on those of the forefeet.

The red fox sleeps out during the winter, but along about January or February mating takes place, and

A hollow log may be a fox den. Telltale signs are hairs at the entrance or animal leftovers—tufts of rabbit fur or feathers.

the female, called the vixen, digs or prepares a den. This might be one she has dug herself in the loose ground or it may be the enlarged hole of one of the burrowing animals such as the woodchuck. In any event, such fox homes are not easy to discover because the animals make sure there is no earth outside of them to indicate their presence.

If you find a hole 10 to 20 inches across, you may be looking at a fox den. Hairs around its entrance may be a giveaway, as may be nearby odds and ends of animal leftovers such as tufts of rabbit fur or inedible feathers. If a mild, skunklike odor is present also, you can be sure you've spotted a fox den.

The dog fox roams fairly far afield after the pups are born, but the vixen stays quite close to her den area, sometimes all her life. The dog fox barks in a short yelp, but the female is more shrill and yaps. During mating season, that yap is apt to be more of a scream.

While the red fox lives over much of the United States and Canada, the gray fox is native to the eastern section of the country and parts of the West and Southwest. This little creature prefers to roam at night more than the red fox, and he likes the brushy areas of the wooded lowlands and swamps more than does his more gregarious, red-haired cousin. He also climbs trees.

In the plains and dry areas of the West and Midwest lives the swift, or kit, fox. He is quite small and, like another desert fox—the long-eared fox—is rarely seen, spending much of his time below ground.

Patches of earth showing through the snow in coyote country are often places where the animal dug for a warm bed.

THE COYOTE

At dusk or daylight in the desert areas of the West and Southwest, one may hear from his bedroll a sudden, eerie, high-pitched noise that sounds like a cry of anguish from some soul lost in hell. *Yip, yip, yip, yowroooooooooo!* This long-drawn-out wail, often taken up by another animal, is the aria of the coyote. It is one of the most thrilling of wilderness sounds.

Tracks of the coyote—he weighs from 20 to 50 pounds—follow the canine pattern laid down by wolves and dogs, and, like them, the coyote has front feet larger than those in the back. The animal tends to pick out a prominent spot for his droppings, a spot that is sure to be investigated by other passersby of the same general family. This may be a trail crossing, rock, stump, or any place not easily missed by, say, a fox or another coyote.

Young are born in a hollow log, in the rocks, a cave, or in a burrow. This latter is dug in loose soil or is the remodeled home of a skunk, badger, or fox. A tip-off to coyote occupancy is that the earth pushed out of the entrance in digging or enlarging is pushed back to the entrance and shaped around it into a fairly low heap, usually somewhat fan shaped. Another tip-off is that the 5- to 30-foot burrow is apt to have a ventilation hole in the roof of the chamber at its end. If you are near a coyote den, you might hear the grown-ups inside barking.

Mating takes place in January or February, and about sixty days later the young are born in litters that range from three pups to well over a dozen. At this time the male does the hunting, dropping food

Coyote den is characterized by semicircle of dirt around entrance, formed by animal after digging hole.

Coyote tracks follow canine pattern of wolf's. Heel pads of fore and hind feet are slightly different in shape.

at the entrance to the den for his mate and progeny.

Coyotes eat just about everything, but their favorite foods are rabbits and rodents, with generous helpings of carrion. They're very partial to watermelons.

In spite of being shot, poisoned, and trapped for their occasional misdemeanors among domestic stock, coyotes are surviving and extending their range east and north. They are now found in some Canadian provinces, a few of the western states, and Alaska.

THE COUGAR

Not too long ago, while hunting deer on the Jicarilla Apache Indian Reservation in New Mexico, two of us heard the most horrible cry of anguish imaginable not over a quarter of a mile away. It was a highpitched *Ya-a-a-a-a! Ya-a-a-a-a-a!* dying in intensity and into silence, quite like a man screaming in the agony of death. Later we talked to the hunter who had shot the animal responsible for this death cry and found that it had been a large cougar, a beast long believed never to scream. It does scream, however, and the sound has been likened to a roaring, a yowling, or the scream of a woman in mortal terror. This cry is not often heard, though, as these big cats—a huge one would go 200 pounds—are almost entirely nocturnal and usually very quiet. They have to be, at least when hunting, as they are beasts of prey whose victims, principally deer, would be spooked by caterwauling and yowling. As cats, however, they do vocalize to some extent, making the same sort of sounds house cats do, only louder and deeper.

There are several visual signs of cougars, or mountain lions. Tracks are quite distinctive. Claws seldom show, and the widths of the prints vary from about 3 to over 4 inches. Front-foot tracks are larger

Cougar tracks are easily identified by their catlike appearance. Even in soft mud, as here, claws do not register.

Deer carcass buried under sticks and foliage is sure sign
that cougar has been in the area and will return to finish
his meal.

than those of the rear feet, and the toes tend to spread
when the animal puts on speed. In winter, tracks are
apt to show foot drags in the snow, and there might
be evidence of where the tail has brushed the white
fluff on either side of the tracks.

During his nightly travels the cougar leaves another sign—scratchings. In common with other cats,
mountain lions cover their droppings with earth, and

Scratchings are another sign to watch for in cougar
country.

these sign heaps, coupled with tracks, clearly show the trail a cougar has taken.

When one of these tree-climbing animals has killed a deer and eaten all he wants of it, he drags it to a spot of his own choosing and covers it with anything handy, such as sticks, leaves, branches, or other forest litter where it remains until he has finished eating it. If you should find a partially eaten carcass so buried, you can be sure a cougar is in the vicinity. But don't be frightened. These huge cats are timid and far more afraid of humans than humans are of them.

In this country these handsome, tawny animals range principally in the West, north to south, and in parts of Texas, Louisiana, and Florida. A full-grown male will stretch up to 8 feet, including its black-tipped tail. It kills by leaping on its victim's back and biting into the neck. The cougar occasionally kills farm stock, but deer are by far the preferred diet.

Favored lair of the cougar, a cave offers shelter from the cold and a place for the mother to give birth in the spring.

THE BOBCAT

Living all over the conterminous United States, with the exception of sections of the mid-South and parts of the corn-belt region, the bobcat resembles an overgrown alley cat with a short tail and tufted ears. He is called variously the wild cat, bay lynx, and other local names. He is light with black spots and averages 20 to 25 pounds, though a really big one will go 10 pounds more. He leaves definite signs, and since he is thriving in a world of encroaching civilization, these signs are of more than passing interest.

His tracks are rather rounded, more so than those of dogs and coyotes, and there is hair between the toes in winter. His larger northern neighbor, the lynx, also has this hair between the toes when cold weather sets in. The bobcat shows no claw marks on the ground, and when the animal is really moving, the front toes tend to spread more than those of the hind feet. Prints are about 8 to 14 inches apart, unless the animal is bounding.

Bobcats often hunt by stretching out on a branch over a game trail, where they wait to pounce on some luckless animal passing below. When they do this, they approach the tree from the side away from the trail.

The bobcat's tracks are slightly smaller than the cougar's. Absence of claw marks distinguishes them from coyote's.

Bits of bark at the base of a tree, as well as claw marks on trunk, are signs of bobcat's claw-sharpening habit.

In summer, these cats, as do all of their tribe, bury their droppings by scratching dirt over them. In the case of the bobcat, however, this is apt to be a haphazard operation, so knowledge of the scats is of value. In very dry areas of the country, these droppings are likely to be marked by constricted segments, and sometimes they appear as pellets. Where the climate is more damp, the scats can be confused with the waste of dogs or coyotes. If you see claw marks around droppings, however, and signs of attempts to bury them with earth are present, chances are better than good that a bobcat has been your predecessor on the trail.

Another sign of these animals can occasionally be seen at the bases of trees. Since bobcats sharpen their claws on trees and stumps, bits of bark are scraped off and drop to the ground. The claw marks themselves, of course, are another sign.

The bobcat is a noisy fellow during mating season, usually January or February. His howling and screeching at that time can be fearsome. At other times his noises are similar to those of the house cat, but with more volume.

This deceptively gentle looking cat is a rarely seen nocturnal wanderer who dens in the rocks, occasionally in a hollow tree, and once in a while in an abandoned fox's den. His basic diet consists of small animals such as rabbits and rodents, but now and then he'll pull down a deer, usually a fawn or sick adult. Sometimes he'll turn his attention to livestock and domestic fowl. But he is a sign of the wilds, and that he is increasing in numbers, in spite of the enthusiasm with which he is hunted, is an indication of his adaptability and courage.

THE BEAVER

Pile of chips and a partially cut tree tell the passerby that a beaver has been hard at work building a lodge or a dam.

A thrilling night sound for the autumn camper near water—especially after ice begins to form—is the *slap-plunk* of a beaver at work. A noisier form of beaver communication can be heard when the animal is alerted—a sound like someone slapping water hard with the flat of a paddle. This warning tells all the beavers in the colony to dive for safety. To make this noise, the animal brings his flat, scaly tail over his back and slaps it quickly down on the water. The resultant *crack* can be heard for incredible distances.

The most common visual sign of the beaver is his dam. Of logs, branches, stones, and mud, it keeps the water behind it at a constant level. Here, in the center of the pond backed up by the 3- to 4-foot-high structure, the one-chamber lodges are built. These lodges, which are 6 to 8 feet across, have subterranean entrances and house an entire family. Occasionally, these stick houses will be erected on the banks of lakes and streams.

An expert engineer, the beaver builds an efficient dam across a stream to protect his intricately constructed lodge behind it.

To build his strong dams and lodges, and to get the branches on which he most often feeds, the beaver cuts down many trees. He can fell a tree 2 feet thick with his chisel-shaped teeth. The woodland wanderer who comes across stumps and chips bordering a stream or pond should recognize them as evidence of beavers.

Still another sign might be a canal. When trees are far from the water's edge, the animals dig canals from the woods area to the water. They are up to 3 feet wide and 18 inches deep. The beavers cut their wood to the lengths required—usually 2 to 6 feet—and float it down the canals to their building sites.

Any spot where beavers are working is crisscrossed with their tracks. The front feet are handlike, have long claws, and are not used when swimming. The

When in danger, the beaver warns his colony by slapping the water with his tail. The noise can be heard far away.

large hind feet are webbed and used as paddles. When the animals are cutting wood, they often stand on their hind feet and use their heavy tails as supports.

Beavers are dark and squat, weighing up to 60 pounds or more. They have valves in their nostrils and ears that close automatically when they submerge. Young are born in late April, May, or early June in litters of six. Favored food is the bark of aspen, willow, birch, poplar, and alder, slender branches of which they store under water for winter eating. When ice forms on the ponds, the animals travel from the dry chambers of their houses, via the subsurface entrances, to their food caches. Selecting a succulent branch, the hungry beaver brings it back and eats its bark by holding it in his front feet and chewing on it as a man eats corn on the cob.

Canals leading to river are sign of beaver's ingenuity. When trees are scarce on river, he cuts trees inland and floats logs down.

THE BADGER

This rather flattened animal with the white stripe running from its nose back over its head is the prime excavator of the western states. He favors the plains country from Mexico into southwest Canada, but he can occasionally be found in the woodlands where there's no heavy brush to impede his rapid digging. He also inhabits parts of the Great Lakes country.

The principal signs of this energetic creature are often encountered by horsemen. A badger digs good-sized holes, and a rider whose cantering mount steps

Foot-wide holes in the ground, with piles of dirt around the edge, are signs of a badger's hunting trips into marmot dens.

Badger tracks are characterized by a toed-in pattern. Front and hind feet appear close together.

into one is apt to have a bad fall. The horse is liable to break its leg.

Beginning to hunt late in the afternoon and continuing through the night, the badger seeks out prairie-dog villages, and pocket-gopher or ground-squirrel dens. Boring like an auger through the burrows of these little fellows in quest of his dinner, he throws huge quantities of dirt outside of the burrows and leaves an elliptical hole almost a foot in diameter behind him. Where the hunting is good, the badger will leave quite a few enlarged holes as testimony to his digging ability and his appetite.

The badger uses for his home one of the burrows he has enlarged, or else he digs one of his own up to 30 feet long with a chamber 2 to 6 feet below the ground at the end of it. He digs with unbelievable speed, and in the large pile of excavated earth outside of the hole his tracks are generally visible. They're usually over 2 inches long, toed in, and the imprint of the long claws on the front feet is apt to be in evidence. When the animal is running, his hind feet, which have shorter claws that rarely show on the ground, are put down in front of the forefeet. In certain areas, you may observe marks left on trees where badgers have honed their front claws.

The badger makes little noise, at least little noise that would carry far enough to be considered a sign. He is a wheezy fellow, and if he is in a fight he hisses, growls, and emits a musk somewhat like that of a skunk but not as strong.

Besides dining on burrowing rodents, the badger eats insects in tremendous quantities, lizards, snakes, and ground-nesting birds. He loves honey and digs up many a nest of bees to get it. He likes rabbits too, and if he kills more than he needs to eat at any given time, he buries whatever is left for the future.

In the northern part of his range, the badger hibernates, often going below the frost line and plugging up his tunnel with earth to protect himself from the cold. Young, numbering anywhere from one to five, are born in spring.

Series of cuts in bark of a tree might be a badger sign in certain areas. He hones his claws needle-sharp this way.

Clam shells strewn along water's edge may be evidence of recent raccoon feast. Animal opens them with claws and eats contents.

THE RACCOON

This 15- to 20-pound animal with the masked face and ringed tail is native, in one form or another, to every state from the Atlantic Ocean to the Pacific and from the southern United States to the southern part of Canada.

His tracks, rather handlike in appearance with the five toes showing on each foot, are generally paired, left hind foot coming down beside the right front one. Hind feet are larger than the forefeet.

The raccoon likes woods, swamps, and partly cleared land, though he is fond of wet places like the edges of tidal creeks, swamps, marshes, and bottom lands. Coons favor hollow trees to live in, however, and you can often spot a coon's home by looking carefully for any tree, such as an old oak, elm, or sycamore that has a downward-sloping hole in it some 6 inches in diameter. These cavities are frequently caused by the butt of a broken-off limb having rotted out. Once you've found a likely looking hole, look for two other signs for positive identification of its occupant. Around the edges of the opening you should see some grayish-black or brown hairs, and if the hole is one used by a coon there will also be scratches that the animal has made in the bark with the claws of his powerful feet. Lacking a hole in a tree, a coon will sometimes live in a hollow log or a cleft in the rocks.

When wandering along by any water, keep an eye out for discarded clam shells and the remains of crawfish. Coons love the latter. The former they open dextrously, eating the insides with relish. If you should happen to see a duck's nest that has been torn apart, and bits of eggshell around, look for coon tracks.

Besides eggs, crawfish, and clams, coons like all sorts of fruits and berries as well as nuts, insects, and the various grains. They'll raid cornfields too, ripping

Raccoon droppings, like those of skunks and opossums, are granular. However, they are usually found on logs and limbs.

Rotted hole in a tree could be a raccoon den; to be sure, check entrance for traces of grayish-black or brown hairs, and claw marks.

off and partly eating the ears, which they leave strewn all over the place.

Scats of this animal aren't easy to identify, though they tend to be even in circumference, granular, and may contain berry seeds. A better tip-off on the droppings, which may be confused with those of skunks and possums, is that often they're deposited on logs or the bigger branches of trees.

Coons don't knock themselves out vocally, but they do make gutteral chatterings. If you're in the woods at night and think you hear a screech owl, listen carefully. If the sound comes from ground level, it's probably the *hoo-hoo-hooing* of a coon setting out on his nocturnal search for sustenance.

THE MUSKRAT

A dome-shaped lodge bulking about 3 feet above
the surface of a shallow pond or marsh is one sign
that this ratlike aquatic animal is in the area. Built
of sticks, the roots and stalks of water plants, and
chinked with mud, these houses have several underwater exits and contain a dry chamber inside. Near
these houses will be found several feeding shelters—
smaller, rounder, and more uniform in shape.

Another interesting visual sign of the muskrat,
whose range extends over most of United States, is
the breather, or push-up. This is found in more
northerly areas and is a hole in the ice packed with
roots and vegetation. The animal digs out a hollow

Shallow ponds or marshes often contain muskrat lodges,
domes of mud and sticks with several underwater exits.

Breather hole in ice is unique muskrat sign.

in this packing and uses it as a breather or as a temporary shelter. The mass formed on the ice above the hole is about the size of a volley ball.

Muskrats living along the edges of watercourses dig burrows in the bank, but they're hard to spot unless you're looking for them. Occasionally, however, you might see a small pile of vegetation well back from the bank. This is the loose wadding that hides the surface entrance to the bank burrow.

Other visual signs of the muskrat are particles of chewed plants and stems floating on the water and possibly air bubbles under the ice. Tracks, of course, are a good identification, and the muskrat has a refinement to his that make evidence of his passage unmistakable. Hind feet, much larger than the front ones, are partially webbed, and the tracks are small

Muskrat burrows along rivers often have entrances away from the bank camouflaged with small pile of vegetation.

and handlike. But more important, he drags his long, vertically flattened, scaly tail and leaves a continuous imprint with it half an inch wide.

The muskrat gets his name from a musky odor that is particularly strong in males at mating time—and three or more litters are born each year! Mature animals are 10 to 14 inches long with a tail that reaches almost a foot in length. They feed on aquatic plants mostly but occasionally grab off crawfish, crabs, mussels, and small fish not fast enough to get away.

Muskrat's hind-foot tracks show partial webbing, and long, flat tail leaves drag mark half an inch wide.

THE PORCUPINE

This grunting, slow, and rather purposeful creature with the barbed quills lives over most of northern North America where there are woodlands that will support him. He makes his home in rocky crevices, hollow logs, or brush piles.

Bark chewed in large patches high on tree trunk, with edges neatly trimmed, is usually porcupine's work.

Porcupine's tracks are spaced about 6 inches apart, and toes point in. On soft ground or snow tail drag shows

Tracks of the porcupine show short steps with the toes pointed in, and the prints themselves look like miniature bearpaw snowshoes with long claw marks quite far ahead of the main pads. If there is deep snow, or if the porky is walking on something soft there will be marks on the trail as if someone had been following the tracks and wielding a broom lightly. These marks, of course, come from the stiff awkward tail as it swings back and forth with the animal's slow, plodding gait.

The generally bean-shaped droppings of the quill pig can be confused with those of deer, though often they are connected and sometimes somewhat irregular in shape.

Perhaps the most obvious sign of the porcupine's presence is the readily seen evidence of chewing on the bark of such trees as beech, maple, birch, pine, fir, and spruce. The porky eats only the inner bark, chipping off the outer layer with his beaverlike teeth and letting it drop to the ground. He generally chews bark in large patches, which are readily recognizable because they are too high for a nonclimbing animal

o have made and because they show carefully trimmed
dges with neat tooth prints. Frequently a porcupine
will girdle a tree, thus killing it.

Signs the porkies leave on the ground are the
cast-off bits of outer bark, droppings, and the cone-
bearing twigs the creatures cut off and let fall.

Though porcupines gnaw trees, this is principally a
winter activity. In spring this destructive animal eats
catkins and flowers, and in summer he turns his attention to leaves and plants.

Another sign that porky has been around can be
seen if you wake up some morning in camp and find
that your ax handle or canoe paddle has been ap-
preciably reduced in size. The animals love salt, and
they will spend a lot of time working on any piece of
wood that has been subjected to sweat.

Porcupines seem like quiet, dignified animals, but
they can make a variety of noises. They bark, snort,
and moan in a manner that occasionally sounds quite
human. During mating season the male goes falsetto,
and the female indulges in squalls.

Incidentally, porcupines cannot shoot their quills.
However, an angry porky swings his tail with great
vehemence, and any loose quills will sail through the
air with high velocity.

A porcupine will not attack, but he is of danger to
livestock and dogs, none of which seem able to resist
taking a close look at him. A slap with that vicious
tail will drive dozens of quills into the face of the
curious.

THE WOODCHUCK

This brown, lumbering chap of the summer field who hibernates in the winter is well known to farmer country boys, and varmint shooters throughout the eastern half of the United States, extreme souther portion excepted.

One of the first signs of the woodchuck that mo people see is the hole leading to his den. This orific in the ground, 8 inches or so in diameter, may be i the woods or on a hillside, but the animal who dig it prefers a spot on the brushy border of a clover-fille field. Outside of his hole is usually a huge pile c excavated earth. Actually, the chuck digs several bu rows, some distance apart. Aside from this, eac

Most obvious sign of a woodchuck is his den, a hole in field or on a hillside and rimmed with excavated dirt.

Tracks of the chuck are placed close together. Hind foot has five toes, forefoot only four.

burrow has more than one opening. If you see a fairly sizeable hole with no earth around it, look for one nearby with the telltale earth mound. The holes without the earth are plunge holes and are dug from underneath.

A woodchuck's tracks show four toes on each forefoot and five on each of the hind ones. When walking, the chuck, or groundhog, puts his hind feet down close to the front ones.

One other visual sign of the chuck may be bits of the chuck himself. Like most of the rabbit clan, the woodchuck gets pretty violent in his courtship period, which occurs right after he comes out of hibernation in early spring. Males contend bitterly for the favors of females, and in the ensuing fights the combatants often rip hunks out of one another, and on occasion tails are bitten off to lie on the ground as mute testimony to the violence.

The woodchuck is also known as the whistlepig, and the reason isn't hard to figure. He whistles. Another audible sign of the animal is a chattering and gritting of teeth when he is disturbed.

In the West, a crevice rock formation may turn to be den of rockch cousin of the woodchuc

The woodchuck's favorite diet is clover, though he also eats the stems of buttercups, daisies, and thistles as well as leaves and flowers. He relishes farm produce and often attacks melon patches with gusto.

Most people don't realize it, but chucks once in a while climb trees.

Cousins of the eastern woodchuck are the rockchucks of the West and the hoary marmots of the western mountains and the mountains of Alaska and western Canada. Tracks of all three are quite similar, though in the hoary marmot prints of the hind feet have a tendency to register in the prints of the front ones.

The marmot is about twice as big as the woodchuck, an animal reaching a maximum of only about 14 pounds, and he also gives out with a whistle, one that can be heard for incredible distances on a still day. He also is a hibernating and burrowing creature, and he digs shallow holes along his various pathways that serve as emergency shelters when danger threatens. Another visual sign of the hoary marmot is his slide. Before the snow has melted in spring, he likes to toboggan down steep banks and hillsides.

The rockchuck is similar to the woodchuck in habits, though his favored denning areas are rocky caves and crevices.

THE GREY SQUIRREL

This handsome little creature, who has a western cousin known as the western gray squirrel, is found throughout the eastern states from Florida to Ontario and west to Texas and the Dakotas. Rare is the person living in this area who has never seen one.

Tracks show long hind feet, with five toes, placed side by side in front of four-toed front feet when the animal is bounding. When walking, however, hind feet and front feet alternate.

Another visual sign of this prolific little rodent is his home. The gray squirrel likes oaks, hickories, and beeches, and his dens and leafy nests are usually found in stands of these hardwoods, though sometimes such stands are mixed in with pine trees. A den can be an abandoned woodpecker's hole or other suitable tree cavity. It is in this den that the female brings forth an average litter of four or five young, usually during

Squirrel tracks are slightly over an inch long; hind feet register in front of forefeet when animal is bounding.

early spring in the North and a month or so earlier in the South.

The gray also makes two types of leaf nest, and they're readily seen in the woods when the leaves are off the trees. They sit on branches anywhere from 30 to 60 feet above ground. One type, constructed of bark, leaves, small branches, and built near the trunk of the tree, contains a chamber of about 16 inches across by about a foot high. This is used for warm weather living, in emergencies, when parasites become too thick in the den, or, occasionally, to raise a summer brood.

The other type of leaf nest is usually farther out on a branch and has a side entrance. It is used for resting or loafing, usually by the male.

In his eating habits, the squirrel is somewhat of a slob, and he leaves many signs of his bad table manners throughout the woods. Diet fluctuates with the produce of the season, and clusters of tree buds and flowers, such as those of oaks, elms, and maples, are nipped off and eaten. At that time of year the denuded clusters form cuttings beneath these types of trees that may pile up several inches deep. Look for these signs where squirrels abound.

In summer, diet may include mushrooms, fruits and berries, tree seeds, and insect cocoons. Come late summer, early fall, and winter, the squirrel's intake switches to the type of food for which he is most noted —nuts. These may be butternuts, acorns, walnuts, hickory nuts, pecans. Look for their hulls at the bases of trees for an indication of what sort of animal has been dining above.

All squirrels bury nuts, but the gray, unlike the red, buries each nut separately in a fist-size hole. Evidence of the squirrel digging these holes in the forest floor

Telltale signs of the squirrel's dining habits are nibbled pine cones and acorns at the base of a tree.

is often easily seen. Also easily seen is the stirred-up appearance of the dead leaves in fall and winter when the animals are scurrying around digging their holes or scratching around trying to find the food they've already buried. Since these animals don't dig up all the nuts they've hidden, they can be considered responsible for much of the forest's new growth.

Another sign of the squirrel's thoughtlessness in eating is found in the mess he occasionally makes of young conifers. Grays, as well as fox squirrels and red squirrels, look for the sap and layer of cambium beneath the bark and chew lustily on limbs and trunks, often girdling young trees. Evidence of this can occasionally be seen at the root line. Porcupines munch bark too, but porcupine teeth are larger than those of squirrels. If you see a tree with eaten bark, check for the size of the dentures that have done the work. Droppings too should be a tip-off. Those of porcupines, while somewhat deerlike, are usually a bit larger than the rather similarly shaped scats of squirrels.

Squirrels have several signs that can be easily heard, and even the inexperienced outdoorsman can soon learn to identify them quickly. If you're wandering through the fall hardwoods and hear something like a small, intermittent rain pattering through the trees, you can be assured that one of these little rodents is nearby eating nuts and that the shells are filtering down through the branches.

Another sound, usually associated with fall, is the rustling of the dead leaves on the forest floor, made as the squirrels scoot here and there burying nuts.

The voice of the gray is deeper than that of the red squirrel and is commonly a loud, fast, chatter. The gray squirrel barks too, with a rather impatient sound at times and at times with a rather soft, questioning quality. Quiet chatterings take place when the animals are conversing with one another. When predators, such as owls and hawks, are around, the squirrels cry in terror as they streak for cover.

The western gray squirrel is much like his eastern counterpart, but he lives in the mountain ranges of the West Coast, mostly in the higher altitudes up to 8,000 feet. He sometimes journeys to lower reaches in the fall, however, when the acorns are about ready for him to harvest. This little chap is more readily at home in conifers than is the eastern gray.

The fox squirrel, though larger, is also very similar to the eastern gray, even to his tracks and his habit of storing nuts individually.

Two beautiful tree squirrels are the tassel-eared squirrels—the Abert (correct) and Kaibab—which are about the size of a big gray. The Abert lives from the Grand Canyon east to New Mexico and north to northern Colorado. The Kaibab is known only on Arizona's Kaibab Plateau.

THE RED SQUIRREL

Noisiness is perhaps the greatest sign of this red-coated forest busybody, who's also called the chickaree and pine squirrel in the West. Smaller than the gray squirrel, this almost unbelievably agile little rodent lives in the coniferous forests of North America from Virginia up through Canada and west to the West Coast and Alaska.

He leaves a track that shows repeated runnings back and forth, crisscrosses, and all the irregularities of an inquisitive, active, little animal. Prints, like those of the gray squirrel, show larger, five-toed hind feet tending to be placed parallel in front of the four-toed front ones. However, don't count on this placement all the time. Sometimes the red will alternate his prints. And sometimes, in snow, the tracks will disappear altogether. This is because the red frequently burrows along under the snow to get to his food caches and to poke around in the ground in search of food.

As far as his home grounds are concerned, the red likes his conifers mixed with hardwoods, and in the latter he prefers tree cavities, often taken over from a woodpecker, for his den. However, if no large-enough hardwoods are available, or if conifers are all he can find, he has to build a nest. This is usually some 30 to 50 feet up (though it may be much lower in areas of stunted trees) and is made of leaves, moss, grass, twigs, bark, or any useful ground litter. Built close to the trunk, it may be 20 inches across and up to a foot deep. The inside chamber is rarely more than 6 inches across. An individual family may build several nests in an area.

While the leaf nests are easy to spot, and the dens

When red squirrel cannot find woodpecker den in hard-wood tree, he builds a leaf nest in a conifer.

in trees aren't easily missed, the red makes still a third
type of home, particularly where suitable trees are
not available, that is not so easy to identify. It may be
in a hollow stump, or the red may make an underground burrow beneath a stump or stone pile. This
burrow may have as many as five tunnels leading from
the surface to the narrow passages and small rooms
that are used for the storage of food or material for

the nest. Look for suspicious holes around stumps, stone piles, or stone walls, and be sure to check the tracks leading to them.

Food habits of the red give an observer a fine opportunity to check his knowledge of the squirrel's presence. For instance, these little animals are very fond of maple and black-birch sap. If you're wandering around the woods in spring and see shallow depressions on the upper sides of the limbs of these trees, you can be sure a red has hollowed out the saucerlike holes to get at the flowing juice. Mushrooms jammed under loose tree bark are a sure sign. These animals love them (even the poisonous ones, which seem to cause no harm) and either wedge them under pieces of bark or place them in the fork of a limb to dry out and be eaten later.

The red squirrel's diet is extremely varied. Besides mushrooms and sap, he likes roots, berries, and the seeds of various grasses. In spring, he nips seeds, flowers, and twig tips from pines, firs, spruces, and all the nut trees. Look for indications of this.

Another thing to look for in this little fellow's country is a midden. This is a pile of pine cones and cone scales—usually built around a rock, tree, or stump in a somewhat damp location—that may contain up to 10 bushels of fresh cones. When the squirrel dines on these cones, which he's cut from the tree, tossed down, and piled up later, he usually sits on the rock or stump around which the midden has been piled. The midden itself and the cone husks on the central protuberance are great tip-offs that a red squirrel is around. Over the years, a midden may grow to as much as 3 feet high and 25 or 30 feet across. Pine squirrels of the Pacific Coast area occasionally store cones in springs or creeks. The moisture tends to keep the cones from losing their seeds by drying out and opening. Damp area of the midden serves the same purpose.

In late summer, the red begins to scamper around in earnest as he collects his winter food. Twigs, nuts, and seeds are high on his list of favorites, and he almost goes beside himself cutting them down. Small seeds and nuts he piles up in various locations, and the cones usually go onto the midden. In the Rocky Mountain area, the pine squirrel often chews on the cast antlers and, when he can find them, the bones of large animals, frequently dragging them to the top of his midden.

The red makes a great deal of racket in the woods. He chatters constantly to himself while working, and if any stranger wanders into his territory, his sharp barks of alarm are interspersed with sputters and growls of indignation as he stamps his feet and scolds with an increasing fury. Should another red cross the boundaries he's laid out for himself, he flies into a rage and attacks without mercy. All these signs are easily heard and quite recognizable.

Another thing to listen for, particularly in late summer and early fall, is the thump made as the severed pine cones hit the forest floor and the rattle of seeds and twigs as they rain down through the trees.

Naturally, as in the case of the gray, the rustling of dead leaves is another tip-off.

THE GROUND SQUIRRELS

Ground squirrels are small, terrestrial rodents found practically all over North America except in the East. There are many species, and the geographic races number more than 100 living in such varying environments as the mountains and the desert.

Burrows of these little creatures, most of whom hibernate, form extensive tunnel work underground, from 6 inches below the surface to many feet down. If you're driving around in western country and suddenly find that one wheel has disappeared beneath the ground, check for a network of subterranean passages and chambers. Many holes in a given area—some with several bushels of dirt and debris in front of them and some with none—are another good indication. Horsemen should be extremely wary in such a locality.

Another sign, besides the holes and the animals themselves, might be a small landslide. The burrows sometimes funnel rainwater into small, underground torrents that loosen the soil and send it cascading downhill. Another visual sign would be a chewed antler or antelope horn.

Ground squirrels have claws that are longer than those of tree squirrels, and you may notice this in the tracks that have been put down on properly receptive ground. Also, there is a difference in the overall pattern. Tree-squirrel pattern is rather squarish, but that of the ground squirrel shows that the front feet are put down more in a line—one nearly behind the other —giving the set of four prints a roughly triangular look. There are other ways to determine whether the tracks you're studying are those of tree squirrels or ground squirrels. For instance, if you see confusing-looking tracks in the snow, you can be pretty sure they were made by a tree squirrel, since the other variety is usually sound asleep in wintertime. Furthermore, tree squirrels generally prefer woodlands, whereas ground squirrels like more open country where tree squirrels are not frequently found.

It is beyond the scope of this book to go deeply into the many races of ground squirrels, but following is a brief description of several of the more well-known varieties.

Columbian Ground Squirrel

One of the largest of this tribe is the Columbian ground squirrel, and he reaches a length of 11 to 15 inches. These animals lives communally in areas of scattered trees and rocky slopes up to 8,000 feet, though they often wander into valleys where they do great damage to hay and grain. Besides eating such farm produce, they dig up wild-onion bulbs and also eat flowers and berries. Water for the Columbian is supplied by the succulence of spring grasses and plants, and when they turn brown and dry out from the summer sun, the squirrel starts to think of hibernation. He may get his winter fur as early as July, and then he goes to sleep in his den for seven or eight months, though in the uplands, where grasses tend to stay green longer, he may be abroad until early fall.

Watch for these animals, and listen for their chirping, along rocky hillsides where there's a scattering of trees. Entrance holes are readily spotted by the huge mounds of earth in front of them, though holes made on leaving hibernation are dug from below and show no such accumulation.

Thirteen-Lined Ground Squirrel

This squirrel is medium size for the species and is sort of buff color with alternating white and dark stripes running down its back. White spots run the length of the dark stripes. This squirrel eats more meat than any of the others—insects, worms, small mice, carrion. If you see the broken eggs and violated nest of a ground-dwelling bird, suspect the thirteen-liner. Aside from meat, this little fellow also consumes just about all kinds of seeds as well as cactus fruits, roots, and acorns.

Burrows of these animals are generally shallow, about 2 inches across, and usually have no earth around them. Most identifiable sound is a high-pitched whistle that can sometimes actually be mistaken for a bird call.

Antelope Squirrel

The antelope squirrel is a small member of the species, averaging about 9 inches. It loves the heat, lives in the hottest part of the Southwest, and generally does not hibernate, except possibly in the highest part of its range, which may be at an altitude of 6,000 feet. These animals are not numerous, and holes indicating the burrows of four or five creatures per acre would be a sign of antelope-squirrel country. Another sign is the shape of the hole itself. It is usually oval and not more than 3 inches across at its widest. Look for burrow entrances in rocky foothills that are near seed-bearing bushes and various greens. You might also find them at the bases of plants or bushes or alongside a big rock, but don't bother to look for an earth mound. The little animal generally carts the dirt away and scatters it. Seeds and grains are the main diet, but he also eats insects, carrion, leaves, twigs, and fruit. A super-cautious, highly nervous, restless little creature, the antelope squirrel can, and does, climb well. He makes a sort of chittering noise that is very rapid and shrill.

GOLDEN-MANTLED GROUND SQUIRREL

The golden-mantled ground squirrel only makes a racket among his own kind, being very quiet when trespassers are wandering around in his territory. When among members of his own species only, however, he chirps and grunts. If in a fight, he is apt to scream, and just before he dives into his burrow in fright he emits a loud, sharp whistle. This little fellow looks something like a chipmunk, is 9 to 12 inches long, and makes a burrow entrance that's about 3 inches across. Look for such entrances in the western mountains at heights up to 13,000 feet. Preferred locations are edges of rock slides or gravelly hillsides. Diet is fruit, nuts, and various grasses. This squirrel also likes mushrooms, insects, and, to some extent, meat.

PRAIRIE DOG

Prairie dogs are pale buff, sociable little animals living in large towns, each creature having its own home except when rearing young. He's fair sized—12 to 16 inches—and he digs a complicated and elaborate burrow with a hallway that may plunge down 16 feet. At the end of this are various passageways and chambers, sometimes even a bathroom. The entrance hole is 6 or 7 inches across and is surrounded by a rim of earth that can be 2 feet high and twice that across. Entrances to burrows may be close but are usually 40 feet or so apart. Only prairie dogs that live in the flatlands build the circular mound around their holes. They're dykes, actually, and serve to keep the water out in the event of hard rains. Dogs living on hillsides toss dirt from their holes downhill the way most digging animals do.

Because these creatures subsist almost completely on succulent grasses and forage, they've been harried and poisoned almost out of existence by cattle raisers. A very small part of the prairie dog's diet is made up of insects.

When conversing, the dogs chirp, chirr, and whistle, but when alarmed, they bark.

THE OPPOSSUM

The possum, as he is more generally called, leaves very little sign. Perhaps that's why he's been around, virtually unchanged, for somewhere around a hundred million years.

His tracks are quite distinctive in that the hind feet resemble human hands, complete with "thumbs" that can move at right angles to the other four toes. The middle three toes on the hind feet tend to be close together. The front feet have five slender toes and leave tracks that look something like those of birds. When the tail drag shows, it is in the shape of a curve.

Full-grown possums resemble giant mice. They are

A sheltered spot like this rock formation may house a possum during his daytime sleeping hours. He prowls for food at night.

2 to 3 feet in length, including the foot-long tail, and an adult can weigh up to 14 pounds. The range of North America's only marsupial, once confined to the Southeast, is expanding. He is now found in Canada and west as far as Colorado. Natives of California, Oregon, and Washington also know him. In fact, he is spreading so far north that occasionally members of his tribe have been found with frostbitten tails and ears.

The possum lives just about anywhere there's shelter, in hollow logs, between rocks, or in tree trunks. He sleeps all day, but in the evening he sallies forth, generally in swamps and wet bottom lands, for whatever is edible—fruits, vegetables, or the flesh of creatures dead or alive. A fine climber, he goes up persimmon trees in the South to feed on the ripe fruit.

Possums are very stupid, and, as every school child knows, play dead when frightened. Perhaps two other reasons why they have survived through the ages are that they smell vile and are very prolific.

THE WEASEL

The first animal I ever shot as a boy with my first .22 was a weasel. On the farm where I grew up we always dreaded their appearance, accompanied by their strong musky odor, in the chicken coop, where the blood-thirsty little killers could destroy dozens of domestic fowl in a single night. This seems odd for an animal only 10 inches long and an inch in diameter, which looks like a loop of rope as it runs on the ground, along a log, or through the brush in a loping bounce.

There are three basic species of weasel, the least weasel, the short-tailed weasel, and the long-tailed weasel. The long-tailed has the widest distribution,

Weasel trail shows animal's habit of burrowing under snow for several yards, then continuing on the surface.

Weasel places hind feet in tracks of forefeet; hence trail consists of series of twin prints. Remains of animal's recent kill are sometimes found nearby.

only southwestern Arizona and part of southern California doing without his presence. He has a long body, short legs, and small head. Like most of his many subspecies, he turns white during winter in his northern range. The tip of his tail remains black, however, and this white-and-black tail was much sought for the robes of royalty.

Tracks of the weasel aren't hard to recognize, because of the prints themselves and because the trail shows swift changes of direction, odd loopings, back tracking, and all sorts of irregularities that attest to the little creature's eagerness and curiosity. Though there are many variations in the weasel's print pattern, usual evidence of a weasel is a series of twin prints. This pattern is most often seen because a running weasel usually plants his hind feet in the tracks made by the front ones. In snow, a tail drag is occasionally seen. Often these animals take alternately long and short leaps.

Sometimes, when following a weasel track in the snow, you'll be astonished to find that it disappears in a neat round hole, only to reappear some distance farther along. This is because these agile little fellows frequently dive under the snow, proceed for some feet under it, then emerge once more. Weasels are mostly nocturnal, but now and then they are seen in daylight.

Many authorities believe a weasel kills just for fun, and it is not unusual to see the corpse of more than one small animal alongside his trail.

If you should ever have occasion to break open a bale of hay, and then find a pile of dead mice in it, you can be sure you've found a spot where a weasel thought he had enough privacy to indulge in his habit of strong food. Besides denning and storing food in hay, these graceful little mammals also live in hollow logs, rabbit holes, beneath rocks, or in the dens of small burrowing animals.

Droppings are another sign of the weasel. They are long, slender, and dark, and they usually contain fur, pieces of bone, and occasionally feathers. Scats are often dropped repeatedly in the same spot, frequently on stones or in easily seen locations beside the trail or even in it.

Another sign of the weasel comes not from the weasel himself but from birds. Birds occasionally attack him, and they make a frightful racket when they do.

Aside from an occasional propensity for cleaning out a hen house, the weasel dines mostly on small mammals—including rabbits—birds, frogs, and snakes. He is an energetic member of a large family, and generally he does more good than harm.

THE MARTEN

Also called the American sable, the marten is found in the northern coniferous forests and the western mountains of the United States. His signs are almost as hard to come by as is the animal himself. He has been extensively trapped, and because of this his numbers have declined, though in areas where martens are protected, such as New York's Adirondack region, they are making a comeback.

The main sign of the marten is his track, and the reason it is not seen as often as those of other animals is that this dark-brown creature with the pale-buff patch on throat and chest spends a lot of time in trees.

Footprints left by the marten are often rather indistinct, particularly in winter, as at that time of year the animal's feet are so fully furred that the toe pads do not show. The size of the tracks varies tremendously, measuring up to 4½ inches long in soft snow. Toward winter's end, the toe pads start to appear, and by summer they're easily seen in the prints. When the marten is going all out, hind prints are in, or slightly ahead of, those of the front feet, and the tracks may be 3 feet apart.

Scats are like those of minks and weasels. Martens, however, are very fond of berries, and the scats, often

Walking tracks of a marten in late-winter snow reveal toe pads clearly. In midwinter, fur on feet conceal toe pads.

The marten often chooses a hollow tree for a den for the female to give birth.

found with previous droppings, sometimes contain their seeds.

These animals den in the hollows of trees and bring forth two or three young a year. Diet, besides berries, includes small mammals, especially pine squirrels, birds, eggs, nuts, and occasionally fish and frogs.

The marten's vocal sounds consist of screams and squeals, but these largely nocturnal creatures are seldom heard.

THE MINK

This lithe, sometimes playful member of the weasel family is dark brown all year long and has a white patch on his chin. Visual signs of the animal are quite numerous.

Prints of hind feet when animal is walking are almost on top of those made by the front ones. The male is larger than his mate, and the tracks show this. Also, tracks differ widely according to the substance on which they're made. In snow, they've been measured at as much as 2½ inches long. In mud, they resemble those of a house cat. Imprint of the heel of the hind foot, which is slightly webbed, is only sometimes visible.

Living in most of North America, with the exception of most of the southwestern United States, the mink prefers for his habitat areas along wooded streams, marshes—even tidal ones—and lakes and ponds. As a result, his tracks are readily discernible in the mud. Minks love muskrat meat and often rip apart muskrat houses to reach their inhabitants. Sometimes, indeed, they take up housekeeping in the dwellings of these animals after they've eaten them.

Minks also den in empty woodchuck holes that are handy to the water, holes in the rocks, hollow logs and stumps, muskrat burrows, and their own dens in the

Tracks of a running mink appear in groups of four slightly spaced prints, with a foot or more separating groups.

Four-inch hole in a river bank is frequently a mink den, which sometimes extends a dozen or more feet into the ground.

bank. These last are about 4 inches in diameter, and they lead to tunnels as long as 10 or 12 feet.

In winter, visual signs of the mink are more numerous. When traveling in snow, he will sometimes push himself along and leave a trough behind him, and once in a while he will coast down a snowy incline like a boy on a toboggan. He will occasionally dive beneath the surface of the snow, and his track will disappear only to reappear some feet farther on. He does this to see what's below the white layer of silence and also, some observers believe, just for fun.

If you happen to see a neat, round hole through the snow and ice of a pond, you can be pretty sure a mink has made it to go foraging underwater. Usually the hole is somewhat muddy, and there may be the remains of aquatic food, such as frogs, scattered nearby.

When the slightest bit upset, the mink lets go with an unmistakeable odor, and it's sometimes evident at his burrow.

Adult male minks run to about 2 feet in length with tails of 6 to 8 inches. Young are born in early spring, and litters average five to eight kits. As they grow older, they play, often making slides on stream banks as they coast down to the water.

Sounds of minks are barks, hisses, deep-toned purrs, and screams. Their food is varied: muskrats, small birds, fish, small mammals, worms, domestic poultry, and turtle eggs.

THE RABBITS

Cottontail

The Eastern cottontail has the greatest distribution of all the nearly seventy species and subspecies of the rabbit family. He ranges to the Midwest, but other forms of cottontail complete the distribution to cover practically all the United States. His familiar tracks with their narrow prints and paired hind feet can be found almost everywhere.

Cottontails pass a lot of the daytime hours relaxing in their "forms," slight depressions in the earth which

In the fall and winter, fruit trees with their bark gnawed at the base are evidence that cottontails have been foraging for food.

The cottontail, like other rabbits, spends much of the day resting in a "form," a rounded depression in the earth which the animal digs under a bush or other shelter.

the rabbits dig themselves. When not in their forms, the creatures may be resting or sleeping in their dens or burrows. These are sometimes abandoned holes, such as those of woodchucks, or are in tangles of protective cover such as hedgerows, briers, or brush piles.

Generally nocturnal, though often seen in early morning and late afternoon, cottontails feed greedily in vegetable gardens that contain leafy produce or practically any new growth, as irate gardeners can readily testify. In fall and winter, these rabbits chew the bark of bushes and fruit trees besides eating various grains and twigs. Bark gnawings are larger than those of mice, with which they are sometimes confused, and are above the snow. Also, bark alongside the chewings will be in strips. When a cottontail chews off a twig, the end of it will show evidence of many bites rather than a clean cut.

Another sign of the cottontail is the nest. In the North, these rabbits breed for about seven months, starting in January, and bring forth as many as five litters a year. In the South, they breed all year. The nests, usually in open fields, are shallow, somewhat oblong depressions, 7 or 8 inches long. The female digs these with her front feet, often simply enlarging a cow track or the scratchings of some other animal. She then lines it with grass as well as with fur she has pulled from her underside with her teeth. If you don't see a nest, you may hear faint squeaks from the hungry fawns therein.

When two bucks, as the males are called, are vying for the favors of the same female, or doe, they may get into a real battle. Bits of fur scattered around are good evidence of this, as the combatants get pretty violent at such times.

Cottontail's hopping gait leaves a trail of prints in groups of four with a foot or more of space between the groups.

Scats of the cottontail are round and smaller than those of the jacks.

Adult cottontails make little noise. They do, however, often indicate danger by thumping with one of their hind feet, and an injured rabbit will sometimes scream.

SNOWSHOE RABBIT

Unlike the cottontail, a rabbit that doesn't like deep snow too much because of his comparatively small feet, the snowshoe is in his element when the white fluff covers the ground. At that time of year, the 13- to 18-inch animal bounds over the snow using his tremendous, well-furred hind feet to keep him from breaking through. Also, the snowshoe turns from brown in summer to white in winter, a transformation that gives him his other name—varying hare.

The snowshoe inhabits the entire northern United States wherever there are forests, brush, and swamps, and his distinctive tracks are a familiar sight to woodsmen in these regions. The huge hind feet always come down in front of the smaller front ones, and, when the animal is going all out, the hind ones are not quite side by side and the front ones are staggered behind them. When the hare is moving at a slow hop, hind feet are paired and the front ones nearly so.

The snowshoe feeds at night and early in the morning. During the day he spends most of his time in a form. In summer this is a depression in the floor of his habitat, and in winter it is a dished-out spot in the snow. Seeing these, along with the tracks, should prove to you that you're in snowshoe country.

While this animal will eat carrion once in a while, his main diet in summer is made up of grasses, clover,

Conifers stripped of their bark up to 2 feet above the ground are sign of snowshoe rabbit's winter browsing.

and other greens. In winter, he likes twigs, conifer needles, and bark. When eating bark, he slices it from the tree with diagonal cuts of his large incisors, and when nipping twigs he makes clean, slanting cuts. Often a snowshoe will kill a conifer by eating all the bark off it to a height of about 2 feet, standing on his hind legs to get every last bit of it he can reach. This bark-eating propensity is, of course, a positive sign. Scats are round and larger than those of the cottontail.

As in the case of the well-known bunny rabbit, snowshoe bucks sometimes fight over coy females.

Young are born in a rather haphazard fashion, the mother then leaving them in some spot not easily

Snowshoe rabbit bounds across deep snow with aid of large hind feet, which register in front of forefeet.

found while she moves off. She feeds them regularly however, and if danger threatens the young ones they make a low, gurgling noise.

Whitetailed Jackrabbit

This long-eared animal is mainly indigenous to the central Northwest, and he is the only jackrabbit with an all-white tail. He weighs from 5 to 10 pounds, and in summer his coat is grayish brown. In winter it turns white in his northern range.

This is a very fast-moving critter, and when he is really pouring on the coal his leaps may be as much as 20 feet, though such extreme spacing between tracks is not often seen. Prints themselves show fairly long hind feet, more or less paired, in front of front feet when the animal is speeding. At slower speeds, extreme length of hind feet doesn't always show. Also, tracks generally show a straight course rather than the zigzag one made by the smaller species.

The whitetailed jack lives in the open prairie as well as on the slopes of the open mountains, and, like most of his kind, feeds at night on just about any available greenery, including snakeweed and sagebrush. Also like others of his ilk, this animal rests in forms during the day. These are scooped-out places in the grass beside a rock or bush or are simply platter-sized depressions in the snow. Occasionally, if the snow is deep, the whitetailed jack will tunnel into it for protection from enemies and weather.

Blacktailed Jackrabbit

This fellow with the 8-inch ears and the black-topped tail mainly inhabits the Southwest, though he is known also from the state of Washington south into Mexico. Grayish to sandy color, he does not turn white in winter.

Because the range of this rabbit and that of his whitetailed cousin overlap in some areas, their tracks can cause some confusion. Usually, however, the blacktail's tracks are somewhat smaller. Also, the blacktail has an interesting pattern as he bounds along. While his regular jumps may be 15 feet along the ground, he occasionally makes leaps 4 feet or so into the air to see what's going on around him. When he lands from one of these observatory take-offs, his front feet are usually in front of the hind ones. Also, this rabbit may leave a tail mark on the trail.

Somewhat smaller than the whitetail, the black-tailed jack feeds on the usual grasses as well as on field crops, sometimes causing widespread destruction. However, he also feeds on cactus plants, occasionally going after those with sharp spines. He gets at the pulp of these by chewing around the thorns, pulling them out, and then sticking his nose in the resultant hole. Watch for this sign on such cacti as the prickly pear. When feeding on desert bushes, he leaves a slanting cut on the small, nipped-off branches.

This rabbit, too, spends much time in forms near any rocks or shrubs that give a little protection. He does not occupy a burrow, but will go down a hole when hotly pursued.

The nests of all jackrabbits are oval, well hidden by grass or brush, and lined with fur. If you find one, you'll doubtless have little trouble recognizing it.

If you find patches of rabbit fur scattered around, you can come to the fairly safe conclusion that a pair of battling bucks has been trying to reach a decision about which will have the favors of some nearby female. When buck jacks fight, they don't fool around. The hind foot of a jackrabbit has a good set of claws, and if he connects with it he can disembowel his luckless opponent. Occasionally grunts and growls can be heard when rabbit battles are going on.

THE SKUNK

Probably the most obvious sign that skunks are in the neighborhood—and their neighborhood is most of North America—is the vile-smelling musk they spray when they are injured or threatened. Once smelled it can never be forgotten. If it hits an eye, it hurts terribly and causes blindness for fifteen or twenty minutes. The fine spray will carry 15 feet or so if the wind is right, and it can be smelled through the woods for half a mile or more.

But evidence of skunks can be determined in other

A small opening in the rocks is a likely place for a skunk to make his home. Watch for traces of hair.

ways. Since the animals feed mostly on insects, look for small pits in the ground—some 2 inches deep and 3 or 4 across—where these nocturnal prowlers have been digging for them.

Hairs around den entrances are another positive sign. These quiet, bulky little animals den in any sort of natural hole or abandoned burrow. One dug by the skunk itself, however, is short and terminated by a round chamber.

Droppings also offer a clear sign of a skunk's passage. These are made up of berry seeds and the indigestible coverings of many types of insects.

Tracks should give no trouble to the observant

Rooted-up area with small pits in the ground indicate that skunk was digging for insect food during nocturnal prowl.

Tracks of the skunk are under 2 inches long; larger hind foot with prominent heel registers in front of forefoot.

woods rover. The hind feet leave imprints in front of the forefeet; both show claw marks in the dirt.

The striped skunk, glossy black with white stripes, has the widest range of North American skunks. Besides him, however, there's the eastern spotted skunk and the hog-nosed skunk. The former weighs only about 1½ pounds, can climb trees, and has a white spot on his forehead as well as one under each ear. He lives mainly in the south and looks spotted because his narrow, white stripes are broken. The hog-nosed skunk, the only South American variety, has a piglike snout, short fur, and lives in parts of Arizona, Colorado, and Texas.

The peccary often dens in clefts in the desert rock formations of the Southwest. The animal leaves a skunklike odor wherever it lives.

THE JAVELINA

The javelina, or peccary, is a bad-smelling, piglike little creature whose signs may be encountered by the outdoorsman in Arizona, New Mexico, and Texas. He is not a true hog in the sense that those of Asia and Africa are, but he is the best we can do in the way of a wild pig native to the United States. The "Russian" boars of Tennessee, North Carolina, and elsewhere are from imported stock.

The little javelina—a big one would weigh 60 pounds—is a gregarious chap traveling in noisy groups of up to sixty or so animals. As the herd wanders along feeding, mostly in early morning and evening, its members keep up a steady grunting and yapping. To the experienced dweller of the Southwest, this rumbling conversation is readily identifiable. If the herd is alerted and takes refuge in flight, some of the more outraged animals will emit shrill grunts as they bounce away for safety.

Visual signs of javelinas have to do with their eating habits and their tracks, the latter being imprinted in pairs with the hind feet falling directly behind the forefeet.

The peccary will eat practically anything edible, including snakes of all sizes. His favored diet, however, is the prickly pear cactus, and an area of chewed-up prickly pears is sure evidence that javelinas have passed through. However, he also enjoys small animals such as mice and lizards, and with his long, flexible, flat-ended snout he digs up tubers and insects. Any spot that shows signs of this rooting around indicates that a band of the little pigs may have passed

Chewed-up prickly pear cactus is reliable proof that javelinas have been feeding on their favorite plant.

Javelina tracks, similar to those of pigs, are slightly over an inch long. Hind foot registers behind forefoot.

by. They like charcoal too, and will poke around where campfires have existed.

A very distinctive sign of the peccary is his odor, particularly pungent when the animal has been frightened. He has a gland on his back, about 8 inches up from his short tail, through which he emits his strong, musky smell. Anyone in javelina country who wanders into a cave or cleft in the rocks and perceives a skunklike aroma in the enclosure can be sure javelinas have been there before him.

The peccary, or more properly the collared peccary, is the only member of his tribe living in the United States, but another species, the white-lipped peccary, lives from southern Mexico south. Our javelina is called a collared peccary because a band of light-grayish hair encircles his thick neck and stands out clearly against the darker gray of the rest of his body.

In spite of tales told with wide-eyed intensity about the ferocity of this big-headed, slender-legged little animal with the fearsome tusks, the javelina is peaceful and only fights when cornered.

THE SNAKES

Though cursed by nature with a repulsive appearance, most snakes are actually beneficial to man, for they control many undesirable rodents and insects. A few species of snakes, however, do have a poisonous bite, and, as with the eating of wild plants, you should stay clear of all species until you are sure they're harmless.

Snakes leave very little sign. They will leave a trail in soft sand or mud that can either be an arrow-straight furrow, a series of curves, or, in the case of the sidewinder, a series of parallel indentations. Occasionally some types can be heard slithering over or through dry brush and leaves; some release a musky odor when frightened; and, of course, the rattler makes a distinct buzzing when agitated.

All snakes shed their skins frequently, and these semitransparent sheds are often found in snake habitat. All snakes hibernate too, and all are totally deaf. Incidentally, dens are usually on south-facing slopes. Colors of snakes vary tremendously, even among a given species. The more northerly and high the habitat, the darker, generally, is the specimen.

Most nonpoisonous snakes found in the United States have slender heads and round pupils.

Black Snake

Also called the black racer, this reptile lives from New England to Florida and west to Ohio and southern Indiana. He averages 4½ feet long, lays eggs, is a plain black color, and eats small animals, frogs, eggs, and other snakes. This snake prefers dry, open places but is also found in woods, meadows, and around loose rock or brush piles. When hibernating, which he does with many companions, he picks stone crevices or the abandoned hole of a ground-burrowing animal. Certain members of his tribe can scoot over the tops of bushes. If you hear a suspicious rustling, look for this snake or any of his cousins—the racers.

Chicken Snake

This reptile lives in Florida and north to lower North Carolina. He averages 4 feet long and has four dark stripes—two on his back and one on each side—running the length of the body on a yellow or tan background. This fellow hunts in trees and the rafters of barns and chicken houses for rats and mice.

Garter Snake

Range is most of the eastern United States for this 20-inch serpent with three light stripes on a darker background running down its back. The common garter bears living young and lives in fields, meadows, gardens, and marshes. It rather prefers damp, open spots and is found from sea level to high mountain slopes. When caught, this snake exudes an unpleasant odor from its musk glands. Diet is largely worms, amphibians, and insects.

Path of a king snake in the dust leaves a long, undulating track, an inch or more in width.

King Snake

The common king snake ranges throughout most of the southern United States in three subspecies—the Eastern, the black, in the Ohio and Tennessee valleys, and the speckled, which lives in and west of the Mississippi Valley. Colors vary tremendously in these fairly long (up to 6 feet) snakes. All of them lay eggs, have relatively small heads, are constrictors, and live in the burrows of other animals. These reptiles are very valuable, eating rats, mice, and poisonous snakes, bites of which don't bother them a bit. When alarmed, they vibrate their tails and hiss.

Water Snake

The common water snake is aptly named. He loves water and commonly lives near it, often sunning himself on a branch hanging over a stream, swamp, or pond. He ranges from South Carolina to Canada and west to eastern Colorado. He is a blotchy-looking snake with crossbands on his foreparts and is sometimes confused with the moccasin. Diet is mostly made up of crawfish, fish, frogs and other amphibians, and occasionally small animals. It bears live young.

POISONOUS SNAKES

Poisonous snakes—the coral snake excepted—have triangular-shaped heads, elliptical pupils, and evident poison sacs.

The Copperheads

The three subspecies of this reptile are well colored with chestnut-brown crossbands on their backs. Head is copper colored without markings. The southern copperhead ranges pretty much throughout the Southeast, the northern takes over for the Northeast, and the broad-banded operates from southern Kansas to the middle of Texas. These are highly poisonous, are members of the pit-viper family, and bear living young.

Coral Snake

This is a highly dangerous creature with bright red,

yellow, and black rings. There are other snakes with the same coloration, but the poisonous coral is the only one with a black nose and the only one that has the red ring touching the yellow. This snake rarely exceeds 45 inches, lives from Florida to North Carolina, burrows, and generally keeps himself hidden underground in fields or, in some cases, near water.

WATER MOCCASIN

Called a cottonmouth in the South because of the white interior of its mouth, it is very fond of water and gives off quite a pungent odor when caught. Look for this creature near the quiet waters of bayous and swamps from Virginia to Florida and west to Texas. He resembles somewhat the water snake and is one of the largest of American poisonous snakes, reaching 6 feet.

Rock crevices are often the homes of copperheads and rattlesnakes. Sometimes several snakes congregate in same place.

The Rattlesnakes

These terrifying serpents come in many forms, but perhaps the best known is the diamondback. Characteristically, it has a diamond-shaped pattern on its back. The western variety lives throughout the Southwest, while the eastern one is known from Florida and Louisiana north to North Carolina. Average length is about 5 feet. As with all pit vipers, young are born live.

The timber rattler, which inhabits the Northeast from Maine to Alabama and Oklahoma, likes to live in timberlands where there are plenty of rocky outcroppings. He's got dark, V-shaped crossbands on his back. They're usually dark on a lighter brown or yellowish background.

The prairie rattler lives in the prairie states and is marked with brown blotches on a background color of anything from greenish yellow to olive. He lives principally in the burrows of other animals, often

Rattle of the rattlesnake is a series of horny cylindrical rings at the end of the tail which knock against each other.

J-shaped tracks in sand show sidewinder's unique method of locomotion, different from undulating course of other snakes. Note clear prints left by belly scales.

those dug by prairie dogs. This is the rattler of the Great Plains region.

The sidewinder is distinguished from other rattlers by the hornlike protuberances over the eyes and the distinctive track. Since he lives in the sandy deserts of Lower California, southern California, Nevada, Utah, and Arizona, this track is readily seen and easily identifiable. It is a series of J-shaped markings in the sand made by the snakes bringing his head through the air, setting it down, then looping the body after it. The snake does not drag its body, and a good track will show the imprints of every belly scale. You'll look a long time before seeing the maker of this track, however, as the sidewinder is nocturnal. He only averages about 18 inches in length, and females are usually larger than the males.

Index

Index

A

Abert squirrel, 342
Acapulco, Mexico, 67
Alaska Highway, 9, 141, 202
Aleutians, 3
amanita, 206
American elm tree, 292, 311
animal pests, 118, 121-122
animal signs, 345-480
animal trails, 12-13, 145
antelope, 373-375
antelope squirrel, 449-450
"Antique," 284
Appalachian Mountains, 4-5, 304
arborvitae tree, 291, 303
arctic birch, 302
Arctic explorer, 148
Arizona whitetail deer, 352
Armalite Ar-7 Explorer, 151

arrowhead plant, 198
ash tree, 291, 293
aspen tree, 296
atmospheric pressure, 91-92, 93, 95
ax, 37, 45, 101
Australian aborigine, 148

B

badger, 345, 424-426
balsam fir tree, 290, 312
barometers, 91
barrel cactus, 147, 198
"baseball tree," 293
basswood tree, 291, 298
Bear-'N-Burlap fly, 179
bearberry, 214
bears, 121, 122, 217-218, 390-405
beaver, 345-346, 421-423
bed camp, 250-251
beech tree, 299
beechnut, 220

485

bergamot, 221

berries, 147, 213-220

big game, preparation of, 172-175

bigleaf maple, 320, 321

binoculars, 37, 144

birch tree, 291, 300-301

birchbark canoe, 61

birchbark kettle, 142, 258-259

bird's-eye maple, 321

bitterroot (purslane), 208-209

Bitterroot Mountains, 4, 208-209

black bear, 99-100, 390-395

black cottonwood tree, 306

black maple tree, 320

black oak tree, 324

black snake, 476

black spruce tree, 336

black walnut tree, 338

black willow tree, 339

blackberry, 214

blacktail deer, 361

blacktailed jackrabbit, 467-468

blue ash tree, 293

blue spruce tree, 290, 336

blueberry, 215

boat, all-purpose, 55-56

boat leaks, 70

boats, 55-58

bobcat, 418-420

boiling game, 169

boiling water, 142

bowline, 231

box trap, 160-161

boxelder maple tree, 292, 320

braiding rope, 227-229

broadleaf trees, 288, 290, 291-292

brown bear, 400-403

Buck-'N-Burlap fly, 179

buckskin, making, 265-268

bullboats, 59

"bullburgers," 175

burdock, 198

buttercups, 213

butternut, 220

butternut tree, 338

C

cactus, 147, 198

camas, 199

camera and film, 37, 40

camp-marking, 83

campsite, selection of, 118-121

candles, 130, 246-248

canoe, development of, 58-62

canoe gear, containers for, 66

canoe-"lining" 68

canoe-loading, 62-65

canoe-packing, 65-67

canoe-portaging, 65-67

canoe-repairing, 69-70

canoe-sailing, 65

canoeing, rough-water, 67-69

canoes, 58-65

canoes, modern, 61-62

caribou, 368-372

Cassiars, British Columbia, 177

catgut, 276-277

cattails, 199

cave-exploration, 118

cave shelters, 117-118

cave varmints, 118

cedar tree, 292, 303

Central Hardwood Belt, 291-292

century plant, 199-200

chestnut, 220

chestnut oak tree, 323

chestnut tree, 291, 304

chicken snake, 476

chicory, 200, 221

chili, 172

chlorine for water, 142

Chlorox, 142, 261

chokecherry, 200-201, 214

chufa, 201, 221

cirrus clouds, 92-93, 102

citrus tree, 202

clock-compass, 256

clothes, hiker's 23-26

clothing materials, 23, 24, 25

cloud ceiling, 98

cloud formations, 92-95

clouds, 92-95, 98

clove hitch, 232

clover, 201, 213

Coastal Range, 4

clothes, hiking, 23-26, 39

Colorado fir tree, 290

Colorado spruce tree, 290, 336

Columbian ground squirrel, 448

compass, 74-75, 80, 256

compass, plant and flower, 86

conifers, 288, 289, 290-291, 292

cooking, no-utensil, 186-187

cooking, outdoor, 129-132, 168-190

cooking practice, 44

cooking small game, 168-175

coolers, camp, 252-254

copperhead snakes, 478

coral snake, 478-479

cord soles, 18

cottonmouth snake (white moccasin), 479

cottontail rabbit, 152, 157, 160, 461-464

cottonwood tree, 306-307
Coues deer, 351, 352
cougar, 415-417
coyote, 412-414
cranberry, 216-217
crane, cooking, 127
Craters of the Moon, 118
creek crossings, 14-15
cumulus clouds, 92, 93
cyclones, 100, 101-103
cypress tree, 292, 308

D

Dall sheep, 383-385
dandelion, 201-202, 221
dangers, outdoor, 9-10
death camass, 213
declination chart, 75
deer, 260-261, 351-360
desert bighorn, 380-382
desert shelters, 115-116
deserts, 7-8, 15, 23, 24, 115-
    116, 119, 146-149, 292,
    345
dew, 97
dewberry, 215
diagonal lash, 237
diamondback snake, 480
dingle stick, 126
Dismal Swamp, 8
dock, 202
donjekberry (silverberry),
    209

Douglas fir tree, 290, 291,
    312
dressing small game, 165-
    168
dugout canoe, 58-59

E

earth's atmosphere, 90-92
eastern cottonwood tree,
    306
elderberry, 215, 221
elderberry bugle, 215
elk, 98-99, 347-350
elm tree, 291, 292, 310
emergency drinks, 221
emergency food, 196-213
emergency kit, 37
emergency lures, 179-185
emergency snowshoes,
    256-258
Englemann spruce tree,
    290, 336
Eskimos, 143, 160, 273-
    276
eucalyptus tree, 314
express hitch, 240-242

F

fiberglass craft, repair of,
    70
finding your way, 71-89
fir trees, 290, 291, 312

fire board, 134-135
fire bow, 134
fire, cooking, 129-132
fire drill, 134-136
fire-extinguishing, 138-139
fire hazards, 123-125
fire platforms, 128
fire rack, 126-127
fire spindle, 134, 135
fire-starters, 129-131
fire tripod, 126, 127
firearms, 150-153
firemaking, 123-139
firemaking, firearm & cartridge, 138
firemaking, flint & steel, 136
firemaking, magnifying glass, 136-137
firemaking, match-less, 134-138
fireplace grid, 128
fireplaces, 125-128, 251
fireplaces, raised, 251
fireweed, 202-203
fish, 176-193
fish, baked, 190
fish-cleaning, 185
fish-fileting, 188-189
fish-frying, 187-188
fish skins, 272-273
fish, smoked, 190-193
fishing rod, 37
fishloaf, 190
flashlight, 246

files, artificial, 176-179
flies, shirt-tail, 176-179
Florida Everglades, 8
food essentials, 42-44
food pack, 43
food packaging, 44
foot care, 22-23
footwear, 18-22
forest areas, 288-292
forests, 5-6, 118-119, 287-292
fox, 410-411
fox squirrel, 441, 442
frame shelters, 110-114
frying game, 169-170
frying pan, 38-39
fuel, cooking-fire, 129
"fuzz sticks," 129-130

G

game, preparation of, 168-175
garter snake, 476
gear, cold-weather, 41-42
gear, go-light, 36
gear, hiking, 36-42
geese, 97
getting lost, 86-89
gloves, 26
going around in circles, 81-83
golden-mantled ground squirrel, 450

goldenrod, 221
gooseberry, 216
grand fir tree, 291
gray fox, 411
gray squirrel, 439-442
gray wolf, 406-409
grayling, 177
greasewood, 213
grizzly bear, 121, 217, 396-399
Ground-Air Emergency Code, 88
ground juniper, 216
ground squirrels, 447-450
groundnut, 203
grouse, 99, 145, 150, 152-153, 166, 168, 170, 171-172
grouse, fricaseed, 171
grouse, fried, 170, 171
grouse with dumplings, 171-172
gum tree, 291, 314

H

H & R 922, 152
hail storm, 98
halo, sun or moon, 97
handgun, 37, 152
handgun lanyard, 152
Harrington & Richardson's Handy Gun, 151
haw, 216

headgear, 25-26
hemlock tree, 291, 315
hemp rope, 222, 223-224, 226-227, 244-245
hickory nut, 220
hickory tree, 291, 317
hiking, 11-46
hiking distance per day, 17-18
hitches, 222, 232, 233-234, 235, 240-242
hog peanut, 203
hog-nosed skunk, 471
huckleberry, 217-218
hunter's stew, 174
hunting regulations, 150

I

Indian cucumber, 203
iodine for water, 142

J

jack pine tree, 290
jacket, hiking, 24, 37
jackrabbit, 157, 163-165, 345, 466-468
javelina, 472-474
Jerusalem artichoke, 204
jimson weed, 213, 214
Joshua tree, 335
juniper tree, 303

K

Kaibab squirrel, 342
kayak, 59-60
Key deer, 351
king snake, 477
kinnikinik (bearberry),
    214
kit fox, 411
knapsack, 29
knots, 222, 229-235

L

Labrador tea, 221
lace-cutting, 269-271
laces, 269-271, 282-284
lacing, 282-284
lamb's quarters (pig-
    weed), 207
landmarks, 78-79, 83, 86-
    87
lantern, gasoline, 246
larch tree, 290, 318
larkspur, 213
lashing poles, 238-239
lashings, 222, 235-243
laundry, 26-27
laurel bay tree, 319
lean-tos, 107-109, 110-114
leather-dyeing, 284
leather pattern, 277
leather soles, 18-19
leathercraft, 277-284

leg tendons, big-game,
    273-276
lichens, 204
lights, camp, 246-248
live oak tree, 324
liver, game, 173
loblolly pine tree, 292, 331
loco weed, 213
locust tree, 291
lodgepole pine tree, 290,
    325
long-eared fox, 411
longleaf pine tree, 292
longneedle pine tree, 325,
    327
looped knots, 234
lupine, 213

M

"mackerel sky," 97
magnolia tree, 320
mahogany tree, 292
mallow, 204
maple tree, 291, 321-322
maps, 72-73
Marble's Game-Getter,
    151
mariposa (sego lily), 209
marmot, 438
marsh marigold, 204-205
marten, 457-458
match container, 132-133
matches, 132-134

meadow mushroom, 206
meat, 150-175
mesquite, 292
milkweed, 205, 213-214
mink, 459-460
mint, 221
moccasins, 19-20
moisture, sources of, 148-149
Mojave Desert, 7
moose, 175, 362-367
moose nose, roasted, 175
morel, 206
mossberry, 218
mountain sorrel, 206
mountains, 3-5, 13-14, 120, 140-141
mukluks, 273
mulberry, 218, 221
mule deer, 358-360
mushrooms, 205-206
muskrat, 430-432
mustard, 207

N

neckerchief, 26
nested aluminum pots, 38
newspaper roll, 130
nimbus clouds, 92, 93
noble fir tree, 291
North Star, finding, 75-77
Northern Forest Belt, 289-290

Norway maple tree, 320
Norway pine tree, 290
Norway spruce tree, 336
nuts, edible, 220-221
nylon rope, 222, 223, 224-225, 244-245

O

oak tree, 291, 292, 323-324
oarlocks, 56-57
oars, 56
odors, 98
oogruk, 60
oonok, 16
opossum, 452-453
Ormond's Bull-'N-Burlap Fly, 179
Owendoff, Bob, 77
owl, 99

P

Pacific Forest Belt, 291
pack, 28-46
pack-shouldering, 45-46
pack basket, 29
pack size, 28-29
packboard lash, 242-243
packboards, 30-34, 36, 242-243
packing the load, 45
pacs, 19, 24

paddles, canoe, 62-63

paddling canoe, 62-65, 69

"palooser," 248

pants, hiking, 24, 25

papaya (pawpaw), 218-219

paper birch tree, 301

paraffined matches, 133-134

pawpaw, 218-219

peanut, 220

pecan, 220

peccary (javelina), 472-474

Penguin Aerial Flare, 88-89

peppermint, 221

persimmon, 219

pheasant, 99

pigweed, 207

pine trees, 207, 290, 291, 292, 325

pinion, 220, 325, 328

pinole, 44, 196-197

pirogue (dugout canoe), 58-59

pitch, 131

pitch pine, 290

plants, edible, 194-221

plants, toxic, 195

pokeweed, 207-208

polar bear, 404-405

poling watercraft, 53, 54, 55, 56

ponderosa pine tree, 290, 325, 328

poplar tree, 291, 296

porcupine, 121, 433-435, 441

Port Orford cedar tree, 303

portaging, 65-67

potato-sack pack, 248-249

"poxy resin," 70

prairie dog, 450-451

prairie rattler, 480

prairie turnip, 208

prickly pear, 147, 213

punt, 55

Purex, 142

purslane, 208-209

pussy willow, 331

Q

quamash (camas), 199

R

rabbit, fried, 170

rabbit pie, 171

rabbit, 152-153, 157, 160, 163-165, 166, 170, 171, 345, 461-468

raccoon, 427-429

raft-building, 47-52

raft propulsion, 53-54

rafts, 47-55

rainbow, 97

raincoat, 37, 39
ram ribs, barbecued, 175
raspberry, 219
rattlesnakes, 480-481
rawhide-making, 261-265
red ash tree, 293
red cedar tree, 292, 303
red fir tree, 291
red fox, 410-411
red gum tree, 314
red maple tree, 320, 321
red oak tree, 292, 323-324
red pine tree, 290, 325-
    326, 330
red spruce tree, 290, 336
red squirrel, 441, 443-446
redwood tree, 291, 334
reeds, 209-210
rescue, 88-89
rifle, 37, 151
ring hitches, 233-234
roasting game, 168-169
rock shelters, 116-117
rockchuck, 438
Rocky Mountain Belt,
    290-291
Rocky Mountain bighorn,
    376-379
Rocky Mountain goat,
    386-389
Rocky Mountains, 4, 290-
    291, 376-379, 386-389
rodents, 121
rope, 222-229, 244-245
rope-burning, 224-225

rope, care of, 244-245
rope-tying under tension,
    235
rope-whipping, 224-225
route-sketching, 77-83
rowing, 56-58
rubber life rafts, 54-55
rucksack, 29
Russian boar, 472

S

saguaro, 335
sassafras, 221
Savage Arms Co., 151
Sawtooth Mountains, 3
scow, 55
scrub oak tree, 324
seacoast shelters, 114, 116
seacoasts, 6-7, 114, 116
sego lily, 209
serviceberry, 220
shadow stick, 77
shagbark tree, 317
shaggy mane, 206
shear-pole lash, 236-237
Sheep-Eater Indians, 84,
    127
sheet bend, 230
shelters, 104-122
shirts, hiker's 23, 24, 25,
    27
shoe soles, 18-19
shoes, hiking, 18-22

shortleaf pine tree, 292
shotgun, 150, 151
sidewinder, 481
signs, natural, 84-86, 95-100
silkweed (milkweed), 205, 213-214
silver maple tree, 320, 321
silverberry, 209
Sitka spruce tree, 291
skiff, flat-bottomed, 55
skin boat, 60
skin canoe, 59-61
skin preservation, 261-276
skinning small game, 163-165
skunks, 122, 469-471
sky color, 97, 102
slash pine tree, 292
sleeping area, preparation of, 120-121
sleeping bag, 37, 38
sling, hunting, 153-154
slingshot, 156-157
slip knot, 230
slippery elm, 210, 292, 311
Smith & Wesson Airweight Kit Gun, 152
smoke direction, 97
smokehouses, 191-192
snake skins, 271-272
snakes, 475-481
snakes, non-poisonous, 476-478

snakes, poisonous, 478-481
snares, 161-163
snow water, 120, 143
snowshoe rabbit, 152-153, 157, 464-466
snowstorms, 100, 103
soap, camper's, 259-261
socks, 21, 22, 23, 24, 27
Sonora whitetail deer, 352
sorrel, 210
Southern Forest Belts, 292
southern pine tree, 325, 331
sow thistle, 210
spearmint, 221
"spread-eagle" fall, 16
spruce tree, 290, 291, 336
square knot, 229
square lash, 238
squirrel, 345-346, 439-450
squirrel, fried, 170
squirrel stew, 171
staff, hiking, 14-15
steel traps, 157-160
stew, go-light, 172
stinging nettle, 210-211
Stone sheep, 383-385
stopper knot, 223-224
stratus clouds, 92, 93
strawberry, 220
striped skunk, 471
succory (chicory), 200, 221
sugar maple tree, 292
sugar pine tree, 291

"sun dogs," 97
sunflower, 211
Surveys and Engineering Branch, Ottawa, Canada, 73
survival, 87-88
swamp ash tree, 293
swamp cedar tree, 303
swamp cottonwood tree, 306
swamp laurel, 319
swamp magnolia tree, 319
swamp oak tree, 323
swampland, 8-9, 15-16, 120
sweet acorn, 220
sweet bay tree, 319
sweet birch tree, 221
sweet william, 213
sweetgum tree, 314
sycamore tree, 291, 337

T

table, camp, 249-250
Tahltan Indians, 84
tallow, deer, 260-261
tamarack tree, 290
tanning, Eskimo, 273-276
tanning hairy skins, 268-269
tarp, 37, 40, 104-110
tarp shelters, 104-110
tenderloin, game, 173
thermal winds, 85

thirteen-lined ground squirrel, 449
thorn apple, 216
thunderstorms, 100-101
tides, 98
timber hitch, 233
timber rattler, 480
tobacco root (purslane), 208-209
toboggan, 41-42
tongue, game, 174
tooling design, 277-282
tornadoes, 100, 101-103
trail-blazing, 83-84
traps, 157-161
treacherous terrain, 14-17
tree classification, 288
tree compass, 85-86
tree identification, 287-340
trees, 85-86, 287-340
tularemia, 165
tule (cattails), 199
tulip tree, 291
tumpline, 29
turkey-head knot, 225-226

U

U.S. Geological Survey, 73
underwear, 23, 24, 37
United States Printing Office, 75

utensils, cooking, 37, 38-39
utensils, eating, 37, 39

V

Vermillion Cliffs, Arizona, 7
vest, down, 37, 39
visibility, 98

W

walnut, 220
walnut tree, 291, 340
Wasatch Mountains, 4
washstands, camping, 254-256
water condensation, 90-91
water cress, 211
water, desert, 146-149
water displacement, 48-50
water, drinking, 120, 140-149
water hemlock, 212-213
water hyacinth, 211-212
water knot, 232
water, mountain, 140-141, 143-146
water purification, 141, 142-143
water snake, 477-478

water travel, 47-70
water trough, 145-146
waterfowl, 99
wax candles, 130
waxed paper, 130
weasel, 454-456
"weather breeders," 100
weather, dangerous, 100-103
weather forecasting, 90-103
weather signs, 95-98
weaving stitch, 239-240
wedge soles, 19
weeping willow, 339-340
wheat, threshed, 197
whistlepig, 437
white ash tree, 292, 293
white cedar tree (arborvitae), 291, 303
white fir tree, 290
white fox, 160
white moccasin snake, 479
white oak tree, 292, 323-324
white pine tree, 290, 291, 325, 332
white spruce tree, 290, 336
whitetail deer, 351-357
whitetailed jackrabbit, 466
wild cherry tree, 291
wild geranium, 213
wild grape, 212
wildlife behavior, 98-100

wild onion, 212
wild parsnip, 212-213
wild potato (prairie turnip), 208
wild rice, 213
wild roses, 213
willow trees, 291, 342-343
wind direction, 84-85
Wind River Mountains, 4
windstorms, 100, 101-103

wolfberry (silverberry), 209
woodchuck, 436-438
Wygant, Ernie, 177

Y

yellow birch tree, 301
yellow pine tree, 290